THE OFFICIAL® 2004 BLACKBOOK PRICE GUIDE TO UNITED STATES PAPER MONEY

THIRTY-SIXTH EDITION

BY MARC HUDGEONS, N.L.G.
& TOM HUDGEONS, Jr.
& TOM HUDGEONS, Sr.

HOUSE OF COLLECTIBLES

Random House Reference • New York

Published by: House of Collectibles
Random House Reference
New York, New York

Distributed by Random House Reference, a division of Random House, Inc., New York, and simultaneously in Canada by Random House of Canada Limited, Toronto.

www.HouseofCollectibles.com.

Printed in the United States of America

ISSN: 0195-3540

ISBN: 1-4000-4806-0

Thirty-sixth Edition: June 2003

10 9 8 7 6 5 4 3 2 1

CONTENTS

OFFICIAL BOARD OF CONTRIBUTORS

The author would like to express a special thank you to:

W.R. "Bill" Rindoné, Bank Notes North West, PO Box 406, Wilsonville, OR 97070, for his collaboration and Market Review,

and **Regina Banks and Larry Felix at the Department of the Treasury,** Bureau of Engraving and Printing, Washington, D.C., for the articles on the BEP, and David Koble of Mid-American Currency.

PUBLISHER'S NOTE

The Official ® Blackbook Price Guide to United States Paper Money is designed as a reference aid for collectors, dealers, and the general public. Its purpose is to provide historical and collecting data, as well as current values. Prices are as accurate as possible at the time of going to press, but no guarantee is made. We are not dealers; persons wishing to buy or sell paper money, or have it appraised, are advised to consult collector magazines or the telephone directory for addresses of dealers. We are not responsible for typographical errors.

NOTE TO READERS

All advertisements appearing in this book have been accepted in good faith, but the publisher assumes no responsibility in any transactions that occur between readers and advertisers.

THE OFFICIAL®

2004 BLACKBOOK PRICE GUIDE TO UNITED STATES PAPER MONEY

Market Review

Currency remains strong! Paper money outperformed most forms of investment last year and remains a favorite among collectors. This field is driven principally by collectors; however, it's nice to know that it's also a sound investment.

At a time when the stock market was reeling and the interest rates on other investments were in the doldrums or worse, collectable currency neither stumbled nor faltered. Values slowly spiraled to the up side and more collectors entered this extremely popular hobby.

Dealer inventories are at all time lows and even small collections are hotly contested for by dealers who hold long customer want lists. Amongst collectors, new notes that surface are quickly absorbed and the current availability of notes does not quench the interest of those who are looking for rare notes.

The greatest variety of notes available today can be found in two places. First, amongst old-time dealers who had the foresight to fill their vaults and resist the temptation of selling off their better notes, and secondly, from a variety of auction houses who offer large selections. Included in the latter are a half dozen major houses that include Ebay, CAA, and others.

For those new to collecting, United States paper money has been collected since its conception in the 13 colonies, but only in the last 30 years has it come into its own as a major hobby available to anyone with disposable income. The last half dozen years has seen the collector fraternity multiply at a rapid rate and even with the so-so economy world wide it continues to attract new collectors.

This year we are pleased to have David Koble of Mid-American Currency helping us with pricing in the field of

Small Size currency. David is not only one of the most knowledgeable dealers in this area, but he also attends all the major auctions.

A word of caution regarding grading. If you like the appearance of a note, others will most likely see it in the same light. Beauty as they say "is in the eye of the beholder." Grading is at best a subjective pursuit rather than a science. Professional grading houses have sprung up in the last few years and although they serve a worthwhile purpose to the unknowledgeable collector, there is no replacement for research and study. It will take a while to become familiar with the nuances of grading and value, but any time invested will pay big dividends. You will have a greater respect for the notes you collect and not have to rely on a service that could have their personal interests placed before yours. This book is an excellent source of information and it is recommended that you read all the articles in it.

New record auction prices have been established during the past year in several fields. The breakdown looks like this:

Large Size Type Notes (1861–1923) This area of expertise remains the number one interest among collectors. Several major auctions were held and radical price changes were seen, particularly in the areas of $50 and larger denominations. Condition and rarity are again the key and near-perfect specimens command big prices. Examples of major price changes can be found in the 1880 Silver Certificates, high grade First Charter notes (1865–75), 1880 $50/100 Legal Tenders and 1914 Red Seal Federal Reserve Notes. There are some underrated areas where bargains can be had. The 1880 $10 and $20 Legal Tender series is a good place to start. Issues where only 11–50 notes are known can still be had in low grade for a few hundred dollars.

Small Size Type Notes (1928–Present) This is a major area of interest with today's new collectors and a wide variety of notes exist. WW2 North African and Hawaii issues, Red seal $1 and $2 series along with the 1928–34 "Funny Money" issues are popular with new collectors. Another favorite amongst collectors is the 1928 Federal Reserve series along with the 1929 Federal Reserve Bank Note series. FRBN's are an interesting collecting anomaly as all notes are dated 1929, have brown seals and although there are 50 notes in the series, ALL can be found by a dilligent collector. There are also an astounding number of advanced collectors looking for "Mules," rare blocks and Star Notes. New esoteric discoveries are still being made in this field.

Fractional Notes (1862–1874) These pieces from the Civil War period are of interest to coin, stamp and currency collectors. Originally issued as a substitute for coins they were printed as "Postage Currency." They are still redeemable at face value from your local post office. As this is written a major collection is being offered at auction and preliminary bids indicate a resurgence in interest in notes that are rare or in superb condition.

Centering plays a major role in value for fractional notes. The first two series were issued in sheets and then cut apart by private parties. Thus a dearth of poorly cut notes went into circulation. Another factor in centering is that the printing presses of the time were notorious for printing the back offset to the front, leaving a partial reverse design after the scissors were used. This issue of notes has seen increasing interest in recent years. A "new" note is included here for the first time. In 1877 the federal government issued $50 bonds which had fractional interest notes attached. Each note had a face value of 50 cents. "United States will pay to the bearer 50¢." Signed by J. Allison, Secretary of the Treasury, they bear the same portrait of W.H. Seward as found on the rare 1891 $50 Silver Certificate.

Specimens and Proof notes of most fractional issues exist and the demand for them has increased radically in the last few years. The specimens have narrow margins as cut by the treasury and were originally attached to "shields" that were purchased by banks from the U.S. Treasury. These shields were used to detect counterfeits and several have survived. The individual notes were removed by collectors/dealers and in many cases suffered damage in the process. Proofs were printed on single sheets and thus have survived with wide margins. Proofs are considerably rarer than specimens and are much sought after.

National Currency (1865–1929) These notes were issued by private banks and secured by deposits in the U.S. Treasury. They represent the financial world of their time and several banks issued only a few notes and are thus very scarce. Others issued large quantities and are easily found today. Most collections are based on geographical areas, be it city, county or state-wide. Rare nationals from large populated areas command correspondingly high prices as demand is the main factor. Another category of interest is in Territorial Issues and all of these are rare. The difficult part of collecting nationals is that complete geographical collections are almost unknown due to the unavailability of some notes. Another apparently life-long pursuit is attempting to acquire a representation of all state capitals.

Error Notes (1862–Present) A wide variety of errors exist and some of them are quite startling. Values have been very stable over the past few years and new error notes are leaving the Bureau of Engraving almost daily. Before getting into this area of collecting, I strongly recommend studying the printing process as fake errors are passed to unsuspecting collectors.

Obsolete Notes (Private Issues 1800–1877) Notes were issued by banks and private merchants to supply much need exchange. The issuers often went broke and the notes became known as "broken bank notes." This area is very healthy and has a multitude of collector-based interests. Unusual denominations such as $6, $7, $25, etc. are available. The chances are strong that notes from the area you live in are available. Cost is generally moderate and a wide variety are available in the $10–$30 range.

Depression Scrip (1907 and 1933) These were issued during the period that the government closed banks because of undue pressure on the financial establishments. They were called "bank holidays" which is a complete misnomer. The reason for closure was to give the government a chance to separate the insolvent institutions from the healthy ones. During this period there was a severe lack of currency available and, in order to continue commerce, cities and merchants banded together and issued their own currency. I highly recommend this area to the new collector as there is still much to discover and the opportunities for purchasing rare notes at low prices still exists.

Often they were secured by warrants or city bonds. Until a few years ago there was little interest in this field. Today, it is a rapidly advancing area of collectibility. Notes are still relatively inexpensive, but this opportunity will probably not last long.

Western Exonumia (1850–1910) During the Western

settlement period, gold was the normal specie for payment. Paper was generally frowned upon and often used to wipe windows and bars. A few remote or otherwise desperate merchants, faced with the lack of "hard" currency, issued their own notes. In some cases they were "company stores" that were otherwise faced with shipping of bullion by wagon or stage. These notes continued to be issued long after the U.S. Government decreed their illegality in 1877. Today we see notes that represent the historical old west from towns like Tombstone, AZ and Walla Walla, WA. They are generally quite rare and command a wide range of prices principally because no definitive book has been written on the subject. At auction it is not uncommon to see notes of this type reach $5000, especially when they represent Territorial Issues. On the other end of the spectrum, I've seen valuable notes change hands for less than five dollars.

Summation: The field of collectible currency is extremely healthy and enjoying an influx of new collectors and investors who enjoy the feel of money, history, and discovery.

PUBLICATIONS

Get a global perspective on paper money collecting from ***The Bank Note Reporter***. This monthly tabloid is devoted entirely to U.S. and world paper money, notes, checks, and all related fiscal paper. Find current prices for national and international bank notes, plus an active buy/sell marketplace. *12 monthly issues are $32.00.*

The ***Numismatic News*** delivers weekly news and information on coin and paper money collecting with exclusive reports from the hobby's only full-time Washington Bureau. Accurate retail/wholesale value guide, current events, and up-to-date calendar make this the most comprehensive numismatic forum available. *52 weekly issues are $32.00.*

For more information, please contact:

Krause Publications
700 East State Street
Iola, WI 54990
Phone 715-445-2214, Subscription Services 1-800-258-0929

COIN AND PAPER MONEY COMPUTER SOFTWARE

By Tom Bilotta,
Carlisle Development Corporation

The use of computer software to assist in organizing a coin or paper money collection is an excellent way to enhance your enjoyment of collecting. In addition to helping you to catalog your collection, coin collection software can aide you in identifying collection objectives that are aligned with your interests and financial resources. Software for coin and paper money collectors can be grouped into two broad categories: inventory software and educational software.

Most commonly when collectors think of using computer software to assist with their collecting, they first think of an inventory program. Their goal is to catalog their collection and then use this information to generate a variety of printed reports. These reports include a variety of sorted and filtered listings to assist in managing your collection, want lists which identify items you are seeking, sales lists of items to be sold or traded, and detailed inventories for insurance purposes, as well as many other purposes.

Once familiar with inventory programs, collectors often seek educational programs to enhance their collecting skills. These include general historical information about their collecting interest, software to assist in grading collectibles, and special topics to extend their effectiveness in acquiring collectibles.

RECENT TECHNOLOGY TRENDS IMPACTING COIN AND CURRENCY COLLECTORS

Over the past several years, usage of the Internet has continued to grow. The number of coin and currency sites has grown exponentially. Web sites may be found covering almost any imaginable specialty of coin or currency collecting. These sites are often maintained by very knowledgeable sources. The American Numismatic Association (ANA) maintains a major website dedicated to coin and currency collecting (www.money.org). This site offers a variety of useful information and links to many other coin and currency related websites. Most major mints have a strong web presence. The United States Mint for example, has a highly successful website (www.usmint.gov) which has become the preferred way for its customers to purchase current offerings.

High quality images of coins for sale have become commonplace and are rapidly becoming expected by many online buyers. Users have more powerful computers with very large storage, allowing them to retain hundreds or thousands of high quality coin images. Printers, inks, and specialty papers are now commonly available which allow collectors to print very high quality images of their collection for the purpose of sharing or cataloging. Scanners have continued to improve in quality such that the average collector can now obtain a high quality digital image of a coin in their collection.

The impact of computer technology on coin and paper money collecting is only limited by your imagination. It can be used to obtain specialized information from numismatists throughout the world, to communicate with collectors you would otherwise never meet, or to buy and sell items from a variety of dealers and collectors.

ORGANIZING YOUR COLLECTION WITH COIN & PAPER MONEY INVENTORY SOFTWARE

Collectors of coins and currency fall into several categories. There is the serious coin collector who enjoys the hobby and pursues personally defined collecting objectives. Accumulators retain many of the coins that they receive in normal commerce and build up large quantities of unsorted coins. Investors use coin collecting to build portfolios intended to produce profits. Inheritors receive a coin collection or accumulation from their families and must decide how they will handle a potentially valuable asset.

All of these collectors have a common need to catalog their items and understand their value. Most collectors also have accumulated many items with a very wide range of values.

A modern inventory program can adapt to meet the needs of all types of users from novice collectors to experienced experts. It will incorporate a comprehensive database of coin and/or paper money to assist the user in identifying and defining their collections as well as a flexible set of functionality to enable them to organize their collection in a manner consistent with their collection methodology.

Most collectors will want to organize their collections into several groupings. The collector will want to create collections that mirror their physical collection. For example, someone with coin albums of common series such as Mercury dimes, statehood quarters, or Buffalo nickels will want to have software albums organized in similar fashion. Other coins might be grouped into coins for sale, duplicates, partial collections for other family members, or any other categorization which suits the collector.

USING YOUR TIME WISELY

When using computer software to catalog a coin or paper money collection it is important to use it in a manner consistent with your purposes and which will enhance your enjoyment. You should spend your time, therefore, working with the portions of your collection in which you have the most interest or where the primary financial value exists.

For example, if you are collecting a complete set of Mercury dimes, you may wish to scan an image of each individual piece so that you can print picture catalogs of your collection. For these coins, you might choose to enter incomplete information including purchase price, source, certification information, origin, etc. For this type of grouping you will also likely want to include coins that you don't have that are required to complete your collection, enabling you to generate want lists. This will also assist you in identifying the cost to complete your collection and planning your approach.

For large quantities of relatively inexpensive items or coins worth only bullion content and where you have no particular collecting interest, you might choose to only enter a single line item and not bother to take the time to list each coin individually. For example, if you have several hundred silver Washington quarters in circulated condition from the 1950s and 1960s you might enter a single line item "225 Washington Quarters" with a date range and average value. In this way, large accumulations can be tracked with minimum effort and your attention can be focused on your real collecting interests. Your coin inventory program should adapt to all of these possible approaches to organizing your collection.

EVALUATING COIN AND PAPER MONEY INVENTORY SOFTWARE

The quality of the software that you purchase will greatly impact the success of your efforts.

One of the most important parts of a coin inventory program is the database. The database contains standard information about coins and paper money and saves the user from having to type this information manually. The greater the amount of information in the standard database, the easier the task of data entry. A modern coin collecting program, at a minimum should include coin type, date, mint mark, denomination, and variety. Comprehensive programs, such as those made by Carlisle Development Corporation also include such information as designer/engraver, coinage metal, size, weight, edge, and mintage. The organization of the database should reflect commonly used groupings and thereby provide user with guidance in organizing their collection.

Some inventory programs include current market values. It is important that these are updated frequently and produced by reliable sources. Coin values should evolve to include areas of high market interest. For example, over the past year, the market interest in high grade recent coin issues has become very high. It is also important to allow the user the ability to extend the database to include items that are not listed. These may be specialized varieties, private mint products, or other coin-related collectibles.

Ability to share data with other programs and people is also very important. Most computerized collectors are connected to the Internet and will want to share some information with other collectors and dealers. The ability to export listings in common text readable formats for transmission over the Internet or for input into a word processor or spreadsheet is of great value in buying and selling coins and paper money.

Carlisle Development's inventory software, Collector's Assistant provides a comprehensive database of all coins ever minted by the United States Mint. This includes all type coins by date and mint mark, bullion coins, sets, old, and new commemoratives. Recent additions to the database are the 50 states circulating quarters and the new Sacagawea Dollar. Coin values are licensed from Coin World, Inc., an industry leader in providing coin valuations. Quarterly updates are available by subscription allowing collectors to maintain trends of their values. Carlisle Development's Currency Collector's Assistant has a complete database based on Friedberg's *Paper Money of the United States,* 16th Edition. This database includes all U.S. Paper Money, including Confederate notes and Encased postage stamps. A relationship with CDN, publisher of the Greensheet, makes value information available to the paper money collector in electronic format.

For collectors of ancient coins, Carlisle offers an add-on database containing color images of several hundred ancient coins and a specialized interface containing data entry fields appropriate for ancient coins. For example, the date field can handle and sort mixed AD/BC dates and has long fields for obverse and reverse inscriptions. The most recent additions to Carlisle Development's databases include the Euro Coin Database and World Currency Database.

REPORT GENERATION

Once you have entered your coin collection into an inventory program, the most important function will become its ability to generate a wide array of reports and/or exports for informational purposes.

You will probably want to have a detailed listing, identifying items, their value, and where they are stored for insurance purposes. You will want to generate partial lists of your collections for sales and trading. You may want to generate labels to aide in identifying your coins. You may want to look at your collection in many different ways such as sorted by value or metal content or collection completeness.

One common need of coin collectors is the printing of inserts for 2" flips. Once catalogued, computer software can allow you to produce customized flip inserts in a standard format of your own design.

Report generation is the subset of an inventory program

which produces the listings that you view on the screen, print on paper, or export to other computer applications. Its flexibility will greatly impact its utility. For example, you may want to generate two listings of coins that you have for sale, one which includes your cost and target price (your copy), and one which does not include this information for general distribution to prospective buyers.

At various times, you will probably want to be able to list any subset of the information fields, filter based on a wide array of parameters and sort using different criteria.

OTHER FUNCTIONALITY YOU SHOULD EXPECT FROM YOUR INVENTORY SOFTWARE

Inventory software should be able to store all of the information in which a collector is interested. Specific fields will vary based on collector interest and purpose. Some will require detailed certification and descriptive information, others comprehensive purchase and sales history. Some collectors will want to have comprehensive recording of storage location and insurance information. Modern programs provide sufficient information fields to meet all of these needs.

Backup and restore functionality should allow the user to easily protect the data they have meticulously entered. History charting enables the user to track the changes of value of a part of their collection over time.

Good software must be easy to use and supported by context sensitive help which provides the user with detailed instructions in a "how-to" format on all of the basic functions that they will wish to perform.

AVAILABILITY OF TIMELY UPDATES

Once you have taken the time to catalog your collection in a computer program, you will want to preserve your investment by having access to database updates incorporating information on new coin releases as well as changes in value. Your supplier of inventory software should have a timely program for availability of annual database and value updates.

INVENTORY SOFTWARE FOR INHERITORS OF COIN COLLECTIONS

The inheritor is usually faced with a daunting task, often having to sort a large number of coins and then decide on their disposition. Often this task is undertaken with little knowledge of coin collecting.

One of the first challenges faced by someone who inherits a collection is the identification of the coins that they have received. Modern inventory programs typically incorporate a comprehensive picture catalog enabling visual identification. Once identified, tables of values assist the heir in deciding which coins may have substantial value and should be analyzed closely and which coins are relatively commonplace and not sufficiently valuable to warrant a significant allocation of time.

Once the coins are divided, time can be focused on the coins with greatest potential value and the remainder quickly sold at a fair price.

Educational computer software can be of particular value to the inheritor, who must build his knowledge of coin collecting in a very short period of time.

EDUCATIONAL SOFTWARE FOR COLLECTORS

Adding significantly to your enjoyment of collections are electronic information sources that exploit the power of the computer to present you with high quality information in an easily accessible format. These programs can provide comprehensive knowledge of all aspects of coin collecting, detailed information on grading coins, and specialized information such as collecting coin varieties.

COIN GRADING

Most coin collectors will want to be able to grade their coins, at least to an approximate grade. This enables them to have an understanding of value as well as identify coins that might be appropriate for certification. Coin grading skill is built up through time and experience.

The Grading Assistant, offered by Carlisle Development is based on the official Grading Guide of the American Numismatic

Association. It enables the user to view side-by-side images of their own coins along with various grades from the ANA grading set. These images are supported by detailed descriptions of the wear points for each grade. Using software such as the Grading Assistant, a user can develop their skill in grading coins and establish approximate grades for their collection.

VARIETY COLLECTING

The collecting of coin varieties is an exciting area of the hobby currently experiencing some growth. Varieties are the result of differences in the minting process or dies which produce design differences and/or errors. These include such effects as doubling of some features or letters, extra pieces of metal on the coin surface and die breaks. Variety collecting requires the collector to identify subtle differences in coin designs.

The Morgan dollar series is one of the most commonly collected and is categorized by many varieties. Carlisle Development offers a Top 100 Morgan Dollar CD, based on the book written by Michael Fey and Jeff Oxman. This work provides pictures, identification information, and values for the most sought after and valuable Morgan dollar varieties. It provides a spectacular set of high quality pictures to assist you in identifying these coins and also the full text and information provided in this work.

GENERAL EDUCATIONAL WORKS ON COLLECTING

There is much to learn about coin collecting, whether it is technical knowledge such as grading and authentication or practical knowledge such as buying and selling coins, attending trade shows, or participating in auctions. Educational computer software offers advantages over printed works in that the contents may be searched and indexed allowing the user to rapidly retrieve valuable information.

Carlisle Development offers the *Coin Collector's Survival Manual,* an interactive edition of the work by Scott Travers. This work provides a set of information that every collector of coins should have. The entire contents of this book are provided in a searchable, interactive format. This allows the user to easily locate information based on word searching, topics, illustrations, bookmarks, a table of contents, or index. In addition to the contents of the book, a set of high quality NGC PhotoProof images have been included for such topics as identifying MS-63, MS-65, and MS-67 coins and toning. An interactive grading calculator brings to life the grading methods described in the book.

WELL DESIGNED COMPUTER SOFTWARE WILL ADD TO YOUR ENJOYMENT OF COLLECTING

Carlisle Development Corporation publishes the most comprehensive line of collector software available, especially regarding coins and paper money.

Central to Carlisle's product line is the Collector's Assistant, the most advanced and comprehensive collection software available. It is sold in a variety of configurations to serve collectors of over thirty collectible types from autographs to toys. Most extensive is support for coins and paper money. The Collector's Assistant family includes:

- **United States Coin Database** - complete listings of all U.S. coinage from 1793 to the present. 50 State quarter program and Sacagawea dollar are recent additions. This also includes Colonial and Hawaiian coinage.
- **World Coin Database** - A listing of over 5000 coin types from over forty-five countries, which may be extended by the user.
- **Ancient Coin Database** - includes several thousand listings of Byzantine, Judaic, Roman, and Greek coinage along with several hundred images. Data entry screens are optimized for ancient coin collectors including long fields for inscriptions and preloaded choice lists of rulers, ancient denominations, towns, mints and others.
- **United States Currency Database** - A complete listing of all United States currency based on Friedberg's 16th Edition, *Paper Money of the United States*. This also includes 120 high quality color images of early US currency.

To learn more about Carlisle Development's product line, visit our website at www.carlisledevelopment.com. You will find current product information and may also place orders. You can reach us by e-mail at support@carlisledevelopment.com or by phone at 800-219-0257.

COLLECTING ORGANIZATIONS

PROFESSIONAL CURRENCY DEALERS ASSOCIATION (PCDA)

Looking for a reliable paper money dealer? . . . Collecting rare paper money can be an enjoyable hobby. Imagine being able to own an example of fractional currency printed during the Civil War era, or a National Bank Note issued by a financial institution in your own state.

Whatever your collecting interests, the members of the Professional Currency Dealers Association (PCDA) will be pleased to assist and guide you. The members of this prestigious trade association specialize in virtually all the areas of paper money collecting.

Once you've started to collect, it can sometimes be a challenge to locate a dealer with a significant inventory. Members of the PCDA are the market makers for currency collectors. Whatever your interest, a PCDA member is certain to be able to supply you. Whether you are a beginner on a limited budget or an advanced collector of many years' experience, you can be certain that you'll find fair, courteous, and reliable treatment with a member of the Professional Currency Dealers Association.

CONTACT INFORMATION

General Information and Correspondence

James A. Simek
PCDA Secretary
P.O. Box 7157
Westchester, IL 60154
(630) 889-8207
E-mail: nge3@attbi.com

PCDA Publication

Ron Horstman
PCDA
P.O. Box 2999
Leslie, MO 63056

Webmaster

Gary Whitelock
whiteloc@ktb.net
(818) 506-6930
E-mail: whiteloc@ktb.net

THE SOCIETY OF PAPER MONEY COLLECTORS (SPMC)

The Society of Paper Money Collectors (SPMC) invites you to become a member of our organization. SPMC was founded in 1961 with the following objectives: (1) Encourage the collecting and study of all paper money and financial documents; (2) Provide collectors the opportunity to meet and enjoy fraternal relations with their fellow collectors; (3) Furnish information and knowledge about paper money; (4) Encourage research about paper money and financial documents and publish the resulting information; (5) Promote legislation favorable to collectors; (6) Advance the prestige of the hobby of numismatics; (7) Promote rational and consistent classification of exhibits, and ENCOURAGE participation by our members; (8) Encourage realistic and consistent market valuations.

Paper Money, SPMC's bimonthly journal now in its 36th year, has repeatedly been selected by the ANA as the Best Specialty Publication in numismatics; the Numismatic Literary Guild has also selected *Paper Money* for first-place recognition. Virtually every article in every issue is written by an SPMC member, who receives no monetary compensation. SPMC coordinates and judges the exhibits at the largest all-paper show every year. SPMC co-sponsors many large all-paper shows held in the U.S. each year.

Information about membership may be obtained by writing to:

Frank Clark
P.O. Box 117060
Carrollton, TX 75011

PCDA MEMBERSHIP DIRECTORY

Rick Allard
Cashmans Currency
3453 Green Pine Place
Simi Valley, CA 93065
(805) 579-0339
Cellular: (805) 279-1641
FAX: (805) 579-0339
E-Mail: cashmanscurrency@aol.com

United States Large Size Type Notes
United States Small Size Type Notes
Fancy and Low Serial Numbers Notes
Error Notes

Robert Azpiazu
First City Currency & Collectibles, Inc.
P.O. Drawer 1629
St. Augustine, FL 32085
(904) 794-0784
Fax: (904) 824-1018
Web Site: www.fstctycurr.com
E-mail: fstctycurr@aug.com

United States Small Size Type Notes
Star Notes
Error Notes
Fancy and Low Serial Number Notes
FRN Blocks
Auction Representation
Estate Appraisals

Richard J. Balbaton
Doric Coins & Currency
Doric Publishing Co., Ltd.
P.O. Box 911
North Attleboro, MA 02761-0911
(508) 699-2266
Fax: (508) 643-1154
E-mail: rabalbaton@aol.com
Colonial And Continental
United States Fractional
United States Large Size Type Notes
United States Small Size Type Notes
Confederate
Obsolete Notes
United States National Bank Notes
Books and Supplies
Military Payment Certificates
World Paper Money
Mail Order Price Lists
Publisher of the Phoenix Currency Album Pages

Pat Barnes
Pat Barnes Paper Money
P.O. Box 25114
Lansing, MI 48909
(517) 333-9980
Fax: (517) 333-9982
E-mail: patbarnes@voyager.net

United States Large Size Type Notes
United States National Bank Notes
United States Small Size Notes - By Type and Variety

Doris Bart
Bart, Inc.
P.O. Box 2
Roseville, MI 48066
(586) 979-3400
Fax: (586) 979-7976
Web Site: www.ErrorNotes.com
E-mail: *bartinccor@aol.com*

Auction Representation
Rare United States Small Size Notes
United States Large Size Type Notes

Error Notes
Autographed Notes

Frederick J. Bart
Bart, Inc.
P.O. Box 2
Roseville, MI 48066
(586) 979-3400
Fax: (586) 979-7976
Web Site: www.ErrorNotes.com
E-mail: bartinccor@aol.com

Error Notes
Serial #1 National Bank Notes
Uncut Sheets
Rare Small Size Notes
Large Size Type Notes

Keith S. Bauman
TNA Associates
P.O. Box 250027
Franklin, MI 48025-0027
(248) 647-8938
E-mail: TNAksbauman@earthlink.net

United States Large Size Type Notes
United States Small Size Type Notes
United States Fractional Currency
United States Military Payment Certificates
Confederate
World Paper Money
Numismatic Related Art Work

David A. Berg
Dave Berg, Ltd.
P.O. Box 348
Portersville, PA 16051
(724) 452-4586
Fax: (724) 452-0276
E-mail: davbergltd@aol.com

Error Notes
Mail Order Price Lists
United States Fractional Currency
United States Large Size Type Notes
United States National Bank Notes
United States Small Size Type Notes

Carl Bombara
P.O. Box 524
New York, NY 10116
(212) 989-9108
(888) 449-9268
Fax: (212) 989-9108
E-mail: CBcurrency@aol.com

United States Large Size Type Notes
United States Small Size Type Notes
United States National Bank Notes
Error Notes
Mail Order Sales
Auction Representation
Want Lists Serviced

Q. David Bowers
P.O. Box 539
Wolfeboro, NH 03896-0539
E-mail: qdbarchive@metrocast.net

United States Currency
Celebrating 50 years in professional numismatics 1953-2003
Past president Professional Numismatists Guild (1977-1979)
Past president American Numismatic Association (1983-1995)

Jennifer Cangeme
Denly's of Boston
P.O. Box 51010
Boston, MA 02205
(617) 482-8477
(800) HI DENLY (Orders Only)
Fax: (617) 357-8163
Web Site: www.denlys.com
E-mail: jen@denlys.com

Colonial and Continental
United States Fractional Currency
United States Large Size Type Notes
United States Small Size Type Notes
Confederate
Obsolete Notes
United States National Bank Notes
Error Notes
Books and Supplies
Military Payment Certificates
World Paper Money
Auction Sales - Bidder Representative
Mail Order Price Lists
Encased Postage
Mylar D† Currency Holders
United States & Foreign Coins

I. Nelson Clark
I. Nelson Clark Banknotes
P.O. Box 883
Los Alamitos, CA 90720
(714) 761-3683
Cell: (714) 809-5120
Fax: (714) 761-3683
E-mail: inellclark@attbi.com

United States Currency
United States National Bank Notes

Arthur D. Cohen
Penfield Note Exchange
P.O. Box 311
Penfield, NY 14526-0311
(585) 377-4677
Fax: (585) 377-4677
E-mail: adcohen@frontiernet.net

World Paper Money
Mail Order Price Lists
Custom Labels For Currency Holders,
Flips and Slabs

Terry Coyle
Alex Perakis Coins & Currency
P.O. Box 246
Lima, PA 19037
(610) 627-1212
Fax: (610) 891-1466

United States National Bank Notes
United States Large Size Type Notes
United States Small Size Type Notes

Paul Cuccia
C $ H Coins & Collectibles, Inc.
P.O. Box 326
Belvidere, NJ 07823
(908) 475-1026

United States Large Size Type Notes
United States Small Size Type Notes
Obsolete Notes
United States National Bank Notes
Error Notes
Small Size Stars

Pat Cyrgalis
A.P. Cyrgalis Currency
P.O. Box 141235
Staten Island, NY 10314-0008
(718) 448-7615
Fax: (718) 448-7615
E-mail: apcyrgalis@att.net

United States Large Size Type Notes
United States Small Size Type Notes
United States National Bank Notes

John DeMaris
P.O. Box 72
Boys Town, NE 68010
(402) 334-2756
E-mail: siramed@aol.com

Colonial and Continental
United States Fractional Currency
United States Large Size Type Notes
United States Small Size Type Notes
Confederate
Obsolete Notes
United States National Bank Notes

Thomas M. Denly
Denly's of Boston
P.O. Box 51010
Boston, MA 02205
(617) 482-8477
(800) HI DENLY (Orders Only)
Fax: (617) 357-8163
Web Site: www.denlys.com
E-mail: denlys@aol.com

Colonial and Continental
United States Fractional Currency
United States Large Size Type Notes
United States Small Size Type Notes
Confederate
Obsolete Notes
United States National Bank Notes
Error Notes
Books and Supplies
Military Payment Certificates
World Paper Money
Auction Sales - Bidder Representative
Mail Order Price Lists
Encased Postage
Mylar D† Currency Holders
United States & Foreign Coins

Tom Durkin
P.O. Box 328
Walland, TN 37886
(865) 448-3290
E-mail: tdurkin@bellsouth.net

United States Large Size Type Notes
United States Small Size Type Notes
Confederate
Obsolete Notes
United States National Bank Notes

Lawrence Falater
P.O. Box 81
Allen, MI 49227
(517) 437-8977
(888) FALTER (Toll Free)
Fax: (517) 437-8978

Stock and Bonds
Obsolete Notes
United States National Bank Notes
United States Currency - All Kinds Including Errors
Confederate
Colonial and Continental
World Paper Money

Specialized Price Lists
Books on Paper Money and Stocks
Specialist: Michigan Paper; Stocks; Automobile,
Aviation, Banking, and Beverages

Don Fisher
Currency Unlimited
P.O. Box 481
Decatur, IL 62525
(217) 692-2825
Fax: (217) 692-2825

Obsolete Notes
United States National Bank Notes
World Paper Money

Tom Flynn
801 Kerper Court
Dubuque, IA 52001
(563) 583-6494
Fax: (563) 583-7453
E-mail: flynngroup@aol.com

United States Small Size Type Notes
Federal Reserve Notes
Auction Representation

Kevin Foley
Currency Auctions of America. Inc.
P.O. Box 370650
Milwaukee, WI 53237
(414) 421-3498
(800) USCOINS, ext. 256
Fax: (414) 423-0343

Auction Sales
Auction Representation
Internet Sales
Colonial and Continental Notes
Confederate Notes
Error Notes
Low and Fancy Serial Numbers
Obsolete Notes
Serial #1 Notes
United States Fractional Currency
United States Large Size Type Notes
United States National Bank Notes
United States Small Size Type Notes
Numismatic Conventions and Show Management

Dennis Forgue
Harlan J. Berk, Ltd.
31 North Clark Street
Chicago, IL 60602
(312) 609-0016
Fax: (312) 609-1305
Web Site: www.harlanjberk.com

United States Large Size Type Notes
United States Small Size Type Notes
Confederate
Obsolete Notes
United States National Bank Notes
Error Notes
Autographs

Stephen Goldsmith
R.M. Smythe & Co., Inc.
26 Broadway, Suite 972
New York, NY 10004-1703
(212) 943-1880
(800) 622-1880
Fax: (212) 908-4670
E-mail: sgoldsmith@smytheonline.com

Auction Sales
Autographs
Colonial and Continental
Confederate
Financial Documents
Mail Order Sales
Mail Order Price Lists
Obsolete Notes
Stocks, Bonds and Fiscal Documents
United States Fractional Currency
United States Large Size Type Notes
United States Small Size Type Notes
United States National Bank Notes
World Paper Money

Bruce R. Hagen
P.O. Box 836
Bowling Green Station
New York, NY 10274-0836
(212) 721-2028

Appraisals
Auction Representation
Colonial and Continental
Consulting Services
Financial Documents
Obsolete Notes and Proofs
United States Federal Proofs, Essays & Vignettes
Stocks, Bonds and Fiscal Documents
Security Printing Archives, Histories & Artifacts
United States National Bank Notes
World Paper Money

Larry Hanks
Hanks & Associates
415 North Mesa
El Paso, TX 79901
(915) 544-8188
Fax: (915) 544-8194

United States Large Size Type Notes
United States Small Size Type Notes
United States National Bank Notes

Quintin H. Hartt
Red River Rarities
P.O. Box 12444
Alexandria, LA 71315
(318) 443-4405
(800) 314-4405
Fax: (318) 484-3939

United States Large Size Type Notes
United States Small Size Type Notes
World Paper Money

James R. Hatch
P.O. Box 978
Londonderry, NH 03053-0978
(603) 434-3635
Web Site: www.frn-ones.com
E-mail:jim61@frn-ones.com

Specializing in High Grade $1 FRN's

Joe L. Hensley
Char's Paper
P.O. Box 234
Madison, IN 47250
(812) 273-1683

United States Large Size Type Notes
United States National Bank Notes

Roland Hill
Rare Choice Currency
P.O. Box 6426
Fort Myers, FL 33911
(239) 549-7267
E-mail: Hillco@aaacoll.com

United States Large Size Type Notes
United States Small Size Type Notes
United States National Bank Notes
United States Fractional Currency
Obsolete Notes
Colonial and Continental
Confederate
Civil War Photos
Rare Autographs
Canadian
Western Americana
Early Railroad
Star Notes
F.R.N. Red Seals

Gregg Hoffman
Premier Precious Metals Coins & Currency
P.O. Box 28100
Santa Fe, NM 87592-8100
(505) 989-7680
(800) 557-9958
Fax: (505) 989-7685
Web Site: www.premierprecious metals.com
E-mail: cindy@premierprecious metals.com

United States Large Size Type Notes
United States Small Size Type Notes
Silver Dollars
Bust Type Silver Dollars
Older Type Coin

Honorary Life Member
Ronald Horstman
P.O. Box 2999
Leslie, MO 63056
(573) 764-4139

St. Louis National Bank Notes
St. Louis Obsolete Notes
St. Louis Checks
St. Louis Merchants and Bank Tokens

Lowell C. Horwedel
P.O. Box 2395
West Lafayette, IN 47996
(765) 583-2748
Fax: (765 583-4584
Web Site: www.horwedelscurrency.com
E-mail: lhorwedel@insightbb.com

United States National Bank Notes
Colonial and Continental
United States Large Size Type Notes
United States Small Size Type Notes
Confederate
Obsolete Notes
Error Notes
Checks
Books and Supplies
World Paper Money
Mail Order Price Lists

Steve Ivy
Heritage / CAA
100 Highland Park Village
Dallas, TX 75205
(214) 528-3500
(800) 872-6467
Fax: (214) 448-8409
Web Site: www.heritagecion.com
E-mail: steve@heritagecoin.com

Auction Sales of:
United States Large Size Type Notes
United States Small Size Type Notes
United States National Bank Notes
United States Fractional Currency
Error Notes
Colonial and Continental
Confederate
Obsolete Notes

Peter Johnson
Staples Numismatics, Inc.
P.O. Box 541255
Lake Worth, FL 33454-1255
(561) 383-6631
Fax: (561) 383-6621
E-mail: staplescoin@earthlink.net

World Paper money
United States Large Size Type Notes
United States Small Size Type Notes

Harry E. Jones
Harry E. Jones Rare Currency
7379 Pearl Road
Cleveland, OH 44130
(440) 234-3330
Fax: (440) 234-3332
E-mail: hjones6671@aol.com

Error Notes
United States Large Size Type Notes
United States Small Size Type Notes
United States National Bank Notes
Obsolete Notes
Serial #1 Notes
Uncut Sheets

Jeffrey S. Jones
The Small Size Shop
P.O. Box 2007
Westerville, OH 43086
(614) 899-1803
Fax: (614) 899-1557
E-mail: jeff.jones@gnorth.com

United States Small Size Type Notes
Especially High Grade and Rare
Ohio National Bank Notes
Ohio Obsolete Notes

Glen I. Jorde
Lake Region Coin & Currency Exchange
323 Fourth Street
P.O. Box 48
Devils Lake, ND 58301
(701) 662-5770
(800) 803-2322
Fax: (701) 662-5775
E-mail: lrcc@stellarnet.com

United States Large Size Type Notes
United States Small Size Type Notes
United States National Bank Notes
Confederate
Obsolete Notes
Checks
Mail Order Price Lists

A.M. "Art" Kagin
A.M. Kagin, NEWCO, Inc.
505 Fifth Avenue, Suite 1001
Des Moines, IA 50309
(515) 243-7363
Fax: (515) 288-8681

United States National Bank Notes
United States Large Size Type Notes and Varieties
Handled over 95% of U.S. Notes in Friedberg
United States Small Size Type Notes and Varieties
Error Notes
Rarities - Gem to VF
Star Notes - Large and Small
Uncut Sheets - Large and Small
Encased Postage
Odd and Unusual Serial Number Notes

Donald H. Kagin
Kagin's
98 Main Street, Suite 201
Tiburon, CA 94920
(415) 435-1627
(888) 8KAGINS
Fax: (415) 435-1627
E-mail: kagins@earthlink.net

Gem United States Type Notes
United States Fractional Currency

Judith Kagin
Kagin's
98 Main Street, Suite 201
Tiburon, CA 94920
(415) 435-1627
(888) 8KAGINS
Fax: (415) 435-1627
E-mail: kagins@earthlink.net

High Quality and Rare United States Paper Money
Mail Order Sales

Allen Karn
Allen's Coin Shop
399 South State Street
Westerville, OH 43081
(614) 882-3937
(800) 848-3966
Fax: (614) 882-0662
Web Site: www.allensinc.com/coins

Colonial and Continental
United States Large Size Type Notes
United States Small Size Type Notes
Confederate
Obsolete Notes
United States National Bank Notes
Books and Supplies
Military Payment Certificates
World Paper Money
United States Fractional Currency
Mail Order Price Lists

Don C. Kelly
Paper Money Institute
P.O. Box 85
Oxford, OH 45056
(513) 312-4760
Web Site: www.donckelly.com
E-mail: don@donckelly.com

United States Paper Money
Colonial and Continental
Obsolete Notes
United States National Bank Notes

Lyn F. Knight
Lyn Knight Currency Auctions
P.O. Box 7364
Overland Park, KS 66207-0364
(913) 338-3779
(800) 243-5211
Fax: (913) 338-4754
Web Site: www.collectors.com/lynknight/
E-mail: lynfknight@aol.com

Auction Sales for National Conventions
United States Large Size Type Notes
United States National Bank Notes
United States Small Size Type Notes
United States Fractional Currency
Mail Bid Sales

David R. Koble
Mid America Currency
P.O. Box 1282
Bartlesville, OK 74005
(918) 335-0847
Cellular: (918) 914-1496
Fax: (918) 335-3110
E-mail: dkoble@cableone.net

United States Large Size Type Notes
United States Small Size Type Notes
United States National Bank Notes
United States Fractional Currency
Error Notes
Auction Representation

Paul L. Koppenhaver
Thalpa, Inc. / The Coin Haven
P.O. Box 34056
Granada Hills, CA 91394
(818) 832-8068
Fax: (818) 832-8987
E-mail: plkopp@as.net

United States Large Size Type Notes
United States Small Size Type Notes
United States National Currency
Sutler Scrip
Western Americana
Autographs
Exonumia

Robert J. Kravitz
Rob's Coins & Currency
P.O. Box 303
Wilton, CA 95693
(916) 687-7219
E-mail: robsfractional@aol.com

Specialist: United States Fractional Currency
All United States Currency
United States Large and Small Size Gold Certificates
Error Notes
Colonial and Continental Currency

Tim Kyzivat
P.O. Box 451
Western Springs, IL 60558
(708) 784-0974
Web Site: www.kyzivatcurrency.com
E-mail: tkyzivat@kyzivatcurrency.com

Chicago Area National Bank Notes
Illinois National Bank Notes
United States Large Size Type Notes
United States National Bank Notes
United States Small Size Type Notes
Confederate Currency
Obsolete Notes
Error Notes

Jay Laws
Scotsman Coins
11262 Olive Blvd.
St. Louis, MO 63141
(314) 692-2646
(800) 642-4305
Fax: (314) 692-0410

United States National Bank Notes
United States Large Size Type Notes
United States Small Size Type Notes
Confederate Currency
Military Payment Certificates

Stuart Levine
P.O. Box 217
Sudbury, MA
(978) 443-9070
E-Mail: smlevine@ix.netcom.com

Colonial and Continental Currency

Scott Lindquist
R.M. Smythe & Co., Inc.
26 Broadway, Suite 973
New York, NY 10004-1703
(212) 943-1880, ext. 4677
(800) 622-1880
Cellular: (602) 741-3385
Fax: (212) 908-4670
E-mail: slindquist@smytheonline.com

United States and Canadian
Currency - Large and Small
Canadian Charter Bank Notes
World Paper Money
Colonial and Continental
United States Fractional Currency
Confederate
Obsolete Notes
United States National Bank Notes
Error Notes
Books and Supplies
Military Payment Certificates
Auction Sales - Bidder
Representative

Dana Linett
Early American Numismatics
P.O. Box 675390
Rancho Santa Fe, CA 92067
Early American History Auctions, Inc.
P.O. Box 3507
Rancho Santa Fe, CA 92067
(858) 759-3290
Fax: (619) 374-7280
Web Site: www.earlyamerican.com
E-mail: dana@earlyamerican.com

Colonial and Continental
United States Fractional Currency
United States Large Size Type Notes
United States Small Size Type Notes
Confederate
Stocks, Bonds and fiscal Documents
Checks
Books and Supplies
Auction Sales
Mail Order Price Lists
Mail Bid Sales
Encased Postage Stamps
Historic Maps
Rare Autographs

Jess Lipka
Numismania
P.O. Box 847
Flemington, NJ 08822
(908) 782-1635
Cellular: (908) 500-1885
Fax: (908) 782-6235

United States National Bank Notes
United States Large Size Type Notes
United States Small Size Type Notes
Rare Coins

William Litt
William Litt Rare Coins & Currency
P.O. Box 6778
San Mateo, CA 94403
(650) 458-8842
Fax: (650) 458-8843
E-mail: billlitt@aol.com

United States National Bank Notes
United States Large Size Type Notes
National Bank Memorabilia

Claire Lobel
Coincraft
44 & 45 Great Russell Street
London WC1B 3LU
ENGLAND
(44) 20 7636 1188
Fax: (44) 20 7323 2860
E-mail: clairlob@aol.com

England, Scotland, Ireland, Channel
Islands, Isle of Man
General World

Ray Marrello
Antique Currency LLC
P.O. Box 807
Mundelein, IL 60060
(847) 566-2620

Fax: (847) 566-2620
Web Site: www.rmcurrency.com
E-mail: rmcurrency@aol.com

United States Large Size Type Notes
United States Small Size Type Notes
United States National Bank Notes

David V. Messner
Constellation Numismatics
P.O. Box 209
Akron, OH 17501-0209
(717) 721-9504

Error Notes
Colonial and Continental
United States Error and Die Variety Coins

James W. Miller
Deuceman Currency . com
P.O. Box 2452
Statesboro, GA 30458
(912) 284-1586
Cellular: (912) 614-4980
Web Site: www.deucemancurrency.com
E-mail: jwmiller11@aol.com

Obsolete Notes
Confederate
Colonial and Continental
United States National Currency
United States Large Size Type Notes
United States Small Size Type Notes
Internet Auction Sales
Auction Bidder Representation

Thomas J. Modzelesky, Jr.
Gemini Coin
P.O. Box 344
Suffield, CT 06078
(860) 668-2838
Fax: (860) 668-2838
E-mail: Geminicoin@aol.com

United States National Currency
United States Large Size Type Notes
United States Small Size Type Notes

Charles D. Moore
Charles D. Moore, Inc.
P.O. Box 5233
Walnut Creek, CA 94596
(925) 946-0150
Fax: (925) 930-7710

Auction Sales
Mail Bid Sales
Canadian and Related Paper Money
Canadian Cheques
Canadian Fiscal Documents

Stanley Morycz
P.O. Box 355
Englewood, OH 45322
(937) 898-0114

United States Large Size Type Notes

V.H."Ossie" Oswald, Sr.
Ossie's Coin Shop
June to December
P.O. Box 304
Emmaus, PA 18049
(610) 965-9485
(610) 433-4474
Fax: (610) 967-5852
January to June
P.O. Box 810423
Boca Raton, FL 33498
(561) 483-9626
Fax: (561) 483-8390

United States Large Size Type Notes
United States Small Size Type Notes
United States National Bank Notes
Error Notes
Confederate
Better Broken Bank Notes
Mail Order Price Lists
Please Send Want Lists

Thomas N. Panichella
Stack's
123 West 57th Street
New York, NY 10019
(212) 582-2580
Fax: (212) 245-5018

Auction Sales
Appraisals
United States Currency of All Types
United States Coins of All Type
World Coins and Paper Money

Charles C. Parrish
P.O. Box 481
Rosemount. MN 55068
(651) 423-1039

United States Large Size Type Notes
United States Small Size Type Notes
United States National Bank Notes
Obsolete Notes
All Minnesota Nationals

Huston Pearson, Jr.
P.O. Box 13559
Arlington, TX 76094-3559
(817) 274-5971

United States Large Size Type Notes
United States Small Size Type Notes
Republic of Texas Notes
Texas National Bank Notes
United States Fractional Currency
Colonial and Continental Currency
Confederate
Military Payment Certificates
Obsolete Notes
Books and Supplies

Alex G. Perakis
Alex Perakis Coins & Currency
P.O. Box 246
Lima, PA 19037
(610) 627-1212
(610) 565-1110
Fax: (610) 891-1466
and
12941 North Pioneer Way
Tucson, AZ 85737
(520) 544-7778
Fax: (520) 544-7779
E-mail: alperakis@aol.com

United States Fractional Currency
United States Large Size Type Notes
United States Small Size Type Notes
United States National Bank Notes
United States Obsolete Notes

Stephen Perakis
Alex Perakis Coins & Currency
P.O. Box 246
Lima, PA 19037
(610) 627-1212
(610) 565-1110
Fax: (610) 891-1466

United States Fractional Currency
United States Large Size Type Notes
United States Small Size Type Notes
United States National Bank Notes

Earl N. Petersen
USA Coins
419 Nebraska Street
Sioux City, IA 51101
(712) 252-9876
(800) 872-2660
Fax: (712) 252-6130
E-mail: usaco@pionet.net

Iowa and Nebraska National Bank Notes
All Midwest National Bank Notes

James Polis
4501 Connecticut Avenue, N.W.
Suite 306
Washington, DC 20008
(202) 363-6650
Fax: (202) 363-4712
E-mail: jpolis7935@aol.com

Colonial and Continental
United States Fractional Currency
United States Large Size Type Notes
United States Small Size Type Notes
Confederate and Southern States Currency
Confederate Bonds
Mail Order Price List

Richard H. Ponterio
Ponterio & Associates, Inc.
1818 Robinson Avenue
San Diego, CA 92103
(619) 299-0400
(800) 854-2888
Fax: (619) 299-6952

World Paper Money
Mexican Paper Money
Auction Sales
Mail Bid Sales

Vern Potter
Vern Potter Rare Fiscal Documents
P.O. Box 10040
Torrance, CA 90505-0740
(310) 326-0406
Fax: (310) 326-0406
E-mail: VernPotter@aol.com

United States Large Size Type Notes
Obsoletes Notes
Confederate Currency
Gold Rush and Civil War Documents
Historic Maps
Western Americana and Paper Ephemera
Stocks, Bonds, Checks and Fiscal Documents
Western Express and Postal History
Mining and Railroad Certificates and Documents

Lou Rasera
Southland Coins & Currency
P.O. Box 403

Woodland Hills, CA 91365
(818) 348-5275
Fax: (818) 348-5275
E-mail: ljrasera@aol.com

United States Large Size Type Notes
United States Small Size Type Notes
United States National Bank Notes
Confederate
Error Notes
Professional Auction Representation

Kent Robertson
U.S. Currency
P.O. Box 631250
Irving, TX 75063
(404) 229-7184

United States Large Size Type Notes
United States Small Size Type Notes
Obsolete Notes
Confederate Notes
Confederate Bonds
Political Memorabilia
Auction Representation

Edward M. Rothberg
Emporium Coin & Currency
P.O. Box 606
Moorhead, MN 56560
(800) 248-9751

United States National Bank Notes
United States Fractional Currency
Colonial and Continental
Errors
Obsoletes Notes
Canadian Currency
United States Coins

John N. Rowe III
Southwest Numismatic Corp.
6301 Gaston Avenue, Suite 650
Dallas, TX 75214
(214) 826-3036
Fax: (214) 823-1923

United States Large Size Type Notes
United States Small Size Type Notes
Confederate
Obsolete Notes
United States National Bank Notes
Republic of Texas

O.E. "Dusty" Royer
Notes of Note
34 Lake Charles
St. Peters, MO 63376
(636) 441-0481
Web Site: www.geocities.com/dusty
royer
E-Mail: dustyIB@netscape.net

World Currency
German Notgeld
Military Items

Bob Rozycki
Sycamore Coin Gallery
320 West State Street
Sycamore, IL 60178
(815) 895-6669
E-mail: sycamorecoin@tbcnet.com

United States Large Size Type Notes
United States Small Size Type Notes
United States National Bank Notes

Gaylen Rust
Rust Rare Coin Co.
252 East 300 South
Salt Lake City, UT 84111
(801) 363-4014
(800) 343-7878
Fax: (801) 364-0929
Web Site: www.rustcoin.com
E-mail: grust@rustcoin.com

Mormon and Related Items
Utah and Intermountain Area Notes

Sergio Sanchez, Jr.
Sergio Sanchez, Jr. Currency
P.O. Box 44-1490
Miami, FL 33144-1490
(305) 567-1515

United States Large Size Type Notes
United States Small Size Type Notes

Joe Sande
Joe Sande - Professional Numismatist
P.O. Box 211
Nichols, FL 33863-0211
(863) 607-6337
Fax: (863) 607-6337

United States Large Size Type Notes
United States Small Size Type Notes
United States National Bank Notes
United States Fractional Currency
Mail Bid Sales

Jim Sazama
Jim Sazama, Inc.
P.O. Box 1235
Southern Pines, NC 28388

(910) 692-9357
Fax: (910) 692-9357
Web Site: www.jimsazama.com
E-mail: jimsazamainc@pinhurst.net

United States Large Size Type Notes
United States Small Size Type Notes
United States National Bank Notes
Obsolete Notes
Confederate

George Schweighofer
Currency Quest
P.O. Box 384
Reynoldsberg, OH 43068
(614) 864-8875
E-mail: currencyquest@aol.com

All United States Currency

Joel Shafer
P.O. Box 170985
Milwaukee, WI 53217
(414) 228-7351
E-mail: grbaypa@aol.com

World Paper Money

Amanda Sheheen
A & O Auctions
P.O. Box 1711
Camdan, SC 29020
(803) 432-2435
Fax: (803) 713-9048
Web Site: www.AOAuctions.com

Confederate Notes
Obsolete Notes and Scrip
South Carolina National Bank Notes
Colonial and Continentals Notes
United States Fractional Currency
Military Payment Certificates
Books and Supplies
Auction Representative

Austin M. Sheheen, Jr.
P.O. Box 428
Camden, SC 29020
(803) 432-1424
Fax: (803) 432-1831

South Carolina Colonial Notes
South Carolina Obsolete Notes
South Carolina National Bank Notes
Eastman College Scrip

Micky Shipley
Lake Region Coin & Currency Exchange
P.O. Box 48
Devils Lake, ND 58301
(701) 662-5770
(800) 803-2322
Fax: (701) 662-5775
E-mail: lrcc@stellarnet.com

United States National Bank Notes
United States Large Size Type Notes
United States Small Size Type Notes

Hugh Shull
P.O. Box 761
Camden, SC 29020
(803) 432-8500
Fax: (803) 432-9958

Confederate Notes
Obsolete Notes and Scrip
South Carolina National Bank Notes
Colonial and Continentals Notes
United States Fractional Currency
Stocks, Bonds and Fiscal Documents
Mail Order Catalogs
Books and Supplies
Auction Sales - Bidder Representative

James A. Simek
Numisgraphic Enterprises
P.O. Box 7157
Westchester, IL 60154
(630) 889-8207
Fax: (630) 889-1130
E-mail: nge3@attbi.com

United States Large Size Type Notes
United States Small Size Type Notes
United States National Bank Notes
Error Notes
Hawaiian Related Material
Autographs and Documents
Numismatic Photography

James Sorn
Family Coins, Ltd.
12232 South Harlem Avenue
Palos Heights, IL 60463
(708) 923-0100
Fax: (708) 923-0151

United States Large Size Type Notes
United States Small Size Type Notes
United States National Bank Notes
Colonial and Continental
Confederate
Obsolete Notes

David Steckling
Gold-N-Silver Rarities
1615 Division Street

St. Cloud, MN 56301
(302) 259-0233

Minnesota National Bank Notes
Minnesota Obsolete Notes
Obsolete Notes
United States Large Size Type Notes
United States Small Size Type Notes

Mike Storeim
Numismatic Professionals, LLC
2922 Evergrenn Parkway, Suite 203
Evergreen, CO 80439
(303) 670-3212
Cellular: (303) 903-9932
Fax: (303) 670-3216
E-mail: mike@numispro.com

United States Large Size Type Notes
United States Small Size Type Notes
United States National Bank Notes

David M. Sundman
Litttleton Coin Company
1309 Mt. Eustis Road
Littleton, NH 03561-3735
(603) 444-3524
Fax: (603) 444-3512
Web Site: www.littletoncoin.com

United States Large Size Type Notes
United States Small Size Type Notes
United States National Bank Notes
United States Fractional Currency
United States Coins
Fixed Price Lists and Catalogs

Allan L. Teal
P.O. Box 429
Chester Heights, PA 19017
(610) 459-5265
Fax: (610) 459-8821
Sunday at Store 7:30 AM - 4 PM
Renninger's Antique Market
Adamstown, PA
(717) 336-6622

Pennsylvania National Bank Notes
Delaware National Bank Notes
Confederate
Obsolete Notes
United States Large Size Type Notes
United States National Bank Notes

Leon Thornton
P.O. Box 726
Eminence, MO 65466
(573) 226-5536

United States Large Size Type Notes
United States Small Size Type Notes
United States National Bank Notes
Obsolete Notes
Confederate
World Paper Money
Foreign Exchange

Robert L. Vandevender II
American Paper Connection, Inc.
P.O. Box 2816
Joliet, IL 60424-2816
(815) 886-9451
E-mail: rvpaperman@aol.com

United States Large Size Type Notes
United States Small Size Type Notes
United States Fractional Currency
United States National Bank Notes

Frank Viskup
Frank Viskup Collectables
P.O. Box 90122
Dayton, OH 45490
(937) 440-8888
E-mail: fviskup@hotmail.com

United States Large Size Type Notes
United States Small Size Type Notes
Mail Order Price List

George K. Warner
P.O. Box 842
Sheridan, WY 82801
(307) 751-3230

United States Small Size Type Notes
Military Payment Certificates
United States Fractional Currency

Harry Warren
Mid-South Coin Co., Inc.
3894 Park Avenue
Memphis, TN 38111
(901) 324-2244
Fax: (901) 324-2249

United States Large Size Type Notes
United States National Bank Notes

Barry Wexler
Numisvalu
P.O. Box 185
Jamison, NY 18929
(215) 444-0550
Fax: (215) 444-0550
E-mail: nimisvalu@bestweb.net

United States Large Size Type Notes
United States Small Size Type Notes

United States National Bank Notes
Colonial
Confederate
Obsolete Notes
Stocks, Bonds and fiscal Documents
Checks

Louis Whitaker
River Hollow Coins
925 South Mason Road #327
Katy, TX 77450
(281) 829-5097
E-mail: Riverholl@pdq.net

All United States Notes

Harlan White
2425 El Cajon Blvd.
San Diego, CA 92104
(619) 298-0137
Fax: (619) 298-7966

United States High Denomination Notes
United States Paper Money

Gary Whitelock
Whitelock Rare Currency
P.O. Box 6263
Lakewood, CA 90714
(562) 731-0562
Cellular: (562) 673-0794
E-mail: whiteloc@ktb.net

All United States Notes

William Crutchfield Williams II
Crutchfield's Currency
P.O. Box 521
Kemah, TX 77565
(281) 334-3297
Fax: (281) 334-3297
Cellular: (281) 455-2511
Web Site: www.crutchwilliams.com
E-mail: crutchfieldwilliams-csa@worldnet.att.net

Republic of Texas
Confederate States of America
Southern States Currency
Mexican Bancos & Revolutionary Paper Money

Scott Winslow
P.O. Box 10240
Bedford, NH 03110
(603) 641-8292
(800) 225-6233
Fax: (603) 641-5583
Web Site: www.scottwinslow.com

Autographs
Stock, Bonds and Fiscal Documents

John Yasuk
Caribbean Sun Gold
P.O. Box 924533
Princeton, FL 33092-4533
(305) 256-7201

Florida Obsolete Currency
United States Large Size Type Notes
United States Small Size Type Notes

William Youngerman
William Youngerman, Inc.
95 South Federal Highway, Suite 203
Boca Raton, FL 33432
(561) 368- 7707
(800) 327-5010 (Outside Florida)
(800) 826-9713 (Within Florida)
Fax: (561) 394-6084
Web Site: www.williamyoungerman.com
E-mail: wymoney@aol.com

Specialist: United States National Bank Notes
Florida National Bank Notes
Florida Obsolete Notes
United States Large Size Type Notes
United States Small Size Type Notes
United States Fractional Currency
Confederate
Mail Order Price Lists

BUYING PAPER MONEY

Browsing in coin shops is the usual way in which beginners start buying paper money. Just about every coin dealer—and many stamp dealers—stock paper money to one degree or another, from a single display album with elementary material to vaults filled with literally millions of dollars worth of specimens. Be observant of condition when shopping from dealers' stocks. Get to know the dealer and become familiar with his grading practices. Some dealers will grade a specimen higher than another dealer, but this may be offset by the fact that they charge a lower price.

Bargains. Is it possible to get bargains in buying paper money? To the extent that prices vary somewhat from dealer to dealer, yes. But if you're talking about finding a note worth $100 selling at $50, this is unlikely to happen. The dealers are well aware of market values, and the slight price differences that do occur are merely the result of some dealers being overstocked on certain notes or, possibly, having made a very good "buy" from the public. What may appear to be a bargain will generally prove, on closer examination, to be a specimen in undesirable condition, such as a washed bill on which the color has faded.

Auction sales. Many coin auctions feature selections of paper money, and there are occasional sales (mostly of the postal-bid variety) devoted exclusively to it. There is much to be said for auction buying if you have some experience and know how to read an auction catalog.

Shows and conventions. Paper money is offered for sale at every coin show and exposition. These present excellent opportunities to buy, as the dealers exhibiting at such shows are generally out-of-towners whose stock you would not otherwise have a chance to examine. As many sellers are likely to be offering the same type of material, you have the opportunity to make price and condition comparisons before buying.

COLLECTING DO'S AND DON'TS

Paper money is not at all difficult to care for, store, and display attractively.

There is not much question that albums are the favorite storage method of nearly all paper money enthusiasts. Many ills to which paper money falls prey result from not being housed in a suitable album, or any album at all. Framing and mounting present some risk, as the item may then be exposed to long periods of direct sunlight, almost sure to cause fading or "bleaching" of its color.

Faded color. There is no known restorative for faded color.

Holes. It is suggested that no effort be undertaken to repair holes, as this will almost certainly result in a further reduction in value.

Missing corners. Missing corners can seldom be restored in a manner that is totally satisfactory. The best that can be done is to secure some paper of approximately the same color and texture, trim a small piece to the proper size, and glue it in place as described below. If a portion of printed matter is missing, this can be hand-drawn, in ink, after restoration. Obviously, this kind of repair is not carried out to "fool" anybody, but simply to give a damaged specimen a less objectionable appearance.

Repairs to paper money. Repair work on damaged or defaced paper money is carried out strictly for cosmetic purposes; to improve its physical appearance. Repairs, even if skillfully executed, will not enhance the value of a specimen, as it will still be classified as defective. Amateurish repair efforts can very possibly make matters worse.

Tears. Tears can be closed by brushing a very small quantity of clear-drying glue to both sides of the tear, placing the note between sheets of waxed kitchen paper, and setting it under a weight to dry. A dictionary of moderate size serves this function well. Allow plenty of drying time and handle gently thereafter.

Wrinkles. Wrinkles, creases, and the like can sometimes be improved by wetting the note (in plain water) and drying it between sheets of waxed paper beneath a reasonably heavy weight—five pounds or more. This should not be done with a modern or recent specimen if there is danger of losing crispness.

SELLING YOUR COLLECTION

Selling to a dealer. All dealers in paper money buy from the public, but not all buy every collection offered to them. Some are specialists and are interested only in collections within their fields of specialization. Some will not purchase (or even examine) collections worth under $100, or $500, or whatever their line of demarcation happens to be. Obviously, a valuable collection containing many hard-to-get notes in VF or UNC condition is easier to interest a dealer in than a beginner-type collection. If a dealer is interested enough to make an offer, this is no guarantee that another dealer would not offer more. In the case of a collection worth $50,000, offers from several dealers might vary by as much as $5,000. This is not an indication that the dealer making the lowest offer is unscrupulous. Dealers will pay as much as the material is worth to them, and one dealer may be overstocked on items that another badly needs. Or one dealer may have customers for certain material that another doesn't. For this reason it makes good sense, if you choose to sell to a dealer, to obtain several offers before accepting any. But should you sell to a dealer at all? The chief advantage is quick payment and reduced risk. The price may not be as high as would be obtained at auction, however, depending on the property's nature and pure luck.

Selling by auction. Auction selling presents uncertainties but at the same time offers the possibility of gaining a much better return than could be had by selling to a dealer. It is no easy matter deciding which route to follow. If your collection is better than average, you may be better advised to sell by auction. This will involve a waiting period of, generally, four to six months between consigning the collection and receiving settlement; over the summer months it may be longer. However, some auctioneers will give a cash advance, usually about 25 percent of the sum they believe the material is worth. In special circumstances a larger advance may be made, or the usual terms and conditions altered. One auctioneer paid $100,000 under a special contract, stipulating that the money was not to be returned regardless of the sale's outcome or even if no sale took place. But this was on a million-dollar collection. Auctioneers' commissions vary. The normal is 20 percent, but some houses take 10 percent from the buyer and 10 percent from the seller. This would appear to work to the seller's advantage, but such a practice may discourage bidding and result in lower sales prices.

Selling to other collectors. Unless the owner is personally acquainted with a large circle of collectors, this will likely involve running ads in periodicals and "playing dealer," which runs into some expense. Unless you offer material at very favorable prices, you are not apt to be as successful with your ads as are the established dealers, who have a reputation and an established clientele.

GLOSSARY

BROKEN BANK NOTE (a.k.a. obsolete note)

Literally, a Broken Bank Note is a note issued by a "broken" bank—a bank that failed and whose obligations could therefore not be redeemed. It may be presumed, by those who recall passing of legislation establishing the Federal Deposit Insurance Corporation, that banks failed only in the financial panic of 1929. During the 19th century, bank failures were common, especially in western and southwestern states. These were generally small organizations set up in frontier towns which suffered either from mismanagement or a sudden decline in the town's fortunes. Some collectors make a specialty of Broken Bank Notes.

DEMAND NOTES

Demand Notes have the distinction of being the first official circulating paper currency of this country, issued in 1861. There are three denominations: $5, $10, and $20, each bearing its own design on front and back. Demand Notes arose out of the coinage shortage brought about by the Civil War. A total of $60,000,000 in Demand Notes was authorized to be printed, amounting to several million individual specimens. Though this was an extraordinary number for the time, it was small compared to modern output, and only a fraction of the total survived. These notes were signed not by any specially designated Treasury Department officers, but a battery of employees, each of whom was given authority to sign and affix his name by hand in a slow assembly-line process, two signatures to each note. Originally the spaces left blank for signatures were marked "Register of the Treasury" and "Treasurer of the United States." As the persons actually signing occupied neither of these offices, they were obliged to perpetually add "for the . . ." to their signatures. In an effort to relieve their tedium, fresh plates were prepared reading "For the Register of the Treasury" and "For the Treasurer of the United States," which required nothing but a signature. This created a rarity status for the earlier specimens, which are now very desirable collectors' items.

ENGRAVING

Engraving is the process by which designs are printed on U.S. paper money. Bank note engraving involves the use of a metal plate, traditionally steel, into which the design is cut with sharp instruments called "burins" or "gravers." Ink is smeared over the surface and allowed to work into the grooves or lines comprising the design. The ink is then cleaned away from raised portions (intended to show blank in the printing). The engraving is pressed against a sheet of moistened paper, and the ink left in these grooves transfers to the paper, resulting in a printed image. When done by modern rotary press, it's a fast-moving process.

FEDERAL RESERVE BANK NOTES

Federal Reserve Bank Notes were issued briefly in 1915 and 1918. Like National Bank Notes they were secured by bonds or securities placed on deposit by each Federal Reserve Bank with the U.S. government. While issued and redeemable by the member banks of the Federal Reserve system, these notes are secured by—and are obligations of—the government.

FEDERAL RESERVE NOTES

Federal Reserve Notes, the notes in current circulation, were authorized by the Federal Reserve Act of December 23, 1913. Issued under control of the Federal Reserve Board, these notes are released through twelve Federal Reserve Banks in various parts of the country. Originally they were redeemable in gold at the U.S. Treasury or "lawful money" (coins) at a Federal Reserve Bank. In 1934 the option of redemption for gold was removed.

FREAK AND ERROR NOTES

These are bills which, by virtue of error or accident, are in some respect different from normal specimens. See the chapter on Error or Freak Notes.

GOLD CERTIFICATES

When gold coinage became a significant medium of exchange, the government decided to hold aside quantities of it and issue paper notes redeemable by the Treasury Department. The first Gold Certificates for public circulation were released in 1882. The series lasted until the era of small-size currency, ending in 1928. In 1933 all were ordered returned to the Treasury Department for redemption, including those in possession of collectors. A new law in 1964 permitted their ownership by collectors, though they can no longer be redeemed for gold.

LARGE SIZE CURRENCY

Large Size currency is the term generally used to refer to U.S. notes issued up to 1929, which were somewhat larger in size than those printed subsequently. The increased size permitted more elaborate design, which seldom fails to endear Large Size currency to beginners. Some of the earlier examples (especially of the 1870s, 1880s, and 1890s) are works of art. Though economic considerations were mainly responsible for the switch to a reduced size, there is no doubt that today's notes are far more convenient to handle and carry. Large Size notes are sometimes referred to as "bedsheet notes."

NATIONAL BANK NOTES

This is the largest group of notes available to the collector. They were issued from 1863 to 1929 and present collecting potential that can only be termed vast. More than 14,000 banks issued notes, in all parts of the country. While the approach to collecting them is usually regional, sets and series can also be built up, virtually without end. The National Banking Act was instituted in 1863, during the Civil War, to permit chartered banks to issue and circulate their own currency. Printing was done at the U.S. Government Printing Office and the designs were all alike, differing only in names of the banks, state seals, bank signatures, and the bank's charter number. Each charter bank was limited to issuing currency up to 90 percent of the value of bonds that it kept on deposit with the government. Charters remained in force for twenty years and could be renewed for an additional twenty years. National Bank Notes circulated in the same fashion as conventional currency and, thanks to the bond-deposit system, gained public confidence. The financial panic of 1929, which brought ruin or near-ruin to many banks, put an end to National Bank Notes.

NATIONAL GOLD BANK NOTES

These notes were issued exclusively by California banks during the 1870s under the same terms as ordinary National Bank Notes, their values backed by bonds deposited with the government. Events surrounding their origins form a unique chapter in the history of American economy. Following the discoveries of substantial quantities of gold in California in the late 1840s, that metal soon became the chief medium of local exchange, largely because it was more readily available in that remote region than coinage. Later, when gold coins and tokens began to circulate heavily in California, banks became so swamped with them that they petitioned Washington for authority to issue Gold Notes that could be substituted for the actual coinage. On July 12, 1870, Congress voted favorably on this measure, giving the right to issue such notes to nine banks in California and one in Boston. The Boston bank, Kidder National Gold Bank, appears not to have exercised its right, as no Gold Notes of this institution have been recorded.

The California banks wasted no time in exercising their authority, the result being a series of notes ranging from $5–$500. All were printed on yellow-toned paper so as to be instantly identifiable. The banks issuing these notes were permitted to redeem them in gold coins.

REFUNDING CERTIFICATES

Refunding Certificates, a sort of hybrid between currency and bonds or securities, were issued under a Congressional Act of February 26, 1879. These were notes with a $10 face value which could be spent and exchanged in the fashion of ordinary money but drew interest at the rate of 4 percent per year. The purposes behind Refunding Certificates were several. They were chiefly designed to encourage saving and thereby curb inflation, which even at that time was becoming a problem. Also, they provided a safe means of saving for persons who distrusted banks (safe so long as the certificates were not lost or stolen), and, probably more important, were readily obtainable in areas of the country not well served by banks. In 1907 the interest was halted. Their redemption value today, with interest, is $21.30.

SERIAL NUMBER

The serial number is the control number placed on all U.S. paper bills, appearing below left-center and above right-center. No two bills in the same series bear repetitive serial numbers. The use of serial numbers is not only an aid in counting and sorting bills as printed, but a deterrent to counterfeiting.

SIGNATURES

The inclusion of signatures of Treasury Department officials on our paper bills, a practice as old as our currency (1861), began as a mark of authorization and as a foil to counterfeiters. The belief was that the handwriting would be more difficult to copy than an engraved design. Persons whose signatures appear on notes did not always occupy the same office. From 1862 to 1923, the two signers were the Treasurer and the Register (or Registrar as it appears in old writings) of the Treasury. Subsequently, the Treasurer and the Secretary of the Treasury were represented. These signatures are of great importance to collectors, as some notes are relatively common with certain combinations of signa-tures and others are rare. A "series" collection is not considered complete until one obtains every existingcombination, even though the specimens may be in other respects identical.

SILVER CERTIFICATES

Silver Certificates were authorized in 1878. America's economy was booming at that time, and the demand for silver coinage in day-to-day business transactions outdistanced the supply. Silver Certificates were not intended to replace coinage but to create a convenient medium of exchange, whereby the government held specific quantities of Silver Dollars (later bullion) and agreed to redeem the notes or certificates against them. In 1934 the Treasury Department ceased redemption of these notes in Silver Dollars, and on June 24, 1968, redemption in all forms was ended. The notes are still, however, legal tender at their face value. When printing of Silver Certificates was discontinued, a flurry of speculation arose and many persons began hoarding them. This was done not only in hope of eventual redemption for bullion but in the belief that such notes would become valuable to collectors. Though Silver Certificates are popular with hobbyists, they have not increased sufficiently in price to yield speculators any great profits—especially since many collectors saved specimens in circulated condition.

STAR NOTES

United States Notes, Silver Certificates, and Gold Certificates sometimes have a star or asterisk in place of the letter in front of the serial number. Federal Reserve Notes and Federal Reserve Bank Notes have it at the end of the serial number. These notes are known as "Star Notes."

When a note is mutilated or otherwise unfit for issue, it must be replaced. To replace it with a note of the same serial numbers would be impractical, and Star Notes are therefore substituted. Other than having their own special serial number and a star, these notes are the same as the others. On United States Notes and Silver Certificates, the star is substituted for the prefix letter; on Federal Reserve Notes, for the suffix letter. All defective notes are accounted for and destroyed by burning them in an incinerator.

Large stars after the serial number on the 1869 Series of United States Notes, and 1890 and 1891 Treasury Notes, do not signify replacement notes as are known in later and present-day Star Notes.

Serial numbers on early Large Size Notes were preceded by a letter and were ended by various odd characters or symbols. These characters are not known to have any significance, except to show that the number was terminated, and prevented any elimination or addition of digits. The suffix characters were replaced by alphabet letters on later issues of notes.

TREASURY OR COIN NOTES

Treasury Notes were authorized by Congress in 1890. Their official title was Coin Notes, as they could be redeemed for silver or gold coins. The series did not prove popular and was discontinued after the issue of 1891.

TREASURY SEAL

The Treasury Seal is the official emblem of the U.S. Treasury Department, which has appeared on all our currency since 1862. It is missing only from the early Demand Notes, issued in 1861, and some Fractional Currency. Two versions have been employed, distinguished readily by the fact that one (the original) bears a Latin inscription, while the current Treasury Seal is in English. The basic motif is the same, a badge displaying scales and a key. The original Seal, somewhat more decorative, was in use until 1968.

UNITED STATES NOTES

Also known as Legal Tender Notes, this substantial and ambitious series followed Demand Notes and constitutes the second earliest variety of U.S. paper currency. There are five distinct issues, running from 1862 to 1923. Though United States Notes are all "Large Size" and their designs not very similar to those in present use, they show in their successive stages the evolutionary advance from this nation's first efforts at paper money to its currency of today. The first issue is dated March 10, 1862. Denominations are $1, $2, $5, $10, $20, $50, $100, $500, $1,000, $5,000 and $10,000. Individuals portrayed included not only presidents but other government officials: Salmon P. Chase (Lincoln's Secretary of the Treasury), Daniel Webster, and Lewis and Clark. Some of the reverse designs are masterpieces of geometrical linework. A number of rarities are to be found among Legal Tender Notes, but in general the lower denominations can be collected without great expense.

WILDCAT NOTES

Wildcat Notes are the notes that were issued by so-called "wildcat banks" in the era of State Bank Notes before the Civil War. Numerous banks sprang up around the middle part of the 19th century, mostly in the west and southwest, operated by persons of questionable integrity. Some never had capital backing and were instituted purely as a front for confidence swindles. After issuing notes, the bank shut down, its directors disappeared, and owners of the notes were left with worthless paper. As news traveled slowly in those days, the same persons could move from town to town and work the scheme repeatedly. Notes issued by these banks, or any banks that became insolvent, are also called Broken Bank Notes. Apparently the origin of the term "wildcat" derives from public sentiment of the time, which held that owners of such banks had no greater trustworthiness than a wild animal. "Wildcat" may also refer to the rapid movement of swindling bank officials from one locality to another.

DEPARTMENT OF THE TREASURY, BUREAU OF ENGRAVING AND PRINTING

Reprinted with permission of the Department of the Treasury, Bureau of Printing and Engraving, Washington, D.C.

BUREAU FACTS

- Since October 1, 1877, all U.S. paper currency has been printed by the Bureau of Engraving and Printing, which began as a six-person operation using steam-powered presses in the Department of the Treasury's basement.
- Now 1,900 Bureau employees occupy 25 acres of floor space in two Washington, D.C. buildings flanking 14th Street. Currency and stamps are designed, engraved, and printed 24 hours a day, 5 days a week on 23 high-speed presses. An additional 600 Bureau employees are at the Western Currency Facility in Fort Worth, Texas, where currency is printed 24 hours a day, 5 days a week on 12 high-speed presses.
- In Fiscal Year 1999, at a cost of 4.5 cents each, the Bureau of Engraving and Printing produced for the Federal Reserve System a record 11.3 billion notes worth approximately $142 billion. Ninety-five percent will replace unfit notes, and five percent will support economic growth. At any one time, $200 million in notes may be in production.
- Of total production, notes currently produced are the $1 (48% of production time), $2 (1 %), $5 (9%), $10 (11%), $20 (19%), $50 (5%), and $100 (7%).
- The Bureau also prints White House invitations and some 500 engraved items, such as visa counterfoils, naturalization documents, commissions, and certificates for almost 75 federal departments and agencies.

TOURS

BEP Public Tour Contact Information
Bureau of Engraving and Printing
14th and C Streets, S.W.
Washington, DC 20228
Telephone: 1.866.874.2330 (toll-free), 202.874.2330 (local)
School Group Tours Fax: 202.874.6331
Congressional Tours Fax: 202.874.0968

VISITORS' CENTER

- At the Visitors' Center, history, production, and counterfeit exhibits showcase interesting information about U.S. currency.
- Many unique items can be purchased at the sales counter. Items include uncut currency sheets of 32, 16, 8, or 4 $1, $2, and $5 notes; a premium portfolio containing a new series 1996 $20 note with a low serial number and one of the last previous series $20 notes; a deluxe single note in the series 1996 with a low serial number; $150 worth of shredded currency in plastic bags that are sold for $1.50; engraved collectors' prints; souvenir cards; and Department of the Interior Duck Stamps.
- If you are planning a trip to Washington, please call our information number at 1.866.874.2330 (toll-free) for updated information or program changes.

MAIL ORDER SALES

The Bureau of Engraving and Printing (BEP) is experiencing extended delays in the delivery of incoming mail. At this moment, it is unknown when timely mail deliveries will resume. In order to get timely delivery of numismatic products, it is recommended that customers order by telephone, fax, or Internet.

- For telephone orders, call toll free at 1-800-456-3408.
- For fax orders, call toll free at 1-888-891-7585.
- For Internet orders, the BEP web site is

INTERNET

The Bureau's **Internet address** is *www.bep.treas.gov/.* We also offer an **interactive website** at www.moneyfactory.com/.

THE FEDERAL RESERVE BANKS

Reprinted with permission of the Department of the Treasury, Bureau of Printing and Engraving, Washington, D.C.

The Federal Reserve System is divided into twelve Federal Reserve districts, in each of which is a Federal Reserve Bank. There are also twenty-four branches. Each district is designated by a number and the corresponding letter of the alphabet. The district numbers, the cities in which the twelve banks are located, and the letter symbols are:

1-A—Boston	5-E—Richmond	9-I—Minneapolis
2-B—New York	6-F—Atlanta	10-J—Kansas City
3-C—Philadelphia	7-G—Chicago	11-K—Dallas
4-D—Cleveland	8-H—St. Louis	12-L—San Francisco

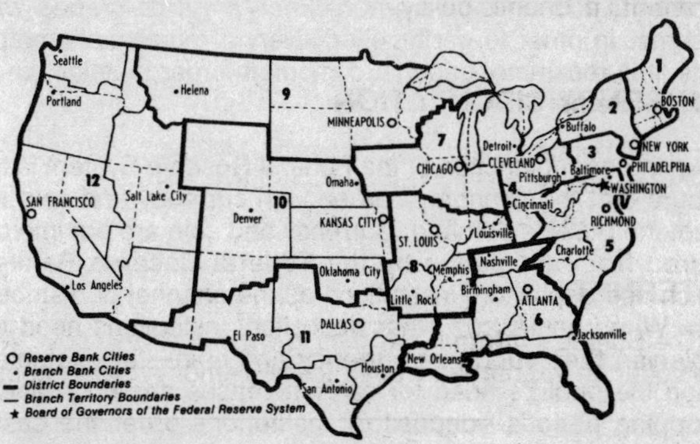

FEDERAL RESERVE SYSTEM

The Federal Reserve System was created by the Federal Reserve Act, which was passed by Congress in 1913, in order to provide a safer and more flexible banking and monetary system. For approximately 100 years before the creation of the Federal Reserve, periodic financial panics had led to failures of a large number of banks, with associated business bankruptcies and general economic contractions. Following the studies of the National Monetary Commission, established by Congress a year after the particularly severe panic of 1907, several proposals were put forward for the creation of an institution designed to counter such financial disruptions. Following considerable debate, the Federal Reserve System was established. Its original purposes were to give the country an elastic currency, provide facilities for discounting commercial credits, and improve the supervision of the banking system.

ECONOMIC STABILITY AND GROWTH

From the inception of the Federal Reserve System, it was clear that these original purposes were aspects of broader national economic and financial objectives. Over the years, stability and growth of the economy, a high level of employment, stability in the purchasing power of the dollar, and a reasonable balance in transactions with foreign countries have come to be recognized as primary objectives of governmental economic policy.

CURRENCY CIRCULATION

An important function of the Federal Reserve System is to ensure that the economy has enough currency and coin to meet the public's demand. Currency and coin are put into or retired from circulation by the Federal Reserve Banks, which use depository institutions as the channel of distribution. When banks and other depository institutions need to replenish their supply of currency and coin—for example, when the public's need for cash increases around holiday shopping periods—depository institutions order the cash from the Federal Reserve Bank or Branch in their area, and the face value of that cash is charged to their accounts at the Federal Reserve. When the public's need for currency and coin declines, depository institutions return excess cash to the Federal Reserve Bank, which in turn credits their accounts.

UNFIT AND COUNTERFEIT NOTES

The Federal Reserve Banks and the U.S. Department of the Treasury share responsibility for maintaining the physical quality of U.S. paper currency in circulation. Each day, millions of dollars of deposits to Reserve Banks by depository institutions are carefully scrutinized. The Reserve Banks are responsible for receiving, verifying, authenticating, and storing currency and shipping it as needed. Currency in good condition is stored for later distribution. Worn or mutilated notes are removed from circulation and destroyed. Counterfeit notes are forwarded to the U.S. Secret Service, an agency of the Treasury Department.

FEDERAL RESERVE NOTES

Virtually all currency in circulation is in the form of Federal Reserve Notes, which are printed by the Bureau of Engraving and Printing of the U.S. Treasury. The Reserve Banks are currently authorized to issue notes in denominations of $1, $2, $5, $10, $20, $50, and $100. Coins are produced by the Treasury's U.S. Mint.

CASH TRANSFERS

Currency and coin are used primarily for small transactions. In the aggregate, such transactions probably account for only a small proportion of the value of all transfers of funds.

32-SUBJECT SHEET LAYOUT

All U.S. currency is now printed with 32 subjects (notes) to a large sheet. The first printing is the greenback. The second printing is the face of the note, in black. This includes the portrait and border, the series year, the check letter and quadrant number, two signatures, and the face plate number. The sheet is then cut in half vertically for the third printing. This includes the black Federal Reserve seal, the four Federal Reserve district numbers, the green Treasury seal, and two green serial numbers.

The 32-subject sheet is divided into four quarters called quadrants for numbering and other controls. Each quadrant has its own numbering sequence for the eight notes, with serial numbers advancing by 20,000 to the next note. The quadrant number and check letter in the upper left section indicate the first, second, third, or fourth quadrant and the position of the note in the quadrant. In the lower right corner the position letter is shown again with a plate number. On the back of the note the same small number in the lower right is the back plate number.

FIRST QUADRANT		THIRD QUADRANT	
A1 A00000001A A100	E1 A00080001A E100	A3 A00320001A A100	E3 A00400001A E100
B1 A00020001A B100	F1 A00100001A F100	B3 A00340001A B100	F3 A00420001A F100
C1 A00040001A C100	G1 A00120001A G100	C3 A00360001A C100	G3 A00440001A G100
D1 A00060001A D100	H1 A00140001A H100	D3 A00380001A D100	H3 A004600001A H100
A2 A00160001A A100	E2 A00240001A E100	A4 A00480001A A100	E4 A005600001A E100
B2 A00180001A B100	F2 A00260001A F100	B4 A00500001A B100	F4 A00580001A F100
C2 A00200001A C100	G2 A00280001A G100	C4 A0050001A C100	G4 A00600001A G100
D2 A00220001A D100	H2 A00300001A H100	D4 A00540001A D100	H4 A00620001A H100
SECOND QUADRANT		FOURTH QUADRANT	

NUMBERING SYSTEM

The system of numbering paper money must be adequate to accommodate a large volume of notes. For security and accountability purposes, no two notes of any one class, denomination, and series may have the same serial number. The two serial numbers on each note have a full complement of eight digits and an alphabetical prefix and suffix letter. When necessary, ciphers are used at the left of the number to make a total of eight digits.

Whenever a numbering sequence is initiated for United States Notes or Silver Certificates, the first note is numbered A 00 000 001 A; the second A 00 000 002 A; the hundredth A 00 000 100 A; the thousandth A 00 001 000 A; and so on through A 99 999 999 A. The suffix letter A will remain the same until a total of twenty-five groups, or "blocks," of 99 999 999 notes are numbered, each group having a different prefix letter of the alphabet from A to Z. The letter "O" is omitted, either as a prefix or as a suffix, because of its similarity to zero. The 100 000 000th note in each group will be a Star Note, since eight digits are the maximum in the mechanical operation of numbering machines.

At this point, the suffix letter changes to B for the next twenty-five groups of 99 999 999 notes, and proceeds in the same manner as the suffix letter A. A total of 62,500,000,000 notes could be numbered before a duplication of serial numbers would occur. However, it has never been required to number that many notes of any one class, denomination, and series.

The Federal Reserve Notes printed for the twelve districts are numbered in the same progression as United States Notes and Silver Certificates, except that a specific alphabetical letter identifies a specific Federal Reserve district. The letter identifying each district is used as a prefix letter at the beginning of the serial numbers on all Federal Reserve Notes and does not change. Only the suffix letter changes in the serial numbers on Federal Reserve currency.

PORTRAITS AND BACK DESIGN ON SMALL SIZE NOTES

DENOMINATION	PORTRAIT	BACK DESIGN
$1	Washington	Great Seal of the United States
$2	Jefferson	Monticello
$5	Lincoln	Lincoln Memorial
$10	Hamilton	United States Treasury
$20	Jackson	The White House
$50	Grant	United States Capitol
$100	Franklin	Independence Hall
$500	McKinley	Five Hundred
$1000	Cleveland	One Thousand
$5000	Madison	Five Thousand
$10,000	Chase	Ten Thousand
$100,000	Wilson	One Hundred Thousand

DATING U.S. CURRENCY

Unlike coins, the date is not changed each year on U.S. currency.

The date appearing on all notes, large or small, is that of the year in which the design was first approved or issued. For instance, Large Size $1 United States Notes of the Series 1880 were issued with the same date until the new Series 1917 was issued. There was no further date change until the Series 1923.

The same rule applies to Small Size Notes. However, in this case a letter is added after the date to designate or indicate a minor change in the main design or probably a change in one or both of the signatures. For example: the $1 Silver Certificate of 1935 was changed to 1935-A because of a change in the size of the tiny plate numbers appearing in the lower right corners of the face and back of the note. It was changed again from 1935-A to 1935-B in 1945 when the signatures of Julian/Morganthau were changed to Julian/Vinson. Subsequent changes in signatures continued in the 1935 Series to the year 1963 when the signatures of Smith/Dillon terminated the issue with the Series 1935-H. Therefore, these notes were issued for twenty-eight years bearing the date 1935.

THE TREASURY SEAL

FORMER DESIGN:
The former design had the Latin inscription *Thesaur. Amer. Septent. Sigil.,* which has several translations. It was the Seal of the North American Treasury.

NEW DESIGN:
This new design drops the Latin and states THE DEPARTMENT OF THE TREASURY, 1789. First used on the $100 Note of the Series 1966.

GRADES AND CONDITIONS OF PAPER MONEY

CONDITION

The physical condition of a note or bill plays an important role in determining its value. There are many notes that have no premium value beyond face value in ordinary condition but are valuable or moderately valuable when uncirculated. Even in the case of scarce early specimens, the price given for an Average example is generally much less than that commanded by Fine or Very Fine condition.

Defects encountered in paper money include:

Creases, folds, wrinkles. Generally the characteristic that distinguishes uncirculated notes from those that almost—but not quite—qualify for such designation is a barely noticeable crease running approximately down the center vertically, resulting from the note being folded for insertion into a wallet or billfold. It may be possible, through manipulation or storage beneath a heavy weight, to remove evidence of the crease; but the knowledge that it once existed cannot be obliterated.

Discoloration. Discoloration is not as easy to recognize as most defects, but it must be classed as one. A distinction should be made between notes printed from underinked rollers and those which originally were normally colored but became "washed out." Sometimes washing is indeed the cause; a well-intentioned collector will bathe a note, attempting to clean it, with the result that its color is no longer strong. This should not happen if warm water is used, without strong cleanser. Atmospheric conditions may play some part in discoloration.

Foxing. Fox spots may sometimes be observed on old notes, especially those of the pre-1890 era, just as on old paper in general. They seem more common to foreign currency than American, but their presence on our notes is certainly not rare. These are tiny brownish-red dots, caused by an infestation of lice attacking the paper fibers.

Holes. Holes are more likely to be encountered in early paper money than specimens of recent origin. In early years it was customary for Federal Reserve Banks to use wire clips in making up bundles of notes for distribution to banking organizations, and these clips or staples often pierced the bills. Another common occurrence years ago was the practice of shop clerks and cashiers in general to impale notes upon holders consisting of nails mounted on stands.

Missing pieces. Missing pieces is a highly undesirable defect which, except in the case of rare specimens, renders the item valueless to collectors. Even if only a blank unprinted corner is torn away, this is called a missing-piece note and hardly anyone will give it a second glance.

Stains. Notes sometimes become stained with ink or other liquids. If the specimen is commonplace and easily obtainable in Very Fine or Uncirculated condition, it will be worthless with any kind of stain. In a note of moderate value, its price will be hurt to a greater or lesser degree depending on the stain's intensity, size, nature, and the area it touches. A stain in an outer margin or at a corner is not so objectionable as one occurring at the center or across a signature or serial number. Ink stains, because of their strong color, are generally deemed the worst, but bad staining can also be caused by oil, crayon, "magic marker," and food substances. Pencil markings, which frequently are found on bank notes, will yield to ordinary erasing with a piece of soft "art-gum" worked gently over the surface and brushed away with an artist's camel-hair brush. Most other stains cannot be so easily removed. With ink there is no hope, as any caustic sufficiently strong to remove the ink will also injure the printing and possibly eat through the paper as well. Oil stains can sometimes be lightened, though not removed, by sprinkling the note on both sides (even if the stain shows only on one) with talcum powder or other absorbent powder, placing it between sheets of waxed kitchen paper, and leaving it beneath a heavy weight for several days in a room where the humidity is not unduly high.

Tears. Tears in notes are very common defects, which may be minute or run nearly the whole length of the bill. As a rule the paper on which American currency is printed is fairly rugged and will not tear as readily as most ordinary paper, but given careless or hurried handling anything is possible. An old worn note is more apt to tear in handling than a new one. Repaired tears are more common in the world of paper money collecting than may be generally supposed. A clean tear—one which does not involve loss of surface—can be patched so as to become virtually unnoticed, unless examined against a light or through a strong magnifying glass. X-ray examination will reveal repairs when all else fails.

CONDITION GRADES

The following condition standards have been used throughout this book and, with slight variations depending upon individual interpretation, are generally current in the trade.

Uncirculated—UNC. A specimen that for all appearances has not been handled or passed through general circulation; a crisp fresh note in "bank" condition. There may be minor blemishes, such as a finger smudge or pinhole, but if these are in any respect severe the condition merits description as "Almost Uncirculated." There is not much satisfaction to be taken in a note fresh and crisp that has gaping holes and fingerprints. Obviously, an 1870 Uncirculated note should not be expected to match a 1970 in appearance or feel.

*Uncirculated—***Unc.** An uncirculated "Star Note."

Almost Uncirculated—A.U. In the case of modern or semimodern notes, this is generally taken to mean a specimen that shows no evidence of having passed through general circulation but, because of some detraction, fails to measure up to a rating of Uncirculated. The problem may be finger smudges, counting crinkles, a light crease, a fold along one or more of the corners, or pinholes. But if more than one of these impairments is present, the item would surely not deserve a classification of Almost Uncirculated.

Extremely Fine—X.F. A note exhibiting little evidence of wear from handling, but not so perfect or near-perfect as to qualify for a rating of Uncirculated or Almost Uncirculated.

On a used note issued before 1900 there may be clear evidence of circulation, but no disfiguring marks.

Very Fine—V.F. A Very Fine note has experienced some circulation but escaped without "being mangled." It is still clean and crisp, and its creases are not offensive.

Fine—F. Here the scale begins sliding down. It is obvious that, being the fifth in rank of condition grades, Fine notes are quite a good deal removed from Uncirculated. They have been handed around pretty thoroughly and suffered the normal consequences, but still are without serious blemishes such as tears, missing corners, serious stains, or holes.

Very Good—V.G. A well-circulated note bearing evidence of much folding, creasing, and wrinkling. It may possibly be lightly stained, smudged, or pin punctured, but major defects—such as a torn-off corner—would drop it into an even lower category.

Good—G. Heavily circulated, worn notes that are possibly stained or scribbled on, edges could be frayed or "dog-eared." There may be holes larger than pin punctures, but not on the central portion of design. This is the lowest grade of condition acceptable to a collector, and only when nothing better is available. Unless very rare, such specimens are considered space-fillers only.

Average Buying Prices—A.B.P. The Average Buying Prices given here are the approximate sums paid by retail dealers for specimens in Good condition. As selling prices vary, so do buying prices, and, in fact, they usually vary a bit more.

RECORD KEEPING

For your convenience, we suggest you use the following record-keeping system to note condition of your paper money in the checklist box:

FAIR	VERY GOOD	VERY FINE	ALMOST UNC
GOOD	FINE	EXTREMELY FINE	UNCIRCULATED

ABOUT THE PRICES IN THIS BOOK

Prices are compiled from offerings made by dealers and from auction sale results. In all cases (except for the Average Buying Price) the prices are retail selling prices. While prices are current at the time of publication, the market can be influenced by buying or selling trends, causing prices to change. All prices, except in the case of seldom-offered rarities, are averages, calculated from numerous sales. The actual prices charged by any individual currency dealer may be slightly higher or lower than those indicated in this book. In any given sale various factors play a role, such as whether the seller is overstocked on notes of that type.

HOW TO USE THIS BOOK

The *Official Blackbook Price Guide to United States Paper Money* provides a convenient reference to prices of all standard U.S. currency, old and new, as well as many unusual issues.

Notes are divided into section by denomination. Within each section can be found the various series of notes for that denomination. The series are arranged chronologically and will vary slightly from section to section, as some notes were issued in one series and not in another. An index page is provided at the beginning of each section.

To familiarize yourself with the various currency terms, the following illustration might be helpful:

To price a note correctly, it is necessary that it be accurately identified and graded. The illustrations will aid in identification, and a grading guide has been provided. In the case of some notes, particularly very old ones, the value depends upon minor details. In all such cases these details have been clearly noted.

Listings include the following information:

Date. This is the "series date," as it appears on the note, and may bear no relation whatsoever to the year in which the note was actually issued. The date of actual issue is not of importance to collectors. If the series date on the note carries a suffix letter, such as 1935A, it will be so indicated in the listing.

Seal. The color of the Treasury Seal will be noted, along with other information if relevant. The following abbreviations are also used: Sm.—small, Lg.—large; w/r—with rays, w/s—with scallops.

Signatures. All U.S. notes carry two signatures, and the names of each signer are given for every note listed. If different signature combinations exist for your note, be sure you refer to the correct signature combination. The listings will show you whether there is just one set of signatures for that note or more than one.

Type. In a small minority of cases, notes were issued in more than one type. For example, a slight change was made in the paper or printing. All recorded types are identified in the listings.

Issuing Bank. This information is provided for Federal Reserve Notes and Federal Reserve Bank Notes only. Check the Federal Reserve seal on your note to identify the issuing bank. In some instances there is a difference in value depending on where the note originated. Space prevents us from listing the numerous local banks issuing National Bank Notes.

A.B.P. The first price column is the A.B.P. or Average Buying Price. This is the approximate sum being paid by dealers for a specimen in the lowest listed grade of condition. The lowest listed grade of condition is the column next to the A.B.P. If the next column is headed "Good," the A.B.P. is for a specimen in Good condition. In all cases the A.B.P. includes the face value of the note. This is an important consideration insofar as U.S. notes, regardless of their age or physical condition, can still be spent as legal tender.

Current Selling Prices. The current selling prices are given in two or three different grades of condition, as indicated at the top of each price column. Different groups of notes are priced in different condition grades, owing to market availability. Some are virtually unobtainable in Uncirculated condition, so it would be pointless to give such a price. Others are of no premium value in less than V.F., hence V.F. is the lowest grade shown.

ONE DOLLAR NOTES

ORDER OF ISSUE

	FIRST LAST ISSUE ISSUE	PAGE
1. UNITED STATES NOTES	1862–1928	66
2. NATIONAL BANK NOTES	1863–75	71
3. SILVER CERTIFICATES	1886–1957B	72
4. TREASURY OR COIN NOTES	1890–91	80
5. FEDERAL RESERVE BANK NOTES	1918 only	82
6. FEDERAL RESERVE NOTES	1963–present	85

ONE DOLLAR NOTES (1862) UNITED STATES NOTES (ALSO KNOWN AS LEGAL TENDER NOTES)

(Large Size)

Face Design: Portrait of Salmon Portland Chase (1808–73), Secretary of the Treasury under Lincoln, red Treasury Seal, signatures of Chittenden and Spinner, lower right.

Back Design: Large circle center with legal tender obligation.

SERIES	SIGNATURES	SEAL	A.B.P.	GOOD	V. FINE	UNC.
1862	Chittenden-Spinner					
□Type I, National Bank Note, American Bank Note without monogram		Red	175.00	250.00	975.00	2200.00
□Type II, National Bank Note, American Bank Note with monogram ABNCO		Red	85.00	145.00	585.00	1750.00
□Type III, National Bank Note, National Bank Note without monogram		Red	80.00	135.00	635.00	1785.00
□Type IV, National Bank Note, National Bank Note with monogram ABNCO		Red	80.00	135.00	585.00	1750.00

ONE DOLLAR NOTES (1869) UNITED STATES NOTES (ALSO KNOWN AS LEGAL TENDER NOTES)

(Large Size)

Face Design: Portrait of President Washington in the center, large red seal to the right. Scene of Columbus in sight of land to left; also called "Rainbow Note" because of the many colors used in printing. Black ink for main design, red seal and serial numbers, green background for the serial number, green shading in upper-half and blue tint in paper left of portrait to deter counterfeiting.

Back Design: Green, ONE DOLLAR and ONE over "1" center, letters U.S. interwoven to left. Legal tender obligation to right of center.

SERIES	SIGNATURES	SEAL	A.B.P.	GOOD	V. FINE	UNC.
☐1869	Allison-Spinner	Red	68.00	125.00	675.00	2000.00
☐1869	Allison-Spinner Water Mark Paper		80.00	150.00	1150.00	2500.00

ONE DOLLAR NOTES (1874–1917)
UNITED STATES NOTES
(ALSO KNOWN AS LEGAL TENDER NOTES)

(Large Size)

Back Design: Large green "X" with UNITED STATES OF AMERICA in the center. Legal tender obligation and counterfeiting warning to right.
Face Design: No blue or green shading and tinting.

SERIES	SIGNATURES	SEAL	A.B.P.	GOOD	V. FINE	UNC.
□1874	Allison-Spinner	Sm. Red	47.00	70.00	385.00	1350.00
□1875	Allison-New	Sm. Red	40.00	68.00	350.00	1050.00
□1875	Same Series A	Sm. Red	120.00	272.00	950.00	2500.00
□1875	Same Series B	Sm. Red	125.00	260.00	935.00	2525.00
□1875	Same Series C	Sm. Red	135.00	275.00	1200.00	2850.00
□1875	Same Series D	Sm. Red	175.00	395.00	995.00	2750.00
□1875	Same Series E	Sm. Red	200.00	590.00	1295.00	3000.00
□1875	Allison-Wyman	Sm. Red	40.00	70.00	210.00	1075.00
□1878	Allison-Gilfillan	Sm. Red	40.00	75.00	210.00	1050.00
□1878	Allison-Gilfillan	Water Marked Paper	50.00	110.00	450.00	1500.00
□1880	Scofield-Gilfillan	Lg. Brown	35.00	75.00	270.00	925.00
□1880	Bruce-Gilfillan	Lg. Brown	35.00	70.00	270.00	975.00
□1880	Bruce-Wyman	Lg. Brown	35.00	70.00	270.00	925.00
□1880	Rosecrans-Huston	Lg. Red	110.00	250.00	975.00	4000.00
□1880	Rosecrans-Huston	Lg. Brown	100.00	175.00	875.00	3900.00
□1880	Rosecrans-Nebeker	Lg. Brown	100.00	175.00	875.00	3900.00
□1880	Rosecrans-Nebeker	Sm. Red	37.00	55.00	260.00	850.00
□1880	Tillman-Morgan	Sm. Red	37.00	55.00	260.00	850.00
□1917	Tehee-Burke	Sm. Red	26.00	48.00	87.00	275.00

Sm.—Small Seal, Lg.—Large Seal

*This note with signatures of Burke and Elliott is an error issue. The regular procedure was to have the signature of the Register of the Treasury on the left, and that of the Treasurer to the right. The signatures were transposed in this instance.

SERIES	SIGNATURES	SEAL	A.B.P.	GOOD	V. FINE	UNC.
□1917	Elliott-Burke	Sm. Red	21.00	26.00	85.00	275.00
□1917	Burke-Elliott*	Sm. Red	62.00	88.00	400.00	1200.00
□1917	Elliott-White	Sm. Red	21.00	26.00	80.00	270.00
□1917	Speelman-White	Sm. Red	21.00	26.00	80.00	270.00

ONE DOLLAR NOTES (1923) UNITED STATES NOTES
(ALSO KNOWN AS LEGAL TENDER NOTES)
(Large Size)

Face Design: Portrait of President Washington in center. Red seal to left, red "1" to the right, red serial numbers.

Back Design: UNITED STATES OF AMERICA and ONE DOLLAR in center. Figures "1" to right and left. This was the last issue of Large Size ONE DOLLAR United States Notes. The last series of Large Size Notes was kept in use until 1929 when the first issue of Small Size Notes was released.

SERIES	SIGNATURES	SEAL	A.B.P.	GOOD	V. FINE	UNC.
□1923	Speelman-White	Red	25.00	35.00	125.00	500.00

ONE DOLLAR NOTES (1928) UNITED STATES NOTES (ALSO KNOWN AS LEGAL TENDER NOTES)

(Small Size)

Face Design: Red seal to left—red serial numbers, large ONE to right. This is the only issue of the $1 United States Note, Small Size. At the present time only the $100 United States Note is current.

Back Design: Large ONE in center with ONE DOLLAR overprint, back printed in green.

SERIES	SIGNATURES	SEAL	A.B.P.	GOOD	V. FINE	UNC.	★UNC.
□1928	Woods-Woodin	Red	27.00	38.00	125.00	465.00	4800.00

*Star Notes: Damaged or unsatisfactory notes were replaced at the Bureau of Engraving with new notes bearing a star (★) in place of the first letter and preceding the serial no. Example: *12345678A

ONE DOLLAR NOTES (1863–1875)
NATIONAL BANK NOTES
FIRST CHARTER PERIOD (Large Size)

Face Design: Name of National Bank top center, maidens at altar below.

Back Design: Landing of Pilgrims center, State Seal of state issuing bank to left, eagle and flag.

SERIES	SIGNATURES	SEAL	A.B.P.	GOOD	V. FINE	UNC.
□Original*	Colby-Spinner	Red w/r	60.00	910.00	500.00	1600.00
□Original*	Jeffries-Spinner	Red w/r	125.00	410.00	1350.00	3050.00
□Original*	Allison-Spinner	Red w/r	60.00	90.00	500.00	1575.00
□1875	Allison-New	Red w/s	60.00	90.00	500.00	1575.00
□1875	Allison-Wyman	Red w/s	60.00	90.00	500.00	1575.00
□1875	Allison-Gilfillan	Red w/s	60.00	90.00	500.00	1575.00
□1875	Scofield-Gilfillan	Red w/s	60.00	90.00	500.00	1575.00

w/r—with Rays, w/s—with Scallops

*Early notes of the First Charter Period did not have the series imprinted on them. They are known by the date on the bill which was usually the date of charter or organization, or as the Original Series. These notes had a seal with rays or small notches. In 1875 the series was imprinted in red, and the seal was changed to have scallops around the border. The charter number was added to later issues of notes of the original series and to all notes of the 1875 series.

ONE DOLLAR NOTES (1886) SILVER CERTIFICATES
(Large Size)

SERIES	SIGNATURES	SEAL	A.B.P.	GOOD	V. FINE	UNC.
□1886	Rosecrans-Jordan	Sm. Red	75.00	110.00	425.00	1375.00
□1886	Rosecrans-Hyatt	Sm. Red	75.00	110.00	425.00	1375.00
□1886	Rosecrans-Hyatt	Lg. Red	75.00	110.00	425.00	1375.00
□1886	Rosecrans-Huston	Lg. Red	75.00	110.00	425.00	1375.00
□1886	Rosecrans-Huston	Lg. Brown	75.00	120.00	475.00	1400.00
□1886	Rosecrans-Nebeker	Lg. Brown	75.00	120.00	475.00	1400.00
□1886	Rosecrans-Nebeker	Sm. Red	75.00	120.00	475.00	1700.00

ONE DOLLAR NOTES (1891) SILVER CERTIFICATES
(Large Size)

Back Design

Face Design: Same as 1886 note.

SERIES	SIGNATURES	SEAL	A.B.P.	GOOD	V. FINE	UNC.
□1891	Rosecrans-Nebeker	Sm. Red	75.00	100.00	340.00	1250.00
□1891	Tillman-Morgan	Sm. Red	75.00	100.00	340.00	1250.00

ONE DOLLAR NOTES (1896) SILVER CERTIFICATES
(Large Size)

Face Design: History instructing youth. To the right, panoramic view of the Capitol and Washington Monument. Constitution on tablet, names of famous Americans on top and side borders.

Back Design: Portrait of Martha Washington to left and President Washington to right with large numeral "1" in center.

There is a story that when this note was issued people objected to it because they said No. "1" (ONE) shouldn't stand between George and Martha Washington. The set consists of $1, $2, and $5 denominations. They all have very beautiful engravings, and they are truly the most beautiful notes ever issued by our government. They were first released in 1896 and replaced by a new issue in 1899. They were short-lived because of objections to the unclad female on the $5 Note.

SERIES	SIGNATURES	SEAL	A.B.P.	GOOD	V. FINE	UNC.
□1896	Tillman-Morgan	Red	80.00	115.00	480.00	1600.00
□1896	Bruce-Roberts	Red	80.00	115.00	480.00	1600.00

ONE DOLLAR NOTES (1899) SILVER CERTIFICATES
(Large Size)

Face Design: Eagle on flag and Capitol background over portraits of Presidents Lincoln and Grant.

Back Design

SERIES	SIGNATURES	SEAL	A.B.P.	GOOD	V. FINE	UNC.
	SERIES OF 1899 (above upper right serial number)					
□1899	Lyons-Roberts	Blue	33.00	48.00	120.00	400.00
	SERIES OF 1899 (below upper right serial number)					
□1899	Lyons-Roberts	Blue	23.00	33.00	115.00	375.00
□1899	Lyons-Treat	Blue	26.00	36.00	110.00	375.00
□1899	Vernon-Treat	Blue	26.00	33.00	110.00	375.00
□1899	Vernon-McClung	Blue	26.00	33.00	105.00	375.00
	SERIES OF 1899 (vertical to right of blue seal)					
□1899	Napier-McClung	Blue	25.00	33.00	100.00	345.00
□1899	Napier-Thompson	Blue	38.00	58.00	275.00	1300.00
□1899	Parker-Burke	Blue	25.00	33.00	95.00	350.00
□1899	Teehee-Burke	Blue	25.00	33.00	95.00	350.00
□1899	Elliott-Burke	Blue	21.00	30.00	95.00	350.00
□1899	Elliott-White	Blue	21.00	30.00	95.00	350.00

SERIES	SIGNATURES	SEAL	A.B.P.	GOOD	V. FINE	UNC.
□1899	Speelman-White	Blue	21.00	30.00	95.00	365.00

ONE DOLLAR NOTES (1923) SILVER CERTIFICATES (Large Size)

Face Design: Portrait of President Washington in center, blue seal left, blue 1 DOLLAR right, blue numbers.

Back Design: Same as 1923 note.

SERIES	SIGNATURES	SEAL	A.B.P.	GOOD	V. FINE	UNC.
□1923	Speelman-White	Blue	14.00	19.00	39.00	95.00
□1923	Woods-White	Blue	14.00	20.00	42.00	95.00
□1923	Woods-Tate	Blue	20.00	30.00	95.00	375.00

ONE DOLLAR NOTES (1928) SILVER CERTIFICATES
(Small Size)

Face Design: Portrait of President Washington, blue seal to the left, ONE to right, blue seal and numbers. ONE SILVER DOLLAR under portrait.

Back Design

First issue of Series 1928. U.S. paper money was reduced in 1928 from the old Large Size to the size presently in use. This was mostly an economy measure. Unlike Large Size Notes, the Small Notes have a letter designation after the date to denote a minor change in design or change of one or both signatures.

SERIES	SIGNATURES	SEAL	A.B.P.	GOOD	V. FINE	UNC.	★UNC.
□1928	Tate-Mellon	Blue	5.00	10.00	20.00	100.00	600.00
□1928A	Woods-Mellon	Blue	5.00	10.00	20.00	100.00	500.00
□1928B	Woods-Mills	Blue	5.00	10.00	20.00	100.00	1500.00
□1928C	Woods-Woodin	Blue	27.00	60.00	300.00	750.00	30000.00
□1928D	Julian-Woodin	Blue	21.00	40.00	100.00	450.00	20000.00
□1928E	Julian-Morgenthau	Blue	80.00	200.00	525.00	2500.00	60000.00

ONE DOLLAR NOTES (1934) SILVER CERTIFICATES
(Small Size)

Face Design: Portrait of President Washington, blue "1" to left. ONE and blue seal to right. ONE DOLLAR IN SILVER under portrait.
Back Design: Same as 1928 note.

SERIES	SIGNATURES	SEAL	A.B.P.	GOOD	V. FINE	UNC.	★UNC.
☐1934	Julian-Morgenthau	Blue	6.50	10.00	25.00	120.00	1500.00

ONE DOLLAR NOTES (1935) SILVER CERTIFICATES
(Small Size)

Face Design: Portrait of President Washington in center. Gray "1" to left, blue seal right, and blue numbers. ONE DOLLAR IN SILVER under portrait.

The following notes are without IN GOD WE TRUST on back.

SERIES	SIGNATURES	SEAL	A.B.P.	GOOD	V. FINE	UNC.	★UNC.
☐1935	Julian-Morgenthau	Blue	3.00	4.50	10.00	36.00	600.00
☐1935A	Julian-Morgenthau	Blue	2.00	3.50	4.00	11.00	115.00
☐1935A	Julian-Morgenthau	Brown	5.00	9.00	25.00	150.00	1500.00

This note was a special issue for use in war zones in the Pacific area during World War II. Brown serial numbers and HAWAII stamped on front and back.

ONE DOLLAR NOTES (1935) SILVER CERTIFICATES
(Small Size)

SERIES	SIGNATURES	SEAL	A.B.P.	GOOD	V. FINE	UNC.	★UNC.
□1935A	Julian-Morgenthau	Yellow	5.50	8.00	30.00	135.00	1800.00

The above note was a special issue for use in war zones in the North African and European areas during World War II. Blue serial numbers and yellow seal.

□1935A	Julian-Morgenthau	Blue	11.00	25.00	75.00	400.00	8000.00

Red "R" between the Treasury Seal and signature of Morgenthau. This was an experimental issue to test wearing qualities of differently treated paper.

□1935A	Julian-Morgenthau	Blue	10.00	22.00	65.00	350.00	7500.00

Above note with red "S" between Treasury Seal and signature of Morgenthau. Experimental issue "R" was for regular paper, "S" for special paper.

□1935B	Julian-Vinson	Blue	2.50	3.00	5.50	18.00	250.00
□1935C	Julian-Snyder	Blue	2.50	3.00	3.50	15.00	75.00
□1935D	Clark-Snyder	Blue	2.50	3.00	3.50	11.00	75.00

Wide design on back. This and all notes of 1935 prior to this have the wide design. See Fig I.

□1935D	Clark-Snyder	Blue	2.00	3.00	3.50	11.00	60.00

Narrow design on back. This and all $1 Notes following have narrow design. See Fig. II.

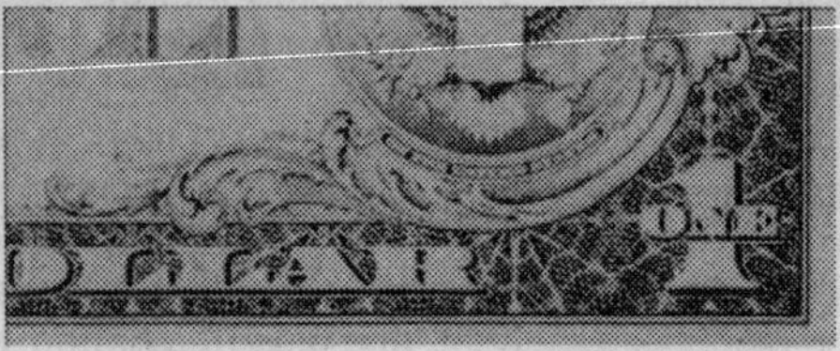

Figure I

Figure II

ONE DOLLAR NOTES (1935) SILVER CERTIFICATES
(Small Size)

SERIES	SIGNATURES	SEAL	A.B.P.	GOOD	V. FINE	UNC.	★UNC.
□1935E	Priest-Humphrey	Blue	1.50	3.00	3.25	11.00	19.00
□1935F	Priest-Anderson	Blue	1.50	3.00	3.50	11.00	19.00
□1935G	Smith-Dillon	Blue	1.50	3.00	3.50	12.00	25.00

IN GOD WE TRUST added. All notes following have the motto.

□1935G	Smith-Dillon	Blue	1.80	5.00	10.00	40.00	200.00
□1935H	Granahan-Dillon	Blue	1.80	3.00	3.25	15.00	40.00

ONE DOLLAR NOTES (1957) SILVER CERTIFICATES
(Small Size)

The following three notes are the last issue of the $1 Silver Certificates. The reason for the change in series from 1935H to 1957 was due to printing improvements. The 1935 Series, up until the issue of Clark and Snyder, was printed in sheets of twelve subjects to a sheet. During the term of Clark and Snyder notes were printed eighteen subjects to a sheet. Starting with Series 1957, new high-speed rotary presses were installed and notes were printed thirty-two subjects to a sheet.

SERIES	SIGNATURES	SEAL	A.B.P.	GOOD	V. FINE	UNC.	★UNC.
□1957	Priest-Anderson	Blue	1.80	2.00	2.15	5.50	15.00
□1957A	Smith-Dillon	Blue	1.80	2.00	2.15	6.50	13.00
□1957B	Granahan-Dillon	Blue	1.80	2.00	2.15	6.00	12.00

The redemption of Silver Certificates by the U.S. Treasury Department ended on June 24, 1968. These notes are now worth only their face value, plus the numismatic value to collectors. Notes in used condition are not regarded as collectors' items.

ONE DOLLAR NOTES (1890)
TREASURY OR COIN NOTES

(Large Size)

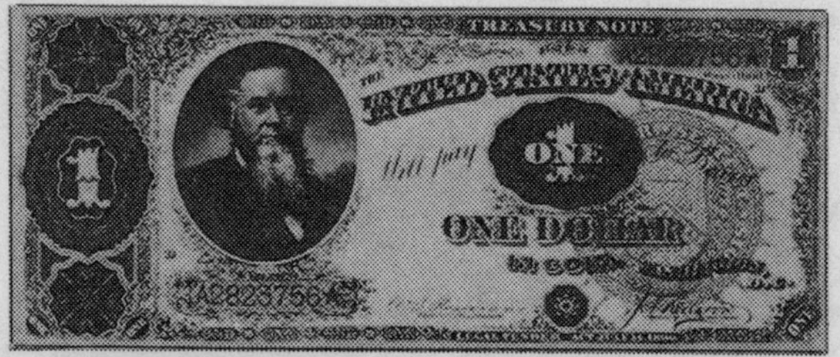

Face Design: Portrait of Stanton, Secretary of War during the Civil War.

Back Design: Green large ornate ONE. Entire back is beautifully engraved.

SERIES	SIGNATURES	SEAL	A.B.P.	GOOD	V. FINE	UNC.
□1890	Rosecrans-Huston	Brown	80.00	120.00	850.00	3000.00
□1890	Rosecrans-Nebeker	Brown	80.00	120.00	850.00	3000.00
□1890	Rosecrans-Nebeker	Red	80.00	120.00	850.00	3000.00

ONE DOLLAR NOTES (1891)
TREASURY OR COIN NOTES

(Large Size)

Face Design: Is similar to 1890 note.

Back Design: More unengraved area, numerous ONES and "1"s.

SERIES	SIGNATURES	SEAL	A.B.P.	GOOD	V. FINE	UNC.
□1891	Rosecrans-Nebeker	Red	60.00	90.00	265.00	950.00
□1891	Tillman-Morgan	Red	60.00	90.00	265.00	950.00
□1891	Bruce-Roberts	Red	60.00	90.00	265.00	950.00

ONE DOLLAR NOTES (1918)
FEDERAL RESERVE BANK NOTES

(Large Size)

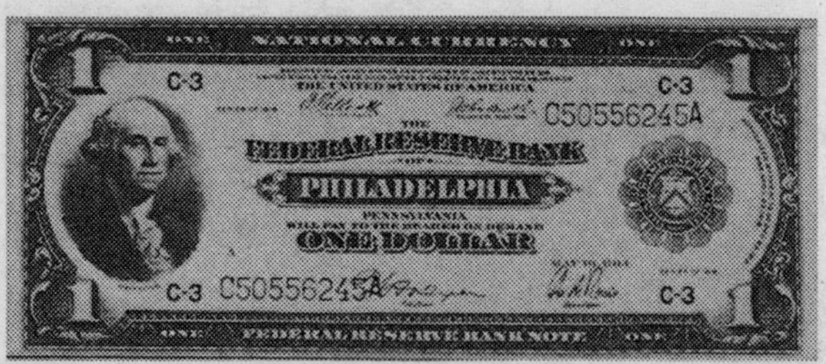

Face Design: Portrait of President Washington, signature to left of center. Bank and city center, blue seal to right. Signatures of government officials above. Signatures of bank officials below. Federal Reserve district letter and numbers in four corners.

Back Design: Flying eagle and flag in center. All are Series 1918 and have blue seals and blue numbers.

BANK	GOV'T SIGNATURES	BANK SIGNATURES	A.B.P.	GOOD	V. FINE	UNC.
☐ Boston	Teehee-Burke	Bullen-Morss	26.00	37.00	95.00	225.00
☐ Boston	Teehee-Burke	Willet-Morss	26.00	37.00	110.00	400.00
☐ Boston	Elliot-Burke	Willet-Morss	26.00	37.00	95.00	225.00

BANK	GOV'T SIGNATURES	BANK SIGNATURES	A.B.P.	GOOD	V. FINE	UNC.
☐ New York	Teehee-Burke	Sailer-Strong	26.00	35.00	90.00	225.00
☐ New York	Teehee-Burke	Hendricks-Strong	26.00	35.00	90.00	225.00
☐ New York	Elliott-Burke	Hendricks-Strong	26.00	35.00	90.00	225.00
☐ Philadelphia	Teehee-Burke	Hardt-Passmore	26.00	35.00	90.00	225.00
☐ Philadelphia	Teehee-Burke	Dyer-Passmore	26.00	35.00	90.00	225.00
☐ Philadelphia	Elliott-Burke	Dyer-Passmore	40.00	60.00	240.00	800.00
☐ Philadelphia	Elliott-Burke	Dyer-Norris	26.00	35.00	90.00	225.00
☐ Cleveland	Teehee-Burke	Baxter-Fancher	26.00	35.00	90.00	225.00
☐ Cleveland	Teehee-Burke	Davis-Fancher	26.00	35.00	90.00	225.00
☐ Cleveland	Elliott-Burke	Davis-Fancher	26.00	35.00	90.00	225.00
☐ Richmond	Teehee-Burke	Keesee-Seay	26.00	35.00	90.00	225.00
☐ Richmond	Elliott-Burke	Keesee-Seay	26.00	35.00	90.00	225.00
☐ Atlanta	Teehee-Burke	Pike-McCord	26.00	35.00	90.00	225.00
☐ Atlanta	Teehee-Burke	Bell-McCord	40.00	55.00	275.00	840.00
☐ Atlanta	Teehee-Burke	Bell-Wellborn	35.00	55.00	250.00	740.00
☐ Atlanta	Elliott-Burke	Bell-Wellborn	26.00	40.00	98.00	230.00
☐ Chicago	Teehee-Burke	McCloud-McDougal	26.00	35.00	90.00	225.00
☐ Chicago	Teehee-Burke	Cramer-McDougal	26.00	35.00	98.00	230.00
☐ Chicago	Elliott-Burke	Cramer-McDougal	26.00	35.00	90.00	225.00
☐ St. Louis	Teehee-Burke	Attebery-Wells	26.00	35.00	90.00	225.00
☐ St. Louis	Teehee-Burke	Attebery-Biggs	40.00	55.00	240.00	770.00

BANK	GOV'T SIGNATURES	BANK SIGNATURES	A.B.P.	GOOD	V. FINE	UNC.
□ St. Louis	Elliott-Burke	Attebery-Biggs	40.00	55.00	245.00	680.00
□ St. Louis	Elliott-Burke	White-Biggs	26.00	35.00	100.00	230.00
□ Minneapolis	Teehee-Burke	Cook-Wold	30.00	35.00	100.00	230.00
□ Minneapolis	Teehee-Burke	Cook-Young	105.00	207.00	470.00	1070.00
□ Minneapolis	Elliott-Burke	Cook-Young	27.00	37.00	100.00	280.00
□ Kansas City	Teehee-Burke	Anderson-Miller	26.00	35.00	95.00	230.00
□ Kansas City	Elliott-Burke	Anderson-Miller	26.00	35.00	95.00	230.00
□ Kansas City	Elliott-Burke	Helm-Miller	26.00	35.00	95.00	230.00
□ Dallas	Teehee-Burke	Talley-VanZandt	26.00	35.00	95.00	225.00
□ Dallas	Elliott-Burke	Talley-VanZandt	36.00	41.00	140.00	330.00
□ Dallas	Elliott-Burke	Lawder-VanZandt	26.00	35.00	95.00	225.00
□ San Francisco	Teehee-Burke	Clerk-Lynch	26.00	35.00	100.00	225.00
□ San Francisco	Teehee-Burke	Clerk-Calkins	36.00	52.00	150.00	430.00
□ San Francisco	Elliott-Burke	Clerk-Calkins	36.00	50.00	125.00	325.00
□ San Francisco	Elliott-Burke	Ambrose-Calkins	26.00	35.00	100.00	230.00

ONE DOLLAR NOTES (1963)
FEDERAL RESERVE NOTES

(Small Size)

Face Design: Portrait of President Washington in center, black Federal Reserve seal with city and district letter to left, green Treasury Seal to right. Green serial numbers, Federal Reserve numbers in four corners.
Back Design: Same as all $1 Notes from 1935.

SERIES OF 1963, GRANAHAN-DILLON, GREEN SEAL

DISTRICT	A.B.P.	UNC.	★UNC.	DISTRICT	A.B.P.	UNC.	★UNC.
☐1A Boston	1.85	4.75	10.00	☐7G Chicago	1.80	4.75	8.00
☐2B New York	1.85	4.75	7.50	☐8H St. Louis	1.80	4.75	8.00
☐3C Philadelphia	1.85	4.75	8.50	☐9I Minneapolis	1.80	4.75	12.00
☐4D Cleveland	1.85	4.75	8.50	☐10J Kansas City	1.80	4.75	8.00
☐5E Richmond	1.85	4.75	8.00	☐11K Dallas	1.80	4.75	8.00
☐6F Atlanta	1.85	4.75	8.00	☐12L San Francisco	1.80	4.75	15.00

The Dallas note of this series as shown, with the letter "K" in the black seal and the number "11" in the four corners, does not have any more significance or value than any other notes with their respective district letter and corresponding number.

A false rumor was circulated several years ago that the "K" was for Kennedy, the "11" was for November (the month in which he was assassinated), and that the note was issued by the Dallas Bank to commemorate the occasion. The entire story is apocryphal.

This note is in no way associated with the late President Kennedy. The notes were authorized by the Act of June 4, 1963. This was five months before Kennedy was assassinated. The Federal Reserve district for Dallas is K-11.

SERIES OF 1963A, GRANAHAN-FOWLER, GREEN SEAL

DISTRICT	A.B.P.	UNC.	★UNC.	DISTRICT	A.B.P.	UNC.	★UNC.
□1A Boston	1.75	4.50	8.00	□7G Chicago	1.75	4.50	8.00
□2B New York	1.75	4.50	8.00	□8H St. Louis	1.75	4.50	8.00
□3C Philadelphia	1.75	4.50	8.00	□9I Minneapolis	1.75	4.50	8.00
□4D Cleveland	1.75	4.50	8.00	□10J Kansas City	1.75	4.50	8.00
□5E Richmond	1.75	4.50	8.00	□11K Dallas	1.75	4.50	8.00
□6F Atlanta	1.75	4.50	8.00	□12L San Francisco	1.75	4.50	8.00

ONE DOLLAR NOTES (1963-B) FEDERAL RESERVE (WITH SIGNATURE OF JOSEPH W. BARR)

(Small Size)

Joseph W. Barr served as Secretary of the Treasury from December 20, 1968, to January 20, 1969, filling the unexpired term of Henry H. Fowler. His signature appears on the $1 Federal Reserve Notes of the Series of 1963-B only.

During the one-month term of Joseph W. Barr, about 471 million notes were printed with his signature. These notes were for the following Federal Reserve Banks.

	REGULAR NUMBERS	A.B.P.	UNC.	★UNC.
□2B New York	123,040,000	1.75	5.00	10.00
□5E Richmond	93,600,000	1.75	5.00	10.00
□7G Chicago	91,040,000	1.75	5.00	10.00
□10J Kansas City	44,800,000	1.75	5.00	—
□12L San Francisco	106,400,000	1.75	5.00	10.00

ONE DOLLAR NOTES (1969)
FEDERAL RESERVE NOTES
(WORDING IN GREEN, TREASURY SEAL CHANGED FROM LATIN TO ENGLISH)

FORMER DESIGN:
The former design had the Latin inscription: *"Thesaur. Amer. Septent. Sigil.,"* which has several translations. It was the Seal of the North American Treasury.

NEW DESIGN:
This new design drops the Latin and states *"The Department of The Treasury, 1789."* First used on the $100 Note of the Series 1966.

ONE DOLLAR NOTES (1969)
FEDERAL RESERVE NOTES

(Small Size)

SERIES OF 1969, SIGNATURES OF ELSTON-KENNEDY, GREEN SEAL

BANK	A.B.P.	V.FINE	UNC.	★UNC.	BANK	A.B.P.	V.FINE	UNC.	★UNC.
☐ Boston	—	1.25	4.00	5.25	☐ Chicago	—	1.25	4.00	5.25
☐ New York	—	1.25	4.00	5.25	☐ St. Louis	—	1.25	4.00	5.25
☐ Philadelphia	—	1.25	4.00	5.25	☐ Minneapolis	—	1.25	4.00	5.25
☐ Cleveland	—	1.25	4.00	5.25	☐ Kansas City	—	1.25	4.00	5.25
☐ Richmond	—	1.25	4.00	5.25	☐ Dallas	—	1.25	4.00	5.25
☐ Atlanta	—	1.25	4.00	5.25	☐ San Francisco	—	1.25	4.00	5.25

SERIES OF 1969A, SIGNATURES OF KABIS-KENNEDY, GREEN SEAL

BANK	A.B.P.	V.FINE	UNC.	★UNC.	BANK	A.B.P.	V.FINE	UNC.	★UNC.
☐ Boston	—	1.25	4.00	8.25	☐ Chicago	—	1.25	4.00	8.25
☐ New York	—	1.25	4.00	8.25	☐ St. Louis	—	1.25	4.00	8.25
☐ Philadelphia	—	1.25	4.00	8.25	☐ Minneapolis	—	1.25	4.00	8.25
☐ Cleveland	—	1.25	4.00	8.25	☐ Kansas City	—	1.25	4.00	8.25
☐ Richmond	—	1.25	4.00	8.25	☐ Dallas	—	1.25	4.00	—
☐ Atlanta	—	1.25	4.00	8.25	☐ San Francisco	—	1.25	4.00	8.25

SERIES OF 1969B, SIGNATURES OF KABIS-CONNALLY, GREEN SEAL

BANK	A.B.P.	V.FINE	UNC.	★UNC.	BANK	A.B.P.	V.FINE	UNC.	★UNC.
☐ Boston	—	1.15	4.00	6.50	☐ Chicago	—	1.15	4.00	6.50
☐ New York	—	1.15	4.00	6.50	☐ St. Louis	—	1.15	4.00	6.50
☐ Philadelphia	—	1.15	4.00	6.50	☐ Minneapolis	—	1.15	4.00	6.50
☐ Cleveland	—	1.15	4.00	6.50	☐ Kansas City	—	1.15	4.00	6.50
☐ Richmond	—	1.15	4.00	6.50	☐ Dallas	—	1.15	4.00	6.50
☐ Atlanta	—	1.15	4.00	6.50	☐ San Francisco	—	1.15	4.00	6.50

SERIES OF 1969C, SIGNATURES OF BANUELOS-CONNALLY, GREEN SEAL

BANK	A.B.P.	V.FINE	UNC.	★UNC.	BANK	A.B.P.	V.FINE	UNC.	★UNC.
☐ New York	—	1.15	5.00	6.25	☐ Chicago	—	1.15	3.30	6.25
☐ Cleveland	—	1.15	5.00	6.25	☐ St. Louis	—	1.15	3.30	6.25
☐ Richmond	—	1.15	5.00	6.25	☐ Minneapolis	—	1.15	3.30	6.25
☐ Atlanta	—	1.15	5.00	6.25	☐ Kansas City	—	1.15	3.30	6.25
					☐ Dallas	—	1.15	3.30	6.25
					☐ San Francisco	—	1.15	3.30	6.25

SERIES OF 1969D, SIGNATURES OF BANUELOS-SHULTZ, GREEN SEAL

BANK	A.B.P.	V.FINE	UNC.	★UNC.	BANK	A.B.P.	V.FINE	UNC.	★UNC.
☐ Boston	—	1.15	3.75	5.10	☐ Chicago	—	1.15	3.75	5.10
☐ New York	—	1.15	3.75	5.10	☐ St. Louis	—	1.15	3.75	5.10
☐ Philadelphia	—	1.15	3.75	5.10	☐ Minneapolis	—	1.15	3.75	—
☐ Cleveland	—	1.15	3.75	5.10	☐ Kansas City	—	1.15	3.75	5.10
☐ Richmond	—	1.15	3.75	5.10	☐ Dallas	—	1.15	3.75	5.10
☐ Atlanta	—	1.15	3.75	5.10	☐ San Francisco	—	1.15	3.75	5.10

SERIES OF 1974, SIGNATURES OF NEFF-SIMON, GREEN SEAL

BANK	A.B.P.	V.FINE	UNC.	★UNC.	BANK	A.B.P.	V.FINE	UNC.	★UNC.
☐ Boston	—	1.15	3.50	7.00	☐ Chicago	—	1.15	3.50	7.00
☐ New York	—	1.15	3.50	7.00	☐ St. Louis	—	1.15	3.50	7.00
☐ Philadelphia	—	1.15	3.50	7.00	☐ Minneapolis	—	1.15	3.50	30.00
☐ Cleveland	—	1.15	3.50	7.00	☐ Kansas City	—	1.15	3.50	7.00
☐ Richmond	—	1.15	3.50	7.00	☐ Dallas	—	1.15	3.50	7.00
☐ Atlanta	—	1.15	3.50	7.00	☐ San Francisco	—	1.15	3.50	7.00

SERIES OF 1977, SIGNATURES OF MORTON-BLUMENTHAL, GREEN SEAL

BANK	A.B.P.	V.FINE	UNC.	★UNC.	BANK	A.B.P.	V.FINE	UNC.	★UNC.
☐ Boston	—	1.15	3.50	7.00	☐ Chicago	—	1.15	3.50	7.00
☐ New York	—	1.15	3.50	7.00	☐ St. Louis	—	1.15	3.50	7.00
☐ Philadelphia	—	1.15	3.50	7.00	☐ Minneapolis	—	1.15	3.50	7.00
☐ Cleveland	—	1.15	3.50	7.00	☐ Kansas City	—	1.15	3.50	7.00
☐ Richmond	—	1.15	3.50	7.00	☐ Dallas	—	1.15	3.50	7.00
☐ Atlanta	—	1.15	3.50	7.00	☐ San Francisco	—	1.15	3.50	7.00

SERIES OF 1977A, SIGNATURES OF MORTON-MILLER, GREEN SEAL

BANK	A.B.P.	V.FINE	UNC.	★UNC.	BANK	A.B.P.	V.FINE	UNC.	★UNC.
☐ Boston	—	1.10	3.50	6.50	☐ Chicago	—	1.10	3.50	6.50
☐ New York	—	1.10	3.50	6.50	☐ St. Louis	—	1.10	3.50	6.50
☐ Philadelphia	—	1.10	3.50	6.50	☐ Minneapolis	—	1.10	3.50	10.00
☐ Cleveland	—	1.10	3.50	6.50	☐ Kansas City	—	1.10	3.50	6.50
☐ Richmond	—	1.10	3.50	6.50	☐ Dallas	—	1.10	3.50	6.50
☐ Atlanta	—	1.10	3.50	6.50	☐ San Francisco	—	1.10	3.50	6.50

SERIES OF 1981, SIGNATURES OF BUCHANAN-REGAN, GREEN SEAL

BANK	A.B.P.	V.FINE	UNC.	★UNC.	BANK	A.B.P.	V.FINE	UNC.	★UNC.
☐ Boston	—	1.10	3.50	10.00	☐ Chicago	—	1.10	3.50	10.00
☐ New York	—	1.10	3.50	10.00	☐ St. Louis	—	1.10	3.50	10.00
☐ Philadelphia	—	1.10	3.50	10.00	☐ Minneapolis	—	1.10	3.50	10.00
☐ Cleveland	—	1.10	3.50	10.00	☐ Kansas City	—	1.10	3.50	10.00
☐ Richmond	—	1.10	3.50	10.00	☐ Dallas	—	1.10	3.50	10.00
☐ Atlanta	—	1.10	3.50	10.00	☐ San Francisco	—	1.10	3.50	10.00

SERIES OF 1981A, SIGNATURES OF ORTEGA-REGAN, GREEN SEAL

★Notes not issued for all banks

BANK	A.B.P.	V.FINE	UNC.	★UNC.	BANK	A.B.P.	V.FINE	UNC.	★UNC.
☐ New York	—	1.10	3.50	6.00	☐ Chicago	—	1.10	4.00	6.00
☐ Richmond	—	1.10	3.50	6.00	☐ Dallas	—	1.10	4.00	250.00
					☐ San Francisco	—	1.10	4.00	6.00

SERIES OF 1981A or 1985 (REVERSE #129 LEFT), SIGNATURES OF ORTEGA-REGAN, GREEN SEAL

BANK	A.B.P.	V.FINE	UNC.	★UNC.	BANK	A.B.P.	V.FINE	UNC.	★UNC.
☐ Boston	—	26.00	42.00	—	☐ Chicago	—	26.00	42.00	—
☐ New York	—	26.00	42.00	—	☐ St. Louis	—	26.00	42.00	—
☐ Philadelphia	—	26.00	42.00	—	☐ Minneapolis	—	26.00	42.00	—
☐ Cleveland	—	26.00	42.00	—	☐ Kansas City	—	26.00	42.00	—
☐ Richmond	—	26.00	42.00	—	☐ Dallas	—	26.00	42.00	—
☐ Atlanta	—	26.00	42.00	—	☐ San Francisco	—	26.00	42.00	—

SERIES OF 1985, SIGNATURES OF ORTEGA-BAKER, GREEN SEAL

★Notes not issued for all banks

BANK	A.B.P.	V.FINE	UNC.	★UNC.	BANK	A.B.P.	V.FINE	UNC.	★UNC.
☐ Boston	—	1.10	3.00	—	☐ Chicago	—	1.10	3.00	8.00
☐ New York	—	1.10	3.00	—	☐ St. Louis	—	1.10	3.00	250.00
☐ Philadelphia	—	1.10	3.00	—	☐ Minneapolis	—	1.10	3.00	10.00
☐ Cleveland	—	1.10	3.00	—	☐ Kansas City	—	1.10	3.00	—
☐ Richmond	—	1.10	3.00	10.00	☐ Dallas	—	1.10	3.00	8.00
☐ Atlanta	—	1.10	3.00	—	☐ San Francisco	—	1.10	3.00	8.00

SERIES OF 1985 (REVERSE #129 LEFT), SIGNATURES OF ORTEGA-BAKER, GREEN SEAL

BANK	A.B.P.	V.FINE	UNC.	★UNC.	BANK	A.B.P.	V.FINE	UNC.	★UNC.
☐ Boston	—	25.00	36.00	—	☐ Chicago	—	25.00	36.00	—
☐ New York	—	25.00	36.00	—	☐ St. Louis	—	25.00	36.00	—
☐ Philadelphia	—	25.00	36.00	—	☐ Minneapolis	—	25.00	36.00	—
☐ Cleveland	—	25.00	36.00	—	☐ Kansas City	—	25.00	36.00	—
☐ Richmond	—	25.00	36.00	—	☐ Dallas	—	25.00	36.00	—

SERIES OF 1988, SIGNATURES OF ORTEGA-BRADY, GREEN SEAL

★Notes not issued for all banks

BANK	A.B.P.	V.FINE	UNC.	★UNC.	BANK	A.B.P.	V.FINE	UNC.	★UNC.
☐ Boston	—	1.10	3.00	6.00	☐ Chicago	—	1.10	3.50	—
☐ New York	—	1.10	3.00	6.00	☐ St. Louis	—	1.10	3.50	—
☐ Philadelphia	—	1.10	3.00	—	☐ Minneapolis	—	1.10	3.50	—
☐ Cleveland	—	1.10	3.00	—	☐ Kansas City	—	1.10	3.50	6.00
☐ Richmond	—	1.10	3.00	6.00	☐ Dallas	—	1.10	3.50	6.00
☐ Atlanta	—	1.10	3.00	300.00	☐ San Francisco	—	1.10	3.50	6.00

SERIES OF 1988A, SIGNATURES OF VILLALPANDO-BRADY, GREEN SEAL

★Notes not issued for all banks

BANK	A.B.P.	V.FINE	UNC.	★UNC.	BANK	A.B.P.	V.FINE	UNC.	★UNC.
☐ Boston	—	1.10	2.50	—	☐ Chicago	—	1.10	2.50	5.00
☐ New York	—	1.10	2.50	5.00	☐ St. Louis	—	1.10	2.50	5.00
☐ Philadelphia	—	1.10	2.50	—	☐ Minneapolis	—	1.10	2.50	5.00
☐ Cleveland	—	1.10	2.50	5.00	☐ Kansas City	—	1.10	2.50	—
☐ Richmond	—	1.10	2.50	5.00	☐ Dallas	—	1.10	2.50	5.00
☐ Atlanta	—	1.10	2.50	5.00	☐ San Francisco	—	1.10	2.50	5.00

SERIES OF 1993, SIGNATURES OF WITHROW-BENTSEN, GREEN SEAL

★Notes not issued for all banks

BANK	A.B.P.	V.FINE	UNC.	★UNC.	BANK	A.B.P.	V.FINE	UNC.	★UNC.
☐ Boston	—	1.10	2.00	—	☐ Chicago	—	1.10	2.00	4.00
☐ New York	—	1.10	2.00	4.00	☐ St. Louis	—	1.10	2.00	—
☐ Philadelphia	—	1.10	2.00	150.00	☐ Minneapolis	—	1.10	75.00	—
☐ Cleveland	—	1.10	2.00	—	☐ Dallas	—	1.10	2.00	4.00
☐ Richmond	—	1.10	2.00	—	☐ San Francisco	—	1.10	2.00	—
☐ Atlanta	—	1.10	2.00	4.00					

SERIES OF 1995, SIGNATURES OF WITHROW-RUBIN, GREEN SEAL

★Notes not issued for all banks

BANK	A.B.P.	V.FINE	UNC.	★UNC.	BANK	A.B.P.	V.FINE	UNC.	★UNC.
☐ Boston	—	1.10	1.75	6.00	☐ Chicago	—	1.10	1.75	6.00
☐ New York	—	1.10	1.75	6.00	☐ St. Louis	—	1.10	1.75	—
☐ Philadelphia	—	1.10	1.75	6.00	☐ Minneapolis	—	1.10	1.75	6.00
☐ Cleveland	—	1.10	1.75	6.00	☐ Kansas City	—	1.10	1.75	6.00
☐ Richmond	—	1.10	1.75	6.00	☐ Dallas	—	1.10	1.75	6.00
☐ Atlanta	—	1.10	1.75	6.00	☐ San Francisco	—	1.10	1.75	6.00

TWO DOLLAR NOTES

ORDER OF ISSUE

TWO DOLLAR NOTES (1862) UNITED STATES NOTES (ALSO KNOWN AS LEGAL TENDER NOTES)

(Large Size)

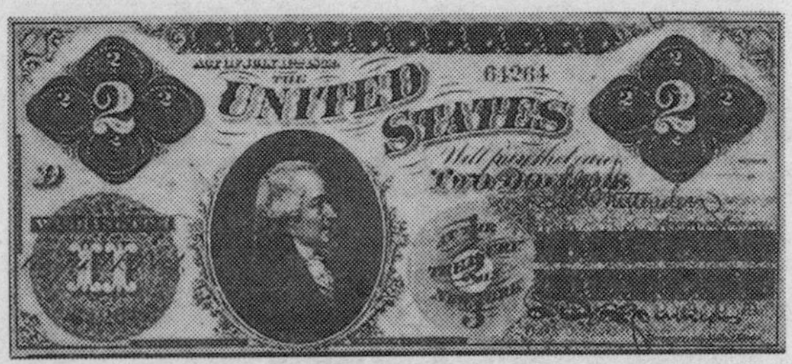

Face Design: Portrait of Alexander Hamilton (1754–1804), cloverleaf "2"s in upper corners, medallion with "II" in lower left, medallion with "1, 2, 3" right of portrait.

Back Design: "2" in each corner, with "2" motif repeated in scallop circles around obligation; back is printed green.

SERIES	SIGNATURES	SEAL	A.B.P.	GOOD	V. FINE	UNC.
□1862	Chittenden-Spinner Type I, American Banknote Company vertical in left border	Red	120.00	170.00	1100.00	2600.00
□1862	Chittenden-Spinner Type II, National Banknote Company vertical in left border	Red	120.00	170.00	1125.00	2600.00

TWO DOLLAR NOTES (1869) UNITED STATES NOTES (ALSO KNOWN AS LEGAL TENDER NOTES)

(Large Size)

Face Design: Portrait of President Jefferson to left, Capitol in center, large red seal to right.

Back Design: Roman "II" left, arabic "2" center, TWO right. This is the companion note to the $1 "Rainbow Note".

SERIES	SIGNATURES	SEAL	A.B.P.	GOOD	V. FINE	UNC.
□1869	Allison-Spinner	Red	105.00	165.00	925.00	3600.00
□1869	Allison-Spinner	Water Mark Paper	120.00	210.00	1375.00	4300.00

TWO DOLLAR NOTES (1874) UNITED STATES NOTES (ALSO KNOWN AS LEGAL TENDER NOTES)

(Large Size)

Face Design: Portrait of President Jefferson; same as 1869 note.

Back Design: Completely revised.

SERIES	SIGNATURES	SEAL	A.B.P.	GOOD	V. FINE	UNC.
☐1874	Allison-Spinner	Red	70.00	110.00	685.00	1950.00
☐1875	Allison-New	Red	75.00	110.00	875.00	2300.00
☐Series A	Allison-New	Red	185.00	320.00	1565.00	5575.00
☐Series B	Allison-New	Red	185.00	320.00	1515.00	5325.00
☐1875	Allison-Wyman	Red	85.00	135.00	675.00	1525.00
☐1878	Allison-Gilfillan	Red	75.00	105.00	575.00	1425.00
☐1878	Scofield-Gilfillan	Red	900.00	1200.00	2900.00	5800.00
☐1880	Scofield-Gilfillan	Brown	40.00	55.00	270.00	995.00
☐1880	Bruce-Gilfillan	Brown	40.00	55.00	260.00	995.00
☐1880	Bruce-Wyman	Brown	40.00	55.00	240.00	975.00
☐1880	Rosecrans-Huston	Red	275.00	550.00	1270.00	6400.00
☐1880	Rosecrans-Huston	Brown	375.00	1250.00	2190.00	7000.00
☐1880	Rosecrans-Nebeker	Red	35.00	55.00	190.00	775.00
☐1880	Tillman-Morgan	Red	35.00	57.00	190.00	775.00

SERIES	SIGNATURES	SEAL	A.B.P.	GOOD	V. FINE	UNC.
□1917	Teehee-Burke	Red	18.00	26.00	80.00	280.00
□1917	Elliott-Burke	Red	18.00	26.00	80.00	280.00
□1917	Elliott-White	Red	18.00	26.00	80.00	280.00
□1917	Speelman-White	Red	18.00	26.00	80.00	280.00

TWO DOLLAR NOTES (1928) UNITED STATES NOTES (ALSO KNOWN AS LEGAL TENDER NOTES)

(Small Size)

Face Design: Portrait of President Jefferson, red seal left, TWO right, red serial numbers.

Back Design: Jefferson Home—Monticello.

SERIES	SIGNATURES	SEAL	A.B.P.	GOOD	V. FINE	UNC.	★UNC.
□1928	Tate-Mellon	Red	4.00	10.00	16.00	125.00	850.00
□1928A	Woods-Mellon	Red	8.00	20.00	75.00	450.00	8000.00
□1928B	Woods-Mills	Red	26.00	60.00	150.00	1200.00	50000.00
□1928C	Julian-Morgenthau	Red	4.00	10.00	20.00	150.00	2000.00
□1928D	Julian-Morgenthau	Red	3.50	6.00	15.00	60.00	500.00
□1928E	Julian-Vinson	Red	3.50	9.00	20.00	100.00	7500.00
□1928F	Julian-Snyder	Red	3.50	5.00	11.00	50.00	450.00
□1928G	Clark-Snyder	Red	3.50	5.00	10.00	45.00	400.00

TWO DOLLAR NOTES (1953) UNITED STATES NOTES (ALSO KNOWN AS LEGAL TENDER NOTES)

(Small Size)

Face Design: Portrait of President Jefferson, gray "2" to left, red seal to right over TWO.
Back Design: Same as 1928 note.

SERIES	SIGNATURES	SEAL	A.B.P.	GOOD	V. FINE	UNC.	★UNC.
□1953	Priest-Humphrey	Red	2.50	3.75	5.00	20.00	45.00
□1953A	Priest-Anderson	Red	2.50	3.75	5.00	16.00	75.00
□1953B	Smith-Dillon	Red	2.50	3.75	5.00	15.00	50.00
□1953C	Granahan-Dillon	Red	2.50	3.75	5.00	16.00	85.00

Back Design: IN GOD WE TRUST on back.
Face Design: Same as previous note.

SERIES	SIGNATURES	SEAL	A.B.P.	GOOD	V. FINE	UNC.	★UNC.
□1963	Granahan-Dillon	Red	2.25	3.00	4.00	12.00	25.00
□1963A	Granahan-Fowler	Red	2.25	3.00	4.00	15.00	40.00

Production of $2 United States Notes was discontinued on August 10, 1966.

TWO DOLLAR NOTES (1875) NATIONAL BANK NOTES
FIRST CHARTER PERIOD (Large Size)

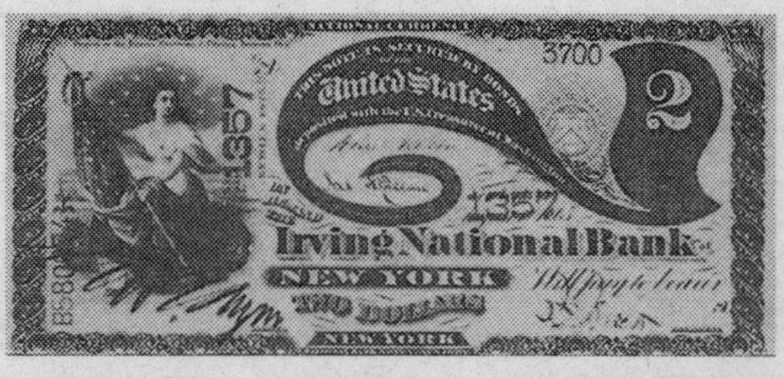

Face Design: This note is known as the "Lazy Two Note" due to the unusual "lying down" shape of the "2" shown on the face. Liberty with flag and red seal.

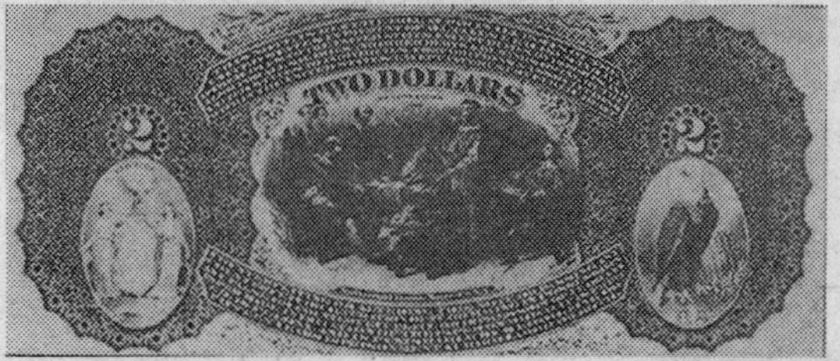

Back Design: Sir Walter Raleigh in England, 1585, exhibiting corn and smoking tobacco from America, State Seal, and eagle.

SERIES	SIGNATURES	SEAL	A.B.P.	GOOD	V. FINE	UNC.
☐Original	Colby-Spinner	Red	250.00	500.00	2000.00	5500.00
☐Original	Jeffries-Spinner	Red	275.00	950.00	2150.00	5750.00
☐Original	Allison-Spinner	Red	250.00	500.00	2000.00	5500.00
☐1875	Allison-New	Red	250.00	500.00	2000.00	5500.00
☐1875	Allison-Wyman	Red	250.00	500.00	2000.00	5500.00
☐1875	Allison-Gilfillan	Red	250.00	500.00	2000.00	5500.00
☐1875	Scofield-Gilfillan	Red	250.00	500.00	2000.00	5500.00

TWO DOLLAR NOTES (1886) SILVER CERTIFICATES
(Large Size)

Face Design: General Hancock portrait left. Treasury Seal to the right of center.

Back Design: "2" left and right, very ornate engraving, obligation in center of note. Note is printed in green.

SERIES	SIGNATURES	SEAL	A.B.P.	GOOD	V. FINE	UNC.
□1886	Rosecrans-Jordan	Red	105.00	150.00	850.00	2000.00
□1886	Rosecrans-Hyatt	Sm.Red	105.00	150.00	850.00	2000.00
□1886	Rosecrans-Hyatt	Lg.Red	105.00	150.00	850.00	2000.00
□1886	Rosecrans-Huston	Red	105.00	150.00	850.00	2000.00
□1886	Rosecrans-Huston	Brown	105.00	150.00	850.00	2000.00

TWO DOLLAR NOTES (1891) SILVER CERTIFICATES
(Large Size)

Face Design: Portrait of William Windom, Secretary of the Treasury 1881–84 and 1889–91, red seal right.

Back Design: "2" left and right, scalloped design center with obligation, printed in green.

SERIES	SIGNATURES	SEAL	A.B.P.	GOOD	V. FINE	UNC.
□1891	Rosecrans-Nebeker	Red	110.00	160.00	775.00	3000.00
□1891	Tillman-Morgan	Red	110.00	160.00	775.00	3000.00

TWO DOLLAR NOTES (1896) SILVER CERTIFICATES (Large Size)

Face Design: Science presenting Steam and Electricity to Industry and Commerce.

Back Design: Portraits of Robert Fulton and Samuel F.B. Morse.

This is the second note of the popular Educational Series.

SERIES	SIGNATURES	SEAL	A.B.P.	GOOD	V. FINE	UNC.
□1896	Tillman-Morgan	Red	145.00	195.00	1050.00	3200.00
□1896	Bruce-Roberts	Red	145.00	195.00	1050.00	3200.00

TWO DOLLAR NOTES (1899) SILVER CERTIFICATES
(Large Size)

Face Design: Portrait of President Washington between figures of Trade and Agriculture, blue "2" left, blue seal right.

Back Design

SERIES	SIGNATURES	SEAL	A.B.P.	GOOD	V. FINE	UNC.
□1899	Lyons-Roberts	Blue	85.00	125.00	250.00	750.00
□1899	Lyons-Treat	Blue	85.00	125.00	250.00	750.00
□1899	Vernon-Treat	Blue	85.00	125.00	250.00	750.00
□1899	Vernon-McClung	Blue	85.00	125.00	250.00	750.00
□1899	Napier-McClung	Blue	85.00	125.00	250.00	750.00
□1899	Napier-Thompson	Blue	100.00	165.00	395.00	1350.00
□1899	Parker-Burke	Blue	85.00	125.00	250.00	750.00
□1899	Teehee-Burke	Blue	85.00	125.00	250.00	750.00
□1899	Elliott-Burke	Blue	85.00	125.00	250.00	750.00
□1899	Speelman-White	Blue	85.00	125.00	250.00	750.00

TWO DOLLAR NOTES (1890-1891)
TREASURY OR COIN NOTES

(Large Size)

Face Design: Portrait of General James McPherson.

Back Design: Large TWO center, over obligation. Large "2" on engraved background right. Intricate engraving, printed green.

SERIES	SIGNATURES	SEAL	A.B.P.	GOOD	V. FINE	UNC.
□1890	Rosecrans-Huston	Brown	185.00	240.00	1750.00	6000.00
□1890	Rosecrans-Nebeker	Brown	185.00	240.00	1750.00	6000.00
□1890	Rosecrans-Nebeker	Red	185.00	240.00	1750.00	6000.00

TWO DOLLAR NOTES (1890-1891)
TREASURY OR COIN NOTES

(Large Size) **NOTE NO. 30**

Face Design: Similar to 1890–1891 note.

Back Design: Revised.

SERIES	SIGNATURES	SEAL	A.B.P.	GOOD	V. FINE	UNC.
□1891	Rosecrans-Nebeker	Red	80.00	120.00	695.00	2200.00
□1891	Tillman-Morgan	Red	80.00	120.00	695.00	2200.00
□1891	Bruce-Roberts	Red	80.00	120.00	695.00	2200.00

TWO DOLLAR NOTES (1918)
FEDERAL RESERVE BANK NOTES

(Large Size)

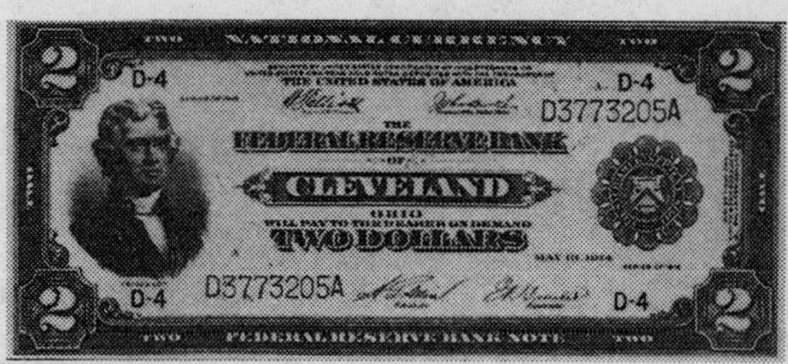

Face Design: Portrait of President Jefferson to left, name of bank in center, blue seal to the right, blue numbers, Federal Reserve district letter and number in four corners.

Back Design: American battleship of World War I.

TWO DOLLAR NOTES (1918)
FEDERAL RESERVE BANK NOTES

(Large Size)

BANK	GOV'T SIGNATURES	BANK SIGNATURES	A.B.P.	GOOD	V. FINE	UNC.
☐ Boston	Teehee-Burke	Bullen-Morss	90.00	145.00	385.00	1200.00
☐ Boston	Teehee-Burke	Willet-Morss	90.00	145.00	385.00	1300.00
☐ Boston	Elliot-Burke	Willet-Morss	90.00	145.00	385.00	1200.00
☐ New York	Teehee-Burke	Sailer-Strong	90.00	145.00	385.00	1200.00
☐ New York	Teehee-Burke	Hendricks-Strong	90.00	145.00	385.00	1200.00
☐ New York	Elliott-Burke	Hendricks-Strong	90.00	145.00	385.00	1200.00
☐ Philadelphia	Teehee-Burke	Hardt-Passmore	90.00	145.00	385.00	1200.00
☐ Philadelphia	Teehee-Burke	Dyer-Passmore	90.00	145.00	435.00	1300.00
☐ Philadelphia	Elliott-Burke	Dyer-Passmore	90.00	145.00	875.00	2175.00
☐ Philadelphia	Elliott-Burke	Dyer-Norris	90.00	145.00	385.00	1200.00
☐ Cleveland	Teehee-Burke	Baxter-Francher	90.00	145.00	385.00	1200.00
☐ Cleveland	Teehee-Burke	Davis-Francher	90.00	145.00	385.00	1200.00
☐ Cleveland	Elliott-Burke	Davis-Francher	90.00	145.00	385.00	1200.00
☐ Richmond	Teehee-Burke	Keesee-Seay	90.00	145.00	385.00	1200.00
☐ Richmond	Elliott-Burke	Keesee-Seay	90.00	145.00	450.00	1425.00
☐ Atlanta	Teehee-Burke	Pike-McCord	90.00	145.00	435.00	1200.00
☐ Atlanta	Teehee-Burke	Bell-McCord	90.00	145.00	875.00	2175.00
☐ Atlanta	Elliott-Burke	Bell-Wellborn	90.00	145.00	825.00	2075.00
☐ Chicago	Teehee-Burke	McCloud-McDougal	90.00	145.00	385.00	1200.00

BANK	GOV'T SIGNATURES	BANK SIGNATURES	A.B.P.	GOOD	V. FINE	UNC.
☐ Chicago	Teehee-Burke	Cramer-McDougal	90.00	134.00	475.00	1200.00
☐ Chicago	Elliott-Burke	Cramer-McDougal	90.00	134.00	450.00	1100.00
☐ St. Louis	Teehee-Burke	Attebery-Wells	90.00	134.00	450.00	1100.00
☐ St. Louis	Teehee-Burke	Attebery-Biggs	90.00	134.00	625.00	1650.00
☐ St. Louis	Elliott-Burke	Attebery-Biggs	90.00	134.00	625.00	1650.00
☐ St. Louis	Elliott-Burke	White-Biggs	90.00	134.00	700.00	1600.00
☐ Minneapolis	Teehee-Burke	Cook-Wold	90.00	134.00	415.00	1150.00
☐ Minneapolis	Elliott-Burke	Cook-Young	90.00	134.00	525.00	1375.00
☐ Kansas City	Teehee-Burke	Anderson-Miller	90.00	134.00	385.00	1150.00
☐ Kansas City	Elliott-Burke	Helm-Miller	90.00	134.00	450.00	1275.00
☐ Dallas	Teehee-Burke	Talley-VanZandt	90.00	134.00	525.00	1150.00
☐ Dallas	Elliott-Burke	Talley-VanZandt	90.00	134.00	525.00	1275.00
☐ San Francisco	Teehee-Burke	Clerk-Lynch	90.00	134.00	450.00	1275.00
☐ San Francisco	Elliott-Burke	Clerk-Calkins	90.00	134.00	450.00	1275.00
☐ San Francisco	Elliott-Burke	Ambrose-Calkins	90.00	134.00	450.00	1275.00

TWO DOLLAR NOTES (1976)
FEDERAL RESERVE NOTES

(Small Size)

Face Design: Portrait of President Jefferson.

Back Design: Signing of the Declaration of Independence.

SERIES OF 1976, NEFF-SIMON, GREEN SEAL

DISTRICT	A.B.P.	UNC.	★UNC.	DISTRICT	A.B.P.	UNC.	★UNC.
☐1A Boston	3.00	6.50	15.00	☐7G Chicago	3.00	6.50	50.00
☐2B New York	3.00	6.00	20.00	☐8H St. Louis	3.00	5.50	15.00
☐3C Philadelphia	3.00	6.00	15.00	☐9I Minneapolis	3.00	10.00	250.00
☐4D Cleveland	3.00	7.00	30.00	☐10J Kansas City	3.00	25.00	275.00
☐5E Richmond	3.00	6.00	40.00	☐11K Dallas	3.00	8.00	20.00
☐6F Atlanta	3.00	6.50	15.00	☐12L San Francisco	3.00	6.00	20.00

SERIES OF 1995, GREEN SEAL

DISTRICT	A.B.P.	UNC.	★UNC.
☐6F Atlanta	2.15	4.00	10.00

FIVE DOLLAR NOTES

ORDER OF ISSUE

	FIRST ISSUE – LAST ISSUE	PAGE
1. DEMAND NOTES	1861 only	108
2. UNITED STATES NOTES	1862–1963	109
3. NATIONAL BANK NOTES	1863–1929	114
4. NATIONAL GOLD BANK NOTES	1870–74	120
5. SILVER CERTIFICATES	1886–1953B	121
6. TREASURY OR COIN NOTES	1890–91	127
7. FEDERAL RESERVE NOTES	1914–present	128
8. FEDERAL RESERVE BANK NOTES	1915–29	140

FIVE DOLLAR NOTES (1861) DEMAND NOTES
(Large Size)

Face Design: Left, Statue of America by Crawford atop United States Capitol. Center, numeral "5" in green. Right, portrait of Alexander Hamilton, statesman, first Secretary of the Treasury.

Back Design: Numerous small "5"s in ovals. This note has no Treasury Seal. The signatures are those of Treasury Department employees who signed for officials.

CITY	A.B.P.	GOOD	V. GOOD
☐Boston (I)	925.00	1675.00	3300.00
☐New York (I)	925.00	1675.00	3300.00
☐Philadelphia (I)	925.00	1675.00	3300.00
☐Cincinnati (I)	2575.00	8075.00	16,600.00
☐St. Louis (I)	2575.00	8075.00	16,600.00
☐Boston (II)	525.00	675.00	1200.00
☐New York (II)	525.00	675.00	1200.00
☐Philadelphia (II)	525.00	675.00	1200.00
☐Cincinnati (II)	3075.00	6075.00	12,100.00
☐St. Louis (II)	3075.00	6075.00	12,100.00

FIVE DOLLAR NOTES (1875–1907)
UNITED STATES NOTES
(ALSO KNOWN AS LEGAL TENDER NOTES)

(Large Size)

Back Design: First Obligation.

Back Design: Second Obligation

SERIES	SIGNATURES	SEAL	A.B.P.	GOOD	V. FINE	UNC.
□1862	Crittenden-Spinner*	Red	80.00	120.00	600.00	1550.00
□1862	Crittenden-Spinner**	Red	80.00	120.00	600.00	1550.00
□1863	Crittenden-Spinner**	Red	80.00	120.00	600.00	1550.00

*First Obligation
**Second Obligation

FIVE DOLLAR NOTES (1869) UNITED STATES NOTES (ALSO KNOWN AS LEGAL TENDER NOTES)

(Large Size)

Face Design: Portrait of President Jackson on left. Pioneer and family in center.

Back Design: Color, green. This is a companion note to the $1 and $2 Notes of 1869 "Rainbow Notes."

SERIES	SIGNATURES	SEAL	A.B.P.	GOOD	V. FINE	UNC.
□1869	Allison-Spinner	Red	90.00	125.00	550.00	1450.00
□1869	Allison-Spinner	Water Marked Paper	95.00	150.00	1050.00	2150.00

FIVE DOLLAR NOTES (1875–1907)
UNITED STATES NOTES
(ALSO KNOWN AS LEGAL TENDER NOTES)

(Large Size)

Back Design: Revised.
Face Design: Similar to 1869 note.

SERIES	SIGNATURES	SEAL	A.B.P.	GOOD	V. FINE	UNC.
□1875	Allison-New	Red	65.00	105.00	275.00	1000.00
□1875A	Allison-New	Red	85.00	140.00	625.00	1900.00
□1875B	Allison-New	Red	65.00	100.00	350.00	975.00
□1875	Allison-Wyman	Red	70.00	100.00	325.00	1075.00
□1878	Allison-Gilfillan	Red	60.00	90.00	370.00	1050.00
□1880	Scofield-Gilfillan	Brown	310.00	710.00	3500.00	7050.00
□1880	Bruce-Gilfillan	Brown	95.00	155.00	750.00	2150.00
□1880	Bruce-Wyman	Brown	65.00	105.00	335.00	950.00
□1880	Bruce-Wyman	Red	70.00	115.00	400.00	1650.00
□1880	Rosecrans-Jordan	Red	65.00	110.00	380.00	1250.00
□1880	Rosecrans-Hyatt	Red	325.00	730.00	3430.00	7100.00
□1880	Rosecrans-Huston	Red	70.00	130.00	605.00	1700.00
□1880	Rosecrans-Huston	Brown	98.00	180.00	650.00	1900.00
□1880	Rosecrans-Nebeker	Brown	50.00	130.00	450.00	1400.00
□1880	Rosecrans-Nebeker	Red	40.00	70.00	225.00	900.00
□1880	Tillman-Morgan	Red	40.00	70.00	210.00	725.00
□1880	Bruce-Roberts	Red	30.00	55.00	185.00	800.00
□1880	Lyons-Roberts	Red	50.00	90.00	805.00	2050.00
□1907	Vernon-Treat	Red	25.00	50.00	200.00	850.00
□1907	Vernon-McClung	Red	25.00	50.00	200.00	850.00
□1907	Napier-McClung	Red	25.00	38.00	150.00	585.00
□1907	Napier-Thompson	Red	45.00	110.00	300.00	730.00
□1907	Parker-Burke	Red	25.00	48.00	150.00	535.00
□1907	Teehee-Burke	Red	25.00	48.00	170.00	535.00
□1907	Elliott-Burke	Red	25.00	48.00	170.00	560.00

SERIES	SIGNATURES	SEAL	A.B.P.	GOOD	V. FINE	UNC.
□1907	Elliott-White	Red	36.00	50.00	175.00	500.00
□1907	Speelman-White	Red	36.00	48.00	135.00	460.00
□1907	Woods-White	Red	36.00	50.00	175.00	510.00

FIVE DOLLAR NOTES (1928) UNITED STATES NOTES (ALSO KNOWN AS LEGAL TENDER NOTES)

(Small Size)

Face Design: Portrait of President Lincoln center. Red seal to left, red serial numbers.

Back Design: Lincoln Memorial in Washington, D.C.

SERIES	SIGNATURES	SEAL	A.B.P	GOOD	V. FINE	UNC.	★UNC.
□1928	Woods-Mellon	Red	6.50	9.00	15.00	90.00	2000.00
□1928A	Woods-Mills	Red	6.50	9.00	25.00	130.00	5000.00
□1928B	Julian-Morgenthau	Red	6.50	9.00	15.00	55.00	1250.00
□1928C	Julian-Morgenthau	Red	6.50	9.00	15.00	55.00	650.00
□1928D	Julian-Vinson	Red	6.50	9.00	35.00	400.00	3000.00
□1928E	Julian-Snyder	Red	6.50	9.00	15.00	50.00	750.00
□1928F	Clark-Snyder	Red	6.50	9.00	15.00	55.00	500.00

FIVE DOLLAR NOTES (1953–1963)
UNITED STATES NOTES

(Small Size)

Face Design: Similar to previous note. Portrait of President Lincoln center. Red seal is moved to the right, red numbers.
Back Design: Similar to 1928 note.

SERIES	SIGNATURES	SEAL	A.B.P.	GOOD	V. FINE	UNC.	★UNC.
□1953	Priest-Humphrey	Red	6.00	7.50	11.00	45.00	250.00
□1953A	Priest-Anderson	Red	6.00	7.50	13.00	30.00	150.00
□1953B	Smith-Dillon	Red	6.00	7.50	11.00	25.00	125.00
□1953C	Granahan-Dillon	Red	6.00	7.50	11.00	50.00	200.00

FIVE DOLLAR NOTES (1953-1963)
UNITED STATES NOTES
(ALSO KNOWN AS LEGAL TENDER NOTES)

(Small Size)

Back Design: The following notes have IN GOD WE TRUST on the back.
Face Design: Similar to 1953–1963 note.

SERIES	SIGNATURES	SEAL	A.B.P.	GOOD	V. FINE	UNC.	★UNC.
□1963	Granahan-Dillon	Red	6.00	7.50	12.00	25.00	60.00

Production of $5 United States Notes ended in 1967.

FIVE DOLLAR NOTES (1863-1875)
NATIONAL BANK NOTES
FIRST CHARTER PERIOD (Large Size)

Face Design: The Columbus Note. The face shows Columbus in sight of land and Columbus with an Indian princess.

Back Design: Christopher Columbus landing at San Salvador, 1492. Also the State Seal left, and American eagle right.

SERIES	SIGNATURES	SEAL	A.B.P.	GOOD	V. FINE	UNC.
□Original	Chittenden-Spinner	Red	80.00	125.00	600.00	1500.00
□Original	Colby-Spinner	Red	80.00	125.00	600.00	1450.00
□Original	Jeffries-Spinner	Red	200.00	540.00	1700.00	3800.00
□Original	Allison-Spinner	Red	80.00	125.00	600.00	1500.00
□1875	Allison-New	Red	80.00	125.00	600.00	1450.00
□1875	Allison-Wyman	Red	80.00	125.00	600.00	1450.00
□1875	Allison-Gilfillan	Red	80.00	125.00	600.00	1450.00
□1875	Scofield-Gilfillan	Red	80.00	125.00	600.00	1450.00
□1875	Bruce-Gilfillan	Red	80.00	125.00	600.00	1450.00
□1875	Bruce-Wyman	Red	80.00	125.00	600.00	1450.00
□1875	Bruce-Jordan	Red			EXTREMELY RARE	
□1875	Rosecrans-Huston	Red	80.00	125.00	600.00	1450.00
□1875	Rosecrans-Jordan	Red	80.00	125.00	600.00	1450.00

FIVE DOLLAR NOTES (1882) NATIONAL BANK NOTES
SECOND CHARTER PERIOD (Large Size)

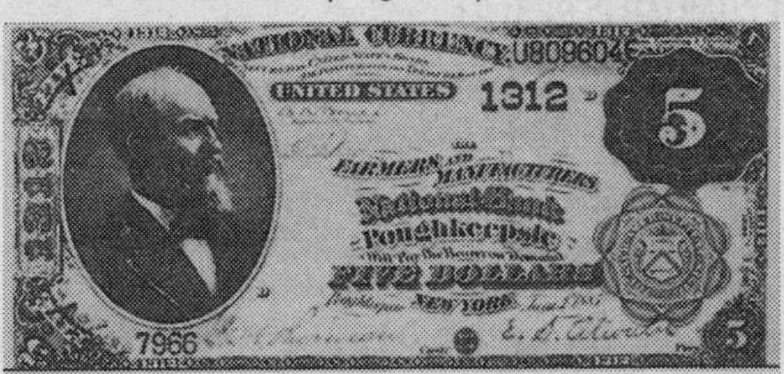

First Issue (Brown seal and brown backs.)
Face Design: Portrait of President Garfield left. Name of bank and city center, brown seal to right. Brown charter number.

Back Design: Brown border design similar to previous note. Center oval now has the bank's charter number in green. The top signatures are those of the Treasury officials. Bottom signatures, usually handwritten or probably rubber-stamped, are bank officials.

SERIES	SIGNATURES	SEAL	A.B.P.	GOOD	V. FINE	UNC.
□1882	Bruce-Gilfillan	Brown	65.00	90.00	360.00	1000.00
□1882	Bruce-Wyman	Brown	65.00	90.00	360.00	1000.00
□1882	Bruce-Jordan	Brown	65.00	90.00	360.00	1000.00
□1882	Rosecrans-Jordan	Brown	65.00	90.00	360.00	1000.00
□1882	Rosecrans-Hyatt	Brown	65.00	90.00	360.00	1000.00
□1882	Rosecrans-Huston	Brown	65.00	90.00	360.00	1000.00
□1882	Rosecrans-Nebeker	Brown	65.00	90.00	360.00	1000.00
□1882	Rosecrans-Morgan	Brown	65.00	188.00	485.00	1350.00
□1882	Tillman-Morgan	Brown	65.00	90.00	360.00	1000.00
□1882	Tillman-Roberts	Brown	65.00	90.00	360.00	1000.00
□1882	Bruce-Roberts	Brown	65.00	90.00	360.00	1000.00
□1882	Lyons-Roberts	Brown	65.00	90.00	360.00	1000.00
□1882	Lyons-Treat		(Unknown in any collection)			
□1882	Vernon-Treat	Brown	65.00	105.00	360.00	1000.00

FIVE DOLLAR NOTES (1882) NATIONAL BANK NOTES
SECOND CHARTER PERIOD, Second Issue (Large Size)

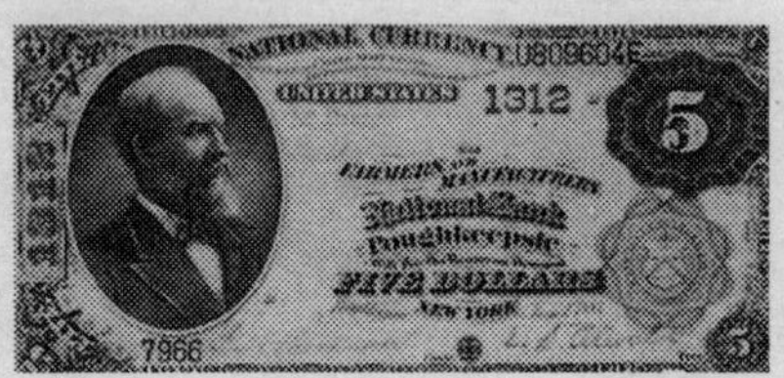

Face Design: Similar to preceding portrait of President Garfield.

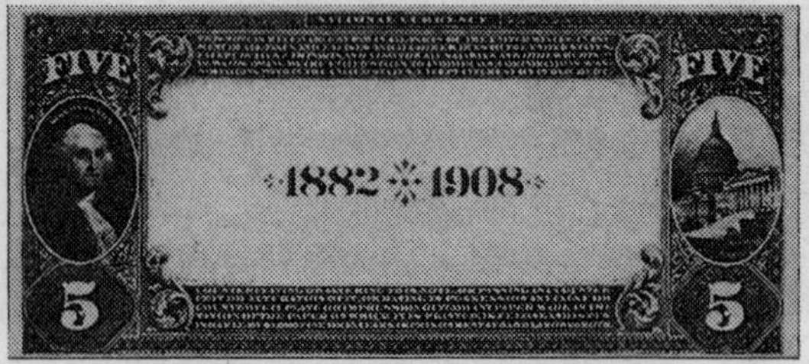

Back Design: Back is now green with date "1882–1908" in center.

SERIES	SIGNATURES	SEAL	A.B.P.	GOOD	V. FINE	UNC.
□1882	Rosecrans-Huston	Blue	55.00	95.00	300.00	900.00
□1882	Rosecrans-Nebeker	Blue	55.00	95.00	300.00	900.00
□1882	Rosecrans-Morgan	Blue	115.00	235.00	830.00	1965.00
□1882	Tillman-Morgan	Blue	55.00	95.00	300.00	900.00
□1882	Tillman-Roberts	Blue	55.00	95.00	300.00	900.00
□1882	Bruce-Roberts	Blue	55.00	95.00	300.00	900.00
□1882	Lyons-Roberts	Blue	55.00	95.00	300.00	900.00
□1882	Vernon-Treat	Blue	55.00	95.00	300.00	900.00
□1882	Vernon-McClung	Blue				RARE
□1882	Napier-McClung	Blue	90.00	300.00	950.00	1900.00

FIVE DOLLAR NOTES (1882) NATIONAL BANK NOTES
SECOND CHARTER PERIOD, Third Issue (Large Size)

Face Design: Same as 1882 note. Blue seal.

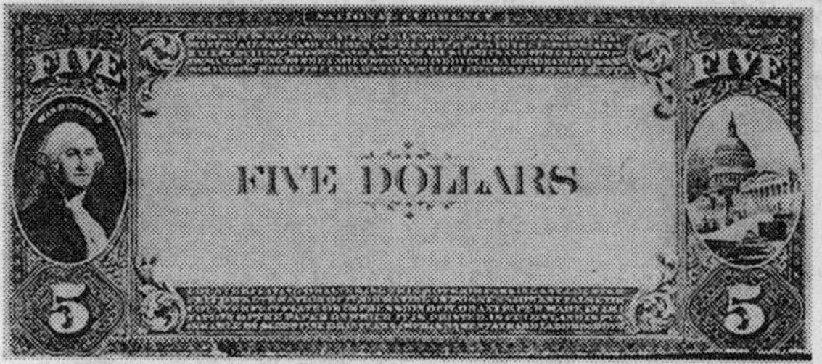

Back Design: Similar to 1882 Second Issue note. FIVE DOLLARS replaces "1882–1908."

SERIES	SIGNATURES	SEAL	A.B.P.	GOOD	V. FINE	UNC.
□1882	Tillman-Morgan	Blue	75.00	105.00	420.00	1400.00
□1882	Tillman-Roberts	Blue	75.00	105.00	420.00	1500.00
□1882	Bruce-Roberts	Blue	75.00	105.00	420.00	1400.00
□1882	Lyons-Roberts	Blue	75.00	105.00	420.00	1500.00
□1882	Vernon-Treat	Blue	75.00	105.00	420.00	1400.00
□1882	Napier-McClung	Blue	75.00	105.00	420.00	1400.00
□1882	Teehee-Burke	Blue	EXTREMELY RARE			

FIVE DOLLAR NOTES (1902) NATIONAL BANK NOTES
THIRD CHARTER PERIOD (Large Size)

First Issue (Red seal and charter numbers.)
Face Design: Portrait of President Harrison left, name of bank and city center, Treasury Seal to right, red seal and charter number.

Back Design: Landing of Pilgrims.

SERIES	SIGNATURES	SEAL	A.B.P.	GOOD	V. FINE	UNC.
□1902	Lyons-Roberts	Red	70.00	115.00	325.00	1200.00
□1902	Lyons-Treat	Red	70.00	115.00	325.00	1200.00
□1902	Vernon-Treat	Red	70.00	115.00	325.00	1200.00

FIVE DOLLAR NOTES (1902) NATIONAL BANK NOTES
THIRD CHARTER PERIOD (Large Size)

SECOND ISSUE

SERIES	SIGNATURES	SEAL	A.B.P.	GOOD	V. FINE	UNC.
□1902	Lyons-Roberts	Blue	19.00	30.00	90.00	425.00
□1902	Lyons-Treat	Blue	19.00	30.00	90.00	425.00
□1902	Vernon-Treat	Blue	19.00	30.00	90.00	425.00
□1902	Vernon-McClung	Blue	19.00	30.00	90.00	425.00
□1902	Napier-McClung	Blue	19.00	30.00	90.00	425.00
□1902	Napier-Thompson	Blue	26.00	40.00	100.00	525.00
□1902	Napier-Burke	Blue	19.00	30.00	90.00	425.00
□1902	Parker-Burke	Blue	19.00	30.00	90.00	425.00
□1902	Teehee-Burke	Blue	19.00	30.00	1100.00	425.00

FIVE DOLLAR NOTES (1902) NATIONAL BANK NOTES
THIRD CHARTER PERIOD (Large Size)
Third Issue (Blue seal and numbers.)

The following notes do not have date of "1902–1908" on the back.

SERIES	SIGNATURES	SEAL	A.B.P.	GOOD	V. FINE	UNC.
□1902	Lyons-Roberts	Blue	19.00	29.00	95.00	375.00
□1902	Lyons-Treat	Blue	19.00	29.00	95.00	375.00
□1902	Vernon-Treat	Blue	19.00	29.00	95.00	375.00
□1902	Vernon-McClung	Blue	19.00	29.00	95.00	375.00
□1902	Napier-McClung	Blue	19.00	29.00	95.00	375.00
□1902	Napier-Thompson	Blue	19.00	29.00	95.00	375.00
□1902	Napier-Burke	Blue	19.00	29.00	95.00	375.00
□1902	Parker-Burke	Blue	19.00	29.00	95.00	375.00
□1902	Teehee-Burke	Blue	19.00	29.00	95.00	375.00
□1902	Elliott-Burke	Blue	19.00	29.00	95.00	375.00
□1902	Elliott-White	Blue	19.00	29.00	95.00	375.00
□1902	Speelman-White	Blue	19.00	29.00	95.00	375.00
□1902	Woods-White	Blue	19.00	29.00	95.00	375.00
□1902	Woods-Tate	Blue	19.00	29.00	95.00	375.00
□1902	Jones-Woods	Blue	66.00	96.00	215.00	575.00

FIVE DOLLAR NOTES (1929) NATIONAL BANK NOTES
(Small Size)

TYPE I

TYPE II

Face Design: Portrait of President Lincoln in center, name of bank to left, brown seal to the right. Type I—charter number in black. Type II—similar; charter number added in brown.

Back Design: Lincoln Memorial.

SERIES	SIGNATURES	SEAL	A.B.P.	GOOD	V. FINE	UNC.
☐1929	Type I Jones-Woods	Brown	10.00	15.00	35.00	140.00
☐1929	Type II Jones-Woods	Brown	10.00	17.00	35.00	145.00

FIVE DOLLAR NOTES (1870)
NATIONAL GOLD BANK NOTES

(Large Size)

Face Design: Vignettes of Columbus sighting land. Presentation of an Indian princess. Red seal. Signatures, Allison-Spinner.

Back Design: California State Seal left, gold coins center, American eagle right.

DATE	BANK	CITY	A.B.P.	GOOD	V. GOOD
□1870	First National Gold Bank	San Francisco	500.00	750.00	1375.00
□1872	National Gold Bank and Trust Co.	San Francisco	500.00	750.00	1375.00
□1872	National Gold Bank of D.O. Mills and Co.	Sacramento	620.00	900.00	1775.00
□1873	First National Gold Bank	Santa Barbara	620.00	900.00	1775.00
□1873	First National Gold Bank	Stockton	620.00	900.00	2175.00
□1874	Farmers National Gold Bank	San Jose	620.00	900.00	2175.00

FIVE DOLLAR NOTES (1886–1891)
SILVER CERTIFICATES

(Large Size)

Face Design: Portrait of President Grant.

Back Design: Five silver dollars.

SERIES	SIGNATURES	SEAL	A.B.P.	GOOD	V. FINE	UNC.
□1886	Rosecrans-Jordan	Red	180.00	260.00	1800.00	4350.00
□1886	Rosecrans-Hyatt	Sm. Red	180.00	260.00	1800.00	4350.00
□1886	Rosecrans-Hyatt	Lg. Red	180.00	260.00	1800.00	4350.00
□1886	Rosecrans-Huston	Lg. Red	180.00	260.00	1800.00	4350.00
□1886	Rosecrans-Huston	Brown	180.00	260.00	1800.00	4350.00
□1886	Rosecrans-Nebeker	Brown	180.00	260.00	1800.00	4350.00
□1886	Rosecrans-Nebeker	Sm. Red	200.00	275.00	1725.00	4850.00

FIVE DOLLAR NOTES (1891) SILVER CERTIFICATES
(Large Size)

Face Design: Similar to previous note.

Back Design: Revised.

SERIES	SIGNATURES	SEAL	A.B.P.	GOOD	V. FINE	UNC.
□1891	Rosecrans-Nebeker	Red	95.00	145.00	800.00	3400.00
□1891	Tillman-Morgan	Red	95.00	145.00	800.00	3200.00

FIVE DOLLAR NOTES (1896) SILVER CERTIFICATES
(Large Size)

Face Design: Portraits of General Grant and General Sheridan.

Back Design: Five females representing Electricity as the dominant force in the world.

This was the last note of the popular Education Series.

SERIES	SIGNATURES	SEAL	A.B.P.	GOOD	V. FINE	UNC.
□1896	Tillman-Morgan	Red	210.00	335.00	1600.00	7400.00
□1896	Bruce-Roberts	Red	210.00	335.00	1600.00	7400.00
□1896	Lyons-Roberts	Red	210.00	335.00	1600.00	7400.00

FIVE DOLLAR NOTES (1899) SILVER CERTIFICATES
(Large Size)

Face Design: Portrait of Indian chief.

Back Design: Green "V" and "5."

SERIES	SIGNATURES	SEAL	A.B.P.	GOOD	V. FINE	UNC.
□1899	Lyons-Roberts	Blue	170.00	235.00	675.00	1900.00
□1899	Lyons-Treat	Blue	170.00	235.00	675.00	1900.00
□1899	Vernon-Treat	Blue	170.00	235.00	675.00	1900.00
□1899	Vernon-McClung	Blue	170.00	235.00	675.00	1900.00
□1899	Napier-McClung	Blue	170.00	235.00	675.00	1900.00
□1899	Napier-Thompson	Blue	170.00	235.00	965.00	2775.00
□1899	Parker-Burke	Blue	170.00	235.00	675.00	1900.00
□1899	Teehee-Burke	Blue	170.00	235.00	675.00	1900.00
□1899	Elliott-Burke	Blue	170.00	235.00	675.00	1900.00
□1899	Elliott-White	Blue	170.00	235.00	675.00	1900.00
□1899	Speelman-White	Blue	170.00	235.00	675.00	1900.00

FIVE DOLLAR NOTES (1923) SILVER CERTIFICATES
(Large Size)

Face Design: Portrait of President Lincoln in oval, nickname "Porthole Note," blue seal left, blue "5" right.

Back Design: Obverse of Great Seal of the United States.

SERIES	SIGNATURES	SEAL	A.B.P.	GOOD	V. FINE	UNC.
□1923	Speelman-White	Blue	140.00	200.00	750.00	2200.00

FIVE DOLLAR NOTES (1934) SILVER CERTIFICATES
(Small Size)

First Issue (Small size of $5 Silver Certificates 1934.)
Face Design: Portrait of President Lincoln, blue "5" to left, blue seal to right.

Back Design: All Small Size $5 Notes have the same back design.

SERIES	SIGNATURES	SEAL	A.B.P.	GOOD	V. FINE	UNC.	★UNC.
□1934	Julian-Morgenthau	Blue	6.00	8.00	13.00	40.00	450.00
□1934A	Julian-Morgenthau	Blue	6.00	8.00	10.00	32.00	350.00
□1934A	Julian-Morgenthau	Yellow	6.50	15.00	40.00	300.00	750.00

This note, with yellow Treasury Seal, was a Special Issue during World War II for military use in combat areas of North Africa and Europe.

SERIES	SIGNATURES	SEAL	A.B.P.	GOOD	V. FINE	UNC.	★UNC.
□1934B	Julian-Vinson	Blue	6.00	8.00	21.00	70.00	450.00
□1934C	Julian-Synder	Blue	6.00	8.00	11.00	30.00	250.00
□1934D	Clark-Snyder	Blue	6.00	8.00	11.00	28.00	300.00

FIVE DOLLAR NOTES (1953) SILVER CERTIFICATES
(Small Size)

Face Design: The following notes are similar to the previous note. The face design has been revised. Gray "5" replaces blue "5" to left of Lincoln. Blue seal is slightly smaller.

Back Design: Same as previous note.

SERIES	SIGNATURES	SEAL	A.B.P.	GOOD	V. FINE	UNC.	★UNC.
☐1953	Priest-Humphrey	Blue	6.25	7.25	10.00	30.00	55.00
☐1953A	Priest-Anderson	Blue	6.25	7.25	10.00	25.00	30.00
☐1953B	Smith-Dillon	Blue	6.25	7.25	10.00	25.00	5000.00

Production of $5 Silver Certificates ended in 1962.

FIVE DOLLAR NOTES (1890) TREASURY OR COIN NOTES
(Large Size)

Face Design: Portrait of General George Henry Thomas (1816–70), the "Rock of Chickamauga."

Back Design:

SERIES	SIGNATURES	SEAL	A.B.P.	GOOD	V. FINE	UNC.
□1890	Rosecrans-Huston	Brown	125.00	180.00	960.00	3750.00
□1890	Rosecrans-Nebeker	Brown	125.00	180.00	960.00	3950.00
□1890	Rosecrans-Nebeker	Red	125.00	180.00	960.00	3750.00

Back Design: Second Issue

SERIES	SIGNATURES	SEAL	A.B.P.	GOOD	V.FINE	UNC.
□1891	Rosecrans-Nebeker	Red	90.00	135.00	540.00	1700.00
□1891	Tillman-Morgan	Red	90.00	135.00	540.00	1700.00
□1891	Bruce-Roberts	Red	90.00	135.00	540.00	1700.00
□1891	Lyons-Roberts	Red	90.00	135.00	540.00	1700.00

FIVE DOLLAR NOTES (1914)
FEDERAL RESERVE NOTES

(Large Size)

Face Design: Portrait of President Lincoln center, Federal Reserve Seal left, Treasury Seal right.

Back Design: Scene of Columbus in sight of land left, landing of Pilgrims right.

SERIES OF 1914, RED TREASURY SEAL AND RED NUMBERS

SERIES	BANK	SIGNATURES	SEAL	A.B.P.	GOOD	V. FINE	UNC.
□1914	Boston	Burke-McAdoo	Red	40.00	50.00	425.00	1750.00
□1914	New York	Burke-McAdoo	Red	40.00	50.00	320.00	1675.00
□1914	Philadelphia	Burke-McAdoo	Red	40.00	50.00	330.00	1725.00
□1914	Cleveland	Burke-McAdoo	Red	40.00	50.00	350.00	1700.00
□1914	Richmond	Burke-McAdoo	Red	40.00	50.00	370.00	1750.00
□1914	Atlanta	Burke-McAdoo	Red	40.00	50.00	330.00	1700.00
□1914	Chicago	Burke-McAdoo	Red	40.00	50.00	475.00	1675.00
□1914	St. Louis	Burke-McAdoo	Red	40.00	50.00	370.00	1700.00
□1914	Minneapolis	Burke-McAdoo	Red	40.00	50.00	415.00	1950.00
□1914	Kansas City	Burke-McAdoo	Red	40.00	50.00	325.00	1700.00
□1914	Dallas	Burke-McAdoo	Red	40.00	50.00	425.00	1775.00
□1914	San Francisco	Burke-McAdoo	Red	40.00	50.00	425.00	1850.00

FIVE DOLLAR NOTES (1914)
FEDERAL RESERVE NOTES

SERIES OF 1914, BLUE TREASURY SEAL AND BLUE NUMBERS

SERIES	BANK	SIGNATURES	SEAL	A.B.P.	GOOD	V. FINE	UNC.
□1914	Boston	Burke-McAdoo	Blue	15.00	44.00	85.00	205.00
□1914	Boston	Burke-Glass	Blue	15.00	44.00	100.00	250.00
□1914	Boston	Burke-Huston	Blue	15.00	44.00	75.00	165.00
□1914	Boston	White-Mellon	Blue	15.00	44.00	75.00	160.00
□1914	New York	Burke-McAdoo	Blue	15.00	44.00	75.00	165.00
□1914	New York	Burke-Glass	Blue	15.00	44.00	85.00	205.00
□1914	New York	Burke-Huston	Blue	15.00	44.00	75.00	165.00
□1914	New York	White-Mellon	Blue	15.00	44.00	75.00	160.00
□1914	Philadelphia	Burke-McAdoo	Blue	15.00	44.00	100.00	250.00
□1914	Philadelphia	Burke-Glass	Blue	15.00	44.00	100.00	250.00
□1914	Philadelphia	Burke-Huston	Blue	15.00	44.00	75.00	165.00

SERIES	BANK	SIGNATURES	SEAL	A.B.P.	GOOD	V. FINE	UNC.
□1914	Philadelphia	White-Mellon	Blue	15.00	22.50	75.00	160.00
□1914	Cleveland	Burke-McAdoo	Blue	15.00	22.50	85.00	205.00
□1914	Cleveland	Burke-Glass	Blue	15.00	22.50	125.00	305.00
□1914	Cleveland	Burke-Huston	Blue	15.00	22.50	75.00	165.00
□1914	Cleveland	White-Mellon	Blue	15.00	22.50	75.00	160.00
□1914	Richmond	Burke-McAdoo	Blue	15.00	22.50	75.00	165.00
□1914	Richmond	Burke-Glass	Blue	15.00	22.50	125.00	320.00
□1914	Richmond	Burke-Huston	Blue	15.00	22.50	75.00	280.00
□1914	Richmond	White-Mellon	Blue	15.00	22.50	75.00	255.00
□1914	Atlanta	Burke-McAdoo	Blue	15.00	22.50	125.00	320.00
□1914	Atlanta	Burke-Glass	Blue	15.00	22.50	285.00	570.00
□1914	Atlanta	Burke-Huston	Blue	15.00	22.50	95.00	250.00
□1914	Atlanta	White-Mellon	Blue	15.00	22.50	75.00	165.00
□1914	Chicago	Burke-McAdoo	Blue	15.00	22.50	125.00	315.00
□1914	Chicago	Burke-Glass	Blue	15.00	22.50	75.00	160.00
□1914	Chicago	Burke-Huston	Blue	15.00	22.50	75.00	160.00
□1914	Chicago	White-Mellon	Blue	15.00	22.50	75.00	160.00
□1914	St. Louis	Burke-McAdoo	Blue	15.00	22.50	95.00	250.00
□1914	St. Louis	Burke-Glass	Blue	15.00	24.00	77.00	185.00
□1914	St. Louis	Burke-Huston	Blue	15.00	22.50	73.00	175.00
□1914	St. Louis	White-Mellon	Blue	15.00	22.50	75.00	165.00
□1914	Minneapolis	Burke-McAdoo	Blue	15.00	24.00	95.00	250.00
□1914	Minneapolis	Burke-Glass	Blue	15.00	24.00	125.00	290.00
□1914	Minneapolis	Burke-Huston	Blue	15.00	22.50	85.00	210.00
□1914	Minneapolis	White-Mellon	Blue	15.00	22.50	75.00	175.00
□1914	Kansas City	Burke-McAdoo	Blue	15.00	22.50	85.00	200.00
□1914	Kansas City	Burke-Glass	Blue	15.00	24.00	95.00	250.00
□1914	Kansas City	Burke-Huston	Blue	15.00	22.50	75.00	200.00
□1914	Kansas City	White-Mellon	Blue	15.00	22.50	75.00	160.00
□1914	Dallas	Burke-McAdoo	Blue	15.00	22.50	130.00	290.00
□1914	Dallas	Burke-Glass	Blue	15.00	25.00	125.00	260.00
□1914	Dallas	Burke-Huston	Blue	15.00	22.50	125.00	255.00
□1914	Dallas	White-Mellon	Blue	15.00	22.50	80.00	175.00
□1914	San Francisco	Burke-McAdoo	Blue	15.00	22.50	135.00	300.00
□1914	San Francisco	Burke-Glass	Blue	15.00	24.00	185.00	365.00
□1914	San Francisco	Burke-Huston	Blue	15.00	22.50	115.00	290.00
□1914	San Francisco	White-Mellon	Blue	15.00	22.50	75.00	165.00

FIVE DOLLAR NOTES (1928)
FEDERAL RESERVE NOTES

(Small Size)

Face Design: Portrait of President Lincoln center, black Federal Reserve Seal with numeral for district in center. City of issuing bank in seal circle. Green Treasury Seal to right.
Back Design: Similar to 1935 note. Lincoln Memorial in Washington, D.C.

SERIES OF 1928, SIGNATURES OF TATE AND MELLON, GREEN SEAL

BANK	A.B.P.	GOOD	V.FINE	UNC.	★UNC.	BANK	A.B.P.	GOOD	V.FINE	UNC.	★UNC.
☐ Boston	10.00	14.00	50.00	350.00	1500.00	☐ Chicago	8.50	12.00	30.00	130.00	975.00
☐ New York	10.00	14.00	30.00	150.00	850.00	☐ St. Louis	8.50	12.00	30.00	200.00	1500.00
☐ Philadelphia	10.00	14.00	30.00	150.00	850.00	☐ Minneapolis	8.50	12.00	125.00	775.00	2500.00
☐ Cleveland	10.00	14.00	30.00	150.00	950.00	☐ Kansas City	8.50	12.00	40.00	200.00	1800.00
☐ Richmond	10.00	14.00	30.00	150.00	1250.00	☐ Dallas	8.50	12.00	30.00	145.00	2000.00
☐ Atlanta	10.00	14.00	30.00	150.00	1500.00	☐ San Francisco	8.50	12.00	30.00	250.00	1500.00

SERIES OF 1928A, SIGNATURES OF WOODS-MELLON, GREEN SEAL

BANK	A.B.P.	GOOD	V.FINE	UNC.	★UNC.	BANK	A.B.P.	GOOD	V.FINE	UNC.	★UNC.
☐ Boston	8.00	13.00	23.00	250.00	1500.00	☐ Chicago	8.00	12.00	24.00	150.00	900.00
☐ New York	8.00	13.00	23.00	125.00	1000.00	☐ St. Louis	8.00	12.00	24.00	150.00	2500.00
☐ Philadelphia	8.00	13.00	23.00	150.00	1000.00	☐ Minneapolis	8.00	12.00	28.00	2000.00	5000.00
☐ Cleveland	8.00	13.00	23.00	150.00	1500.00	☐ Kansas City	8.00	12.00	26.00	200.00	5000.00
☐ Richmond	8.00	13.00	50.00	150.00	1500.00	☐ Dallas	8.00	12.00	52.00	250.00	2000.00
☐ Atlanta	8.00	13.00	23.00	350.00	2500.00	☐ San Francisco	8.00	12.00	26.00	250.00	1500.00

SERIES OF 1928B,
SIGNATURES OF WOODS-MELLON, GREEN SEAL

The black Federal Reserve Seal now has a letter for district in place of the numeral.

BANK	A.B.P.	GOOD	V.FINE	UNC.	★UNC.	BANK	A.B.P.	GOOD	V.FINE	UNC.	★UNC.
☐ Boston	7.00	11.00	20.00	85.00	750.00	☐ Chicago	7.00	11.00	20.00	85.00	750.00
☐ New York	7.00	11.00	20.00	85.00	750.00	☐ St. Louis	7.00	11.00	20.00	85.00	750.00
☐ Philadelphia	7.00	11.00	20.00	85.00	750.00	☐ Minneapolis	7.00	11.00	20.00	200.00	1000.00
☐ Cleveland	7.00	11.00	20.00	85.00	750.00	☐ Kansas City	7.00	11.00	20.00	85.00	1000.00
☐ Richmond	7.00	11.00	20.00	85.00	750.00	☐ Dallas	7.00	11.00	20.00	150.00	1000.00
☐ Atlanta	7.00	11.00	20.00	85.00	750.00	☐ San Francisco	7.00	11.00	20.00	85.00	1000.00

SERIES OF 1928C,
SIGNATURES OF WOODS-WOODIN, GREEN SEAL

BANK	A.B.P.	GOOD	V.FINE	UNC.	★UNC.
☐ Atlanta	80.00	110.00	600.00	3000.00	RARE

SERIES OF 1928D,
SIGNATURES OF WOODS-MILLS, GREEN SEAL

BANK	A.B.P.	GOOD	V.FINE	UNC.	★UNC.
☐ Atlanta	255.00	410.00	1500.00	6500.00	RARE

FIVE DOLLAR NOTES (1934)
FEDERAL RESERVE NOTES
SERIES OF 1934,
JULIAN-MORGENTHAU, GREEN SEAL

"Redeemable in Gold" was removed from obligation over Federal Reserve Seal. Also, the green Treasury Seal on this note is known in a light and dark color. The light seal is worth about 10–20 percent more in most cases.

BANK	A.B.P.	V.FINE	UNC.	★UNC.	BANK	A.B.P.	V.FINE	UNC.	★UNC.
☐ Boston	8.00	13.00	70.00	180.00	☐ St. Louis	8.00	13.00	50.00	180.00
☐ New York	8.00	13.00	50.00	180.00	☐ Minneapolis	8.00	13.00	65.00	180.00
☐ Philadelphia	8.00	13.00	60.00	180.00	☐ Kansas City	8.00	13.00	50.00	180.00
☐ Cleveland	8.00	13.00	50.00	180.00	☐ Dallas	8.00	13.00	80.00	180.00
☐ Richmond	8.00	13.00	70.00	180.00	☐ San Francisco	8.00	13.00	50.00	180.00
☐ Atlanta	8.00	13.00	60.00	180.00	☐ San Francisco*	20.00	100.00	700.00	6000.00
☐ Chicago	8.00	13.00	50.00	180.00					

*This note has brown Treasury Seal and is surprinted HAWAII. For use in Pacific area of operations during World War II.

(Small Size)

Note—1934A (Julian-Morgenthau) is surprinted HAWAII. It was used in the Pacific area during World War II.

SERIES OF 1934A, JULIAN-MORGENTHAU, GREEN SEAL

BANK	A.B.P.	V.FINE	UNC.	★UNC.	BANK	A.B.P.	V.FINE	UNC.	★UNC.
☐ Boston	7.00	13.00	45.00	280.00	☐ Atlanta	7.00	13.00	45.00	600.00
☐ New York	7.00	13.00	45.00	280.00	☐ Chicago	7.00	13.00	45.00	280.00
☐ Philadelphia	7.00	13.00	45.00	280.00	☐ St. Louis	7.00	13.00	45.00	280.00
☐ Cleveland	7.00	13.00	45.00	500.00	☐ San Francisco	7.00	13.00	45.00	280.00
☐ Richmond	7.00	13.00	45.00	400.00	☐ Hawaii*	20.00	75.00	650.00	15000.00

*This note has brown Treasury Seal and is surprinted HAWAII. For use in Pacific area of operations during World War II.

(Small Size)

SERIES OF 1934B, SIGNATURES OF JULIAN-VINSON, GREEN SEAL

BANK	A.B.P.	V.FINE	UNC.	★UNC.	BANK	A.B.P.	V.FINE	UNC.	★UNC.
☐ Boston	7.00	12.00	65.00	500.00	☐ Chicago	6.00	11.00	65.00	500.00
☐ New York	7.00	12.00	65.00	500.00	☐ St. Louis	6.00	11.00	65.00	500.00
☐ Philadelphia	7.00	12.00	65.00	500.00	☐ Minneapolis	6.00	11.00	65.00	500.00
☐ Cleveland	7.00	12.00	65.00	500.00	☐ Kansas City	75.00	1000.00	2500.00	8000.00
☐ Richmond	7.00	12.00	65.00	500.00	☐ Dallas			NOT ISSUED	
☐ Atlanta	7.00	12.00	65.00	500.00	☐ San Francisco	6.00	11.00	65.00	500.00

SERIES OF 1934C, SIGNATURES OF JULIAN-SNYDER, GREEN SEAL

BANK	A.B.P.	V.FINE	UNC.	★UNC.	BANK	A.B.P.	V.FINE	UNC.	★UNC.
☐ Boston	7.00	11.00	75.00	750.00	☐ Chicago	7.00	10.00	75.00	600.00
☐ New York	7.00	11.00	75.00	600.00	☐ St. Louis	7.00	10.00	75.00	600.00
☐ Philadelphia	7.00	11.00	75.00	700.00	☐ Minneapolis	7.00	10.00	75.00	1250.00
☐ Cleveland	7.00	11.00	75.00	500.00	☐ Kansas City	7.00	10.00	75.00	700.00
☐ Richmond	7.00	11.00	75.00	650.00	☐ Dallas	7.00	10.00	75.00	1500.00
☐ Atlanta	7.00	11.00	75.00	750.00	☐ San Francisco	7.00	10.00	75.00	750.00

SERIES OF 1934D, SIGNATURES OF CLARK-SNYDER, GREEN SEAL

BANK	A.B.P.	V.FINE	UNC.	★UNC.	BANK	A.B.P.	V.FINE	UNC.	★UNC.
☐ Boston	6.50	9.00	95.00	650.00	☐ Chicago	6.50	9.00	80.00	500.00
☐ New York	6.50	9.00	85.00	500.00	☐ St. Louis	6.50	9.00	85.00	750.00
☐ Philadelphia	6.50	9.00	90.00	700.00	☐ Minneapolis	6.50	9.00	90.00	1250.00
☐ Cleveland	6.50	9.00	90.00	750.00	☐ Kansas City	6.50	9.00	95.00	750.00
☐ Richmond	6.50	9.00	130.00	750.00	☐ Dallas	6.50	9.00	150.00	750.00
☐ Atlanta	100.00	400.00	2250.00	4500.00	☐ San Francisco	6.50	9.00	95.00	750.00

FIVE DOLLAR NOTES (1950)
FEDERAL RESERVE NOTES
BLACK FEDERAL RESERVE SEAL AND GREEN TREASURY SEALS ARE NOW SMALLER

(Small Size)

SERIES OF 1950, SIGNATURES OF CLARK-SNYDER, GREEN SEAL

BANK	A.B.P.	V.FINE	UNC.	★UNC.	BANK	A.B.P.	V.FINE	UNC.	★UNC.
☐ Boston	6.00	10.00	65.00	500.00	☐ Chicago	6.00	10.00	45.00	400.00
☐ New York	6.00	10.00	55.00	300.00	☐ St. Louis	6.00	10.00	65.00	400.00
☐ Philadelphia	6.00	10.00	55.00	400.00	☐ Minneapolis	6.00	10.00	90.00	750.00
☐ Cleveland	6.00	10.00	50.00	400.00	☐ Kansas City	6.00	10.00	90.00	400.00
☐ Richmond	6.00	10.00	65.00	500.00	☐ Dallas	6.00	10.00	80.00	600.00
☐ Atlanta	6.00	10.00	65.00	500.00	☐ San Francisco	6.00	10.00	65.00	500.00

SERIES OF 1950A, SIGNATURES OF PRIEST-HUMPHREY, GREEN SEAL

BANK	A.B.P.	V.FINE	UNC.	★UNC.	BANK	A.B.P.	V.FINE	UNC.	★UNC.
☐ Boston	6.00	10.00	30.00	75.00	☐ Chicago	6.00	10.00	30.00	65.00
☐ New York	6.00	10.00	30.00	65.00	☐ St. Louis	6.00	10.00	30.00	125.00
☐ Philadelphia	6.00	10.00	30.00	75.00	☐ Minneapolis	6.00	10.00	30.00	175.00
☐ Cleveland	6.00	10.00	30.00	75.00	☐ Kansas City	6.00	10.00	30.00	100.00
☐ Richmond	6.00	10.00	30.00	75.00	☐ Dallas	6.00	10.00	30.00	150.00
☐ Atlanta	6.00	10.00	30.00	75.00	☐ San Francisco	6.00	10.00	30.00	75.00

SERIES OF 1950B, SIGNATURES OF PRIEST-ANDERSON, GREEN SEAL

BANK	A.B.P.	V.FINE	UNC.	★UNC.	BANK	A.B.P.	V.FINE	UNC.	★UNC.
☐ Boston	6.00	9.00	25.00	55.00	☐ Chicago	6.00	9.00	25.00	55.00
☐ New York	6.00	9.00	25.00	55.00	☐ St. Louis	6.00	9.00	25.00	55.00
☐ Philadelphia	6.00	9.00	25.00	55.00	☐ Minneapolis	6.00	10.00	25.00	55.00
☐ Cleveland	6.00	9.00	25.00	55.00	☐ Kansas City	6.00	10.00	25.00	55.00
☐ Richmond	6.00	9.00	25.00	55.00	☐ Dallas	6.00	9.00	25.00	55.00
☐ Atlanta	6.00	9.00	25.00	55.00	☐ San Francisco	6.00	9.00	25.00	55.00

SERIES OF 1950C, SIGNATURES OF SMITH-DILLON, GREEN SEAL

BANK	A.B.P.	V.FINE	UNC.	★UNC.	BANK	A.B.P.	V.FINE	UNC.	★UNC.
☐ Boston	5.75	9.00	25.00	100.00	☐ Chicago	5.75	9.00	25.00	50.00
☐ New York	5.75	9.00	25.00	60.00	☐ St. Louis	5.75	9.00	25.00	150.00
☐ Philadelphia	5.75	9.00	25.00	100.00	☐ Minneapolis	5.75	10.00	25.00	200.00
☐ Cleveland	5.75	9.00	25.00	75.00	☐ Kansas City	5.75	10.00	25.00	100.00
☐ Richmond	5.75	9.00	25.00	100.00	☐ Dallas	5.75	9.00	25.00	250.00
☐ Atlanta	5.75	9.00	25.00	75.00	☐ San Francisco	5.75	9.00	25.00	150.00

SERIES OF 1950D, SIGNATURES OF GRANAHAN-DILLON, GREEN SEAL

BANK	A.B.P.	V.FINE	UNC.	★UNC.	BANK	A.B.P.	V.FINE	UNC.	★UNC.
☐ Boston	5.75	9.00	31.00	95.00	☐ Chicago	5.75	9.00	21.00	60.00
☐ New York	5.75	9.00	21.00	65.00	☐ St. Louis	5.75	9.00	27.00	100.00
☐ Philadelphia	5.75	9.00	31.00	90.00	☐ Minneapolis	5.75	10.00	33.00	155.00
☐ Cleveland	5.75	9.00	23.00	80.00	☐ Kansas City	5.75	9.00	23.00	105.00
☐ Richmond	5.75	9.00	28.00	80.00	☐ Dallas	5.75	9.00	28.00	175.00
☐ Atlanta	5.75	9.00	28.00	100.00	☐ San Francisco	5.75	9.00	21.00	95.00

SERIES OF 1950E, SIGNATURES OF GRANAHAN-FOWLER, GREEN SEAL

BANK	A.B.P.	V.FINE	UNC.	★UNC.	BANK	A.B.P.	V.FINE	UNC.	★UNC.
					☐ Chicago	6.00	9.00	60.00	175.00
☐ New York	6.00	9.00	40.00	85.00					
					☐ San Francisco	6.00	9.00	50.00	225.00

FIVE DOLLAR NOTES (1963)
FEDERAL RESERVE NOTES
(IN GOD WE TRUST IS ADDED ON BACK)

SERIES OF 1963, SIGNATURES OF GRANAHAN-DILLON, GREEN SEAL

BANK	A.B.P.	V.FINE	UNC.	★UNC.	BANK	A.B.P.	V.FINE	UNC.	★UNC.
☐ Boston	5.25	8.00	27.00	50.00	☐ Chicago	5.25	8.00	18.00	50.00
☐ New York	5.25	8.00	18.00	50.00	☐ St. Louis	5.25	8.00	22.00	42.00
☐ Philadelphia	5.25	8.00	20.00	50.00	☐ Minneapolis	5.25	8.00	22.00	50.00
☐ Cleveland	5.25	8.00	18.00	50.00	☐ Kansas City	5.25	8.00	22.00	40.00
☐ Richmond	5.25	8.00	18.00	50.00	☐ Dallas	5.25	8.00	22.00	50.00
☐ Atlanta	5.25	8.00	20.00	50.00	☐ San Francisco	5.25	8.00	22.00	50.00

SERIES OF 1963A, SIGNATURES OF GRANAHAN-FOWLER, GREEN SEAL

BANK	A.B.P.	V.FINE	UNC.	★UNC.	BANK	A.B.P.	V.FINE	UNC.	★UNC.
☐ Boston	5.25	7.00	17.00	30.00	☐ Chicago	5.25	7.00	17.00	30.00
☐ New York	5.25	7.00	17.00	30.00	☐ St. Louis	5.25	7.00	17.00	30.00
☐ Philadelphia	5.25	7.00	17.00	30.00	☐ Minneapolis	5.25	7.00	17.00	30.00
☐ Cleveland	5.25	7.00	17.00	30.00	☐ Kansas City	5.25	7.00	17.00	30.00
☐ Richmond	5.25	7.00	17.00	30.00	☐ Dallas	5.25	7.00	17.00	30.00
☐ Atlanta	5.25	7.00	17.00	30.00	☐ San Francisco	5.25	7.00	17.00	30.00

FIVE DOLLAR NOTES (1969)
FEDERAL RESERVE NOTES
(WORDING IN GREEN TREASURY SEAL IS CHANGED FROM LATIN TO ENGLISH)

SERIES OF 1969, SIGNATURES OF ELSTON-KENNEDY, GREEN SEAL

BANK	A.B.P.	V.FINE	UNC.	★UNC.	BANK	A.B.P.	V.FINE	UNC.	★UNC.
☐ Boston	5.00	6.00	15.00	33.00	☐ Chicago	5.00	6.00	15.00	33.00
☐ New York	5.00	6.00	15.00	33.00	☐ St. Louis	5.00	6.00	15.00	33.00
☐ Philadelphia	5.00	6.00	15.00	33.00	☐ Minneapolis	5.00	6.00	15.00	33.00
☐ Cleveland	5.00	6.00	15.00	33.00	☐ Kansas City	5.00	6.00	15.00	33.00
☐ Richmond	5.00	6.00	15.00	33.00	☐ Dallas	5.00	6.00	15.00	33.00
☐ Atlanta	5.00	6.00	15.00	33.00	☐ San Francisco	5.00	6.00	15.00	33.00

SERIES OF 1969A, SIGNATURES OF KABIS-CONNALLY, GREEN SEAL

BANK	A.B.P.	V.FINE	UNC.	★UNC.	BANK	A.B.P.	V.FINE	UNC.	★UNC.
☐ Boston	5.00	6.00	23.00	45.00	☐ Chicago	5.00	6.00	25.00	41.00
☐ New York	5.00	6.00	23.00	40.00	☐ St. Louis	5.00	6.00	25.00	55.00
☐ Philadelphia	5.00	6.00	23.00	40.00	☐ Minneapolis	5.00	6.00	25.00	45.00
☐ Cleveland	5.00	6.00	23.00	45.00	☐ Kansas City	5.00	6.00	25.00	45.00
☐ Richmond	5.00	6.00	23.00	45.00	☐ Dallas	5.00	6.00	25.00	47.00
☐ Atlanta	5.00	6.00	23.00	45.00	☐ San Francisco	5.00	6.00	25.00	50.00

SERIES OF 1969B, SIGNATURES OF BANUELOS-CONNALLY, GREEN SEAL

BANK	A.B.P.	V.FINE	UNC.	★UNC.	BANK	A.B.P.	V.FINE	UNC.	★UNC.
☐ Boston	5.00	12.00	75.00	—	☐ Chicago	5.00	12.00	50.00	150.00
☐ New York	5.00	8.00	50.00	130.00	☐ St. Louis	5.00	12.00	80.00	—
☐ Philadelphia	5.00	12.00	50.00	—	☐ Minneapolis	5.00	12.00	90.00	—
☐ Cleveland	5.00	12.00	50.00	—	☐ Kansas City	5.00	12.00	80.00	140.00
☐ Richmond	5.00	12.00	50.00	150.00	☐ Dallas	5.00	12.00	50.00	—
☐ Atlanta	5.00	12.00	50.00	175.00	☐ San Francisco	5.00	12.00	50.00	150.00

SERIES OF 1969C, SIGNATURES OF BANUELOS-SHULTZ, GREEN SEAL

BANK	A.B.P.	V.FINE	UNC.	★UNC.	BANK	A.B.P.	V.FINE	UNC.	★UNC.
☐ Boston	5.00	6.00	18.00	40.00	☐ Chicago	5.00	6.00	18.00	—
☐ New York	5.00	6.00	18.00	40.00	☐ St. Louis	5.00	6.00	18.00	40.00
☐ Philadelphia	5.00	6.00	18.00	40.00	☐ Minneapolis	5.00	6.00	18.00	—
☐ Cleveland	5.00	6.00	18.00	40.00	☐ Kansas City	5.00	6.00	18.00	40.00
☐ Richmond	5.00	6.00	18.00	40.00	☐ Dallas	5.00	6.00	18.00	40.00
☐ Atlanta	5.00	6.00	18.00	40.00	☐ San Francisco	5.00	6.00	18.00	40.00

FIVE DOLLAR NOTES (1974)
FEDERAL RESERVE NOTES

SERIES OF 1974, SIGNATURES OF NEFF-SIMON, GREEN SEAL

BANK	A.B.P.	V.FINE	UNC.	★UNC.	BANK	A.B.P.	V.FINE	UNC.	★UNC.
☐ Boston	—	6.00	15.00	25.00	☐ Chicago	—	6.00	15.00	25.00
☐ New York	—	6.00	15.00	25.00	☐ St. Louis	—	6.00	15.00	25.00
☐ Philadelphia	—	6.00	15.00	25.00	☐ Minneapolis	—	7.00	17.00	25.00
☐ Cleveland	—	6.00	15.00	25.00	☐ Kansas City	—	7.00	17.00	25.00
☐ Richmond	—	6.00	15.00	25.00	☐ Dallas	—	7.00	17.00	25.00
☐ Atlanta	—	6.00	15.00	25.00	☐ San Francisco	—	6.00	15.00	25.00

FIVE DOLLAR NOTES (1977)
FEDERAL RESERVE NOTES

SERIES OF 1977, SIGNATURES OF MORTON-BLUMENTHAL, GREEN SEAL

★Notes not issued for all banks

BANK	A.B.P.	V.FINE	UNC.	★UNC.	BANK	A.B.P.	V.FINE	UNC.	★UNC.
☐ Boston	—	6.00	15.00	50.00	☐ Chicago	—	6.00	15.00	26.00
☐ New York	—	6.00	15.00	26.00	☐ St. Louis	—	6.00	15.00	70.00
☐ Philadelphia	—	6.00	15.00	32.00	☐ Kansas City	—	7.00	15.00	35.00
☐ Cleveland	—	6.00	15.00	32.00	☐ Dallas	—	7.00	15.00	35.00
☐ Richmond	—	6.00	15.00	32.00	☐ San Francisco	—	6.00	15.00	35.00
☐ Atlanta	—	6.00	15.00	32.00					

SERIES OF 1977A, SIGNATURES OF MORTON-BLUMENTHAL, GREEN SEAL

BANK	A.B.P.	V.FINE	UNC.	★UNC.	BANK	A.B.P.	V.FINE	UNC.	★UNC.
☐ Boston	—	6.00	12.00	55.00	☐ Chicago	—	6.00	12.00	35.00
☐ New York	—	6.00	12.00	30.00	☐ St. Louis	—	6.00	12.00	60.00
☐ Philadelphia	—	6.00	12.00	30.00	☐ Minneapolis	—	6.00	12.00	75.00
☐ Cleveland	—	6.00	12.00	45.00	☐ Kansas City	—	6.00	12.00	50.00
☐ Richmond	—	6.00	12.00	85.00	☐ Dallas	—	6.00	12.00	45.00
☐ Atlanta	—	6.00	12.00	35.00	☐ San Francisco	—	6.00	12.00	35.00

FIVE DOLLAR NOTES (1981)
FEDERAL RESERVE NOTES

SERIES OF 1981, SIGNATURES OF BUCHANAN-REGAN, GREEN SEAL

★Notes not issued for all banks

BANK	A.B.P.	V.FINE	UNC.	★UNC.	BANK	A.B.P.	V.FINE	UNC.	★UNC.
☐ Boston	—	6.00	20.00	—	☐ Chicago	—	6.00	20.00	45.00
☐ New York	—	6.00	20.00	45.00	☐ St. Louis	—	6.00	20.00	45.00
☐ Philadelphia	—	6.00	20.00	45.00	☐ Minneapolis	—	7.00	20.00	45.00
☐ Cleveland	—	6.00	20.00	45.00	☐ Kansas City	—	7.00	20.00	45.00
☐ Richmond	—	6.00	20.00	45.00	☐ Dallas	—	7.00	20.00	45.00
☐ Atlanta	—	6.00	20.00	45.00	☐ San Francisco	—	6.00	20.00	45.00

SERIES OF 1981A, SIGNATURES OF ORTEGA-REGAN, GREEN SEAL

★Notes not issued for all banks

BANK	A.B.P.	V.FINE	UNC.	★UNC.	BANK	A.B.P.	V.FINE	UNC.	★UNC.
☐ Boston	—	6.00	25.00	—	☐ Chicago	—	6.00	25.00	—
☐ New York	—	6.00	25.00	40.00	☐ St. Louis	—	6.00	25.00	—
☐ Philadelphia	—	6.00	25.00	—	☐ Minneapolis	—	7.00	25.00	—
☐ Cleveland	—	6.00	25.00	—	☐ Kansas City	—	6.00	25.00	—
☐ Richmond	—	6.00	25.00	—	☐ Dallas	—	6.00	25.00	—
☐ Atlanta	—	6.00	25.00	—	☐ San Francisco	—	6.00	25.00	40.00

FIVE DOLLAR NOTES (1985)
FEDERAL RESERVE NOTES

SERIES OF 1985, SIGNATURES OF ORTEGA-BAKER, GREEN SEAL

★Notes not issued for all banks

BANK	A.B.P.	V.FINE	UNC.	★UNC.	BANK	A.B.P.	V.FINE	UNC.	★UNC.
☐ Boston	—	6.00	15.00	30.00	☐ Chicago	—	6.00	15.00	30.00
☐ New York	—	6.00	15.00	30.00	☐ St. Louis	—	6.00	15.00	30.00
☐ Philadelphia	—	6.00	15.00	30.00	☐ Minneapolis	—	6.00	15.00	30.00
☐ Cleveland	—	6.00	15.00	30.00	☐ Kansas City	—	6.00	15.00	30.00
☐ Richmond	—	6.00	15.00	30.00	☐ Dallas	—	6.00	15.00	30.00
☐ Atlanta	—	6.00	15.00	30.00	☐ San Francisco	—	6.00	15.00	30.00

FIVE DOLLAR NOTES (1988)
FEDERAL RESERVE NOTES
SERIES OF 1988, SIGNATURES OF ORTEGA-BRADY, GREEN SEAL

★Notes not issued for all banks

BANK	A.B.P.	V.FINE	UNC.	★UNC.	BANK	A.B.P.	V.FINE	UNC.	★UNC.
☐ Boston	—	6.00	15.00	20.00	☐ Chicago	—	6.00	15.00	20.00
☐ New York	—	6.00	15.00	20.00	☐ St. Louis	—	6.00	15.00	20.00
☐ Philadelphia	—	6.00	15.00	20.00	☐ Minneapolis	—	6.00	15.00	20.00
☐ Cleveland	—	6.00	15.00	20.00	☐ Kansas City	—	6.00	15.00	20.00
☐ Richmond	—	6.00	15.00	20.00	☐ Dallas	—	6.00	15.00	20.00
☐ Atlanta	—	6.00	15.00	20.00	☐ San Francisco	—	6.00	15.00	20.00

SERIES OF 1988A, SIGNATURES OF VILLALPANDO-BRADY, GREEN SEAL

★Notes not issued for all banks

BANK	A.B.P.	V.FINE	UNC.	★UNC.	BANK	A.B.P.	V.FINE	UNC.	★UNC.
☐ Boston	—	6.00	12.00	20.00	☐ Chicago	—	6.00	12.00	20.00
☐ New York	—	6.00	12.00	20.00	☐ St. Louis	—	6.00	12.00	20.00
☐ Philadelphia	—	6.00	12.00	20.00	☐ Minneapolis	—	6.00	12.00	20.00
☐ Cleveland	—	6.00	12.00	20.00	☐ Kansas City	—	6.00	12.00	20.00
☐ Richmond	—	6.00	12.00	20.00	☐ Dallas	—	6.00	12.00	20.00
☐ Atlanta	—	6.00	12.00	20.00	☐ San Francisco	—	6.00	12.00	20.00

FIVE DOLLAR NOTES (1993)
FEDERAL RESERVE NOTES
SERIES OF 1993, SIGNATURES OF WITHROW-BENTSEN, GREEN SEAL

★Notes not issued for all banks

BANK	A.B.P.	V.FINE	UNC.	★UNC.	BANK	A.B.P.	V.FINE	UNC.	★UNC.
☐ Boston	—	6.00	12.00	20.00	☐ Chicago	—	6.00	12.00	20.00
☐ New York	—	6.00	12.00	20.00	☐ St. Louis	—	6.00	12.00	20.00
☐ Philadelphia	—	6.00	12.00	20.00	☐ Minneapolis	—	6.00	12.00	20.00
☐ Cleveland	—	—	—	—	☐ Kansas City	—	6.00	12.00	20.00
☐ Richmond	—	6.00	12.00	20.00	☐ Dallas	—	6.00	12.00	20.00
☐ Atlanta	—	6.00	12.00	20.00	☐ San Francisco	—	6.00	12.00	20.00

FIVE DOLLAR NOTES (1995)
FEDERAL RESERVE NOTES
SERIES OF 1995, SIGNATURES OF WITHROW-RUBIN, GREEN SEAL

★Notes not issued for all banks

BANK	A.B.P.	V.FINE	UNC.	★UNC.	BANK	A.B.P.	V.FINE	UNC.	★UNC.
☐ Boston	—	6.00	8.00	20.00	☐ Chicago	—	6.00	8.00	20.00
☐ New York	—	6.00	8.00	20.00	☐ St. Louis	—	6.00	8.00	20.00
☐ Philadelphia	—	6.00	8.00	20.00	☐ Minneapolis	—	6.00	8.00	20.00
☐ Cleveland	—	6.00	8.00	20.00	☐ Kansas City	—	6.00	8.00	20.00
☐ Richmond	—	6.00	8.00	20.00	☐ Dallas	—	6.00	8.00	20.00
☐ Atlanta	—	0.00	0.00	20.00	☐ San Francisco	—	6.00	8.00	20.00

FIVE DOLLAR NOTES (1918)
FEDERAL RESERVE BANK NOTES
(ALL WITH BLUE SEAL AND BLUE SERIAL NUMBERS)

(Large Size)

Face Design: Portrait of President Lincoln with Reserve City in center.

Back Design: Same as 1914 note.

BANK	SERIES	GOV'T SIGNATURES	BANK SIGNATURES	A.B.P.	GOOD	V. FINE	UNC.
☐Boston	1918	Teehee-Burke	Bullen-Morse	45.00	68.00	290.00	975.00
☐New York	1918	Teehee-Burke	Hendricks-Strong	45.00	68.00	240.00	950.00
☐Philadelphia	1918	Teehee-Burke	Hardt-Passmore	45.00	68.00	290.00	1000.00
☐Philadelphia	1918	Teehee-Burke	Dyer-Passmore	45.00	68.00	290.00	1000.00
☐Cleveland	1918	Teehee-Burke	Dyer-Fancher	45.00	68.00	240.00	975.00
☐Cleveland	1918	Teehee-Burke	Davis-Fancher	45.00	68.00	290.00	875.00
☐Cleveland	1918	Elliott-Burke	Davis-Fancher	45.00	68.00	235.00	800.00
☐Atlanta	1915	Teehee-Burke	Bell-Wellborn	45.00	68.00	300.00	1100.00
☐Atlanta	1915	Teehee-Burke	Pike-McCord	45.00	68.00	290.00	970.00
☐Atlanta	1918	Teehee-Burke	Pike-McCord	45.00	68.00	320.00	975.00
☐Atlanta	1918	Teehee-Burke	Bell-Wellborn	45.00	68.00	320.00	1050.00

BANK	SERIES	GOV'T SIGNATURES	BANK SIGNATURES	A.B.P.	GOOD	V. FINE	UNC.
☐Atlanta	1918	Elliott-Burke	Bell-Wellborn	31.00	57.00	240.00	1050.00
☐Chicago	1915	Teehee-Burke	McLallen-McDougal	31.00	57.00	200.00	975.00
☐Chicago	1918	Teehee-Burke	McCloud-McDougal	27.00	57.00	170.00	975.00
☐Chicago	1918	Teehee-Burke	Cramer-McDougal	27.00	57.00	250.00	1050.00
☐St. Louis	1918	Teehee-Burke	Attebery-Wells	27.00	57.00	170.00	975.00
☐St. Louis	1918	Teehee-Burke	Attebery-Biggs	27.00	57.00	170.00	975.00
☐St. Louis	1918	Elliott-Burke	White-Biggs	27.00	57.00	170.00	975.00
☐Minneapolis	1918	Teehee-Burke	Cook-Wold	27.00	57.00	210.00	975.00
☐Kansas City	1915	Teehee-Burke	Anderson-Miller	29.00	60.00	210.00	975.00
☐Kansas City	1915	Teehee-Burke	Cross-Miller	29.00	60.00	220.00	975.00
☐Kansas City	1915	Teehee-Burke	Helm-Miller	29.00	60.00	240.00	1150.00
☐Kansas City	1918	Teehee-Burke	Anderson-Miller	29.00	60.00	170.00	975.00
☐Kansas City	1918	Elliott-Burke	Helm-Miller	29.00	60.00	215.00	975.00
☐Dallas	1915	Teehee-Burke	Hoopes-VanZandt	29.00	50.00	200.00	975.00
☐Dallas	1915	Teehee-Burke	Talley-VanZandt	29.00	50.00	270.00	1050.00
☐Dallas	1918	Teehee-Burke	Talley-VanZandt	29.00	50.00	210.00	1150.00
☐San Francisco	1915	Teehee-Burke	Clerk-Lynch	29.00	50.00	210.00	1100.00
☐San Francisco	1918	Teehee-Burke	Clerk-Lynch	29.00	50.00	270.00	1200.00

FIVE DOLLAR NOTES (1929)
FEDERAL RESERVE BANK NOTES

(Small Size)
Face Design: Portrait of President Lincoln.

SERIES 1929, BROWN SEAL

BANK & CITY	SIGNATURES	A.B.P.	GOOD	V.FINE	UNC.	*UNC.
☐Boston	Jones-Woods	8.00	13.00	35.00	175.00	3500.00
☐New York	Jones-Woods	8.00	13.00	34.00	150.00	3200.00
☐Philadelphia	Jones-Woods	8.00	13.00	35.00	150.00	3000.00
☐Cleveland	Jones-Woods	8.00	13.00	35.00	140.00	3000.00
☐Atlanta	Jones-Woods	8.00	13.00	33.00	325.00	3500.00
☐Chicago	Jones-Woods	8.00	13.00	33.00	125.00	3200.00
☐St. Louis	Jones-Woods	8.00	13.00	215.00	3000.00	3500.00
☐Minneapolis	Jones-Woods	8.00	13.00	73.00	1000.00	3300.00
☐Kansas City	Jones-Woods	8.00	13.00	34.00	175.00	3000.00
☐Dallas	Jones-Woods	8.00	13.00	38.00	125.00	5000.00
☐San Francisco	Jones-Woods	150.00	235.00	835.00	7500.00	15000.00

TEN DOLLAR NOTES

ORDER OF ISSUE

TEN DOLLAR NOTES (1861) DEMAND NOTES (NO TREASURY SEAL)

(Large Size)

Face Design: Portrait of President Lincoln left, female figure with sword and shield.

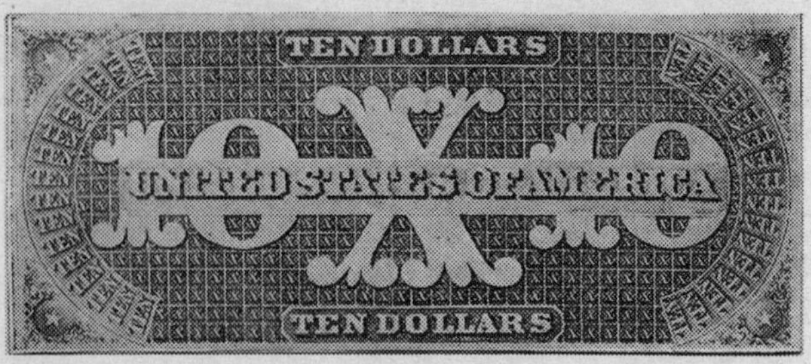

Back Design: Ornate designs of TEN.

PAYABLE AT	A.B.P.	GOOD	V. GOOD	FINE
☐Boston (I)	1000.00	2675.00	8000.00	RARE
☐New York (I)	1000.00	2675.00	8000.00	RARE
☐Philadelphia (I)	1000.00	2675.00	8000.00	RARE
☐Cincinnati (I)	740.00	3650.00	RARE	RARE
☐St. Louis (I)	1540.00	3650.00	RARE	RARE
☐Boston (II)	565.00	1000.00	1600.00	3300.00
☐New York (II)	540.00	950.00	1600.00	3300.00
☐Philadelphia (II)	540.00	950.00	1600.00	3300.00
☐Cincinnati (II)	4200.00	7800.00	18,000.00	RARE
☐St. Louis (II)	4500.00	8200.00	25,000.00	RARE

TEN DOLLAR NOTES (1862–1863) UNITED STATES NOTES (ALSO KNOWN AS LEGAL TENDER NOTES)

(Large Size)

Back Design

Face Design: Similar to 1861 note.

SERIES	SIGNATURES	SEAL	A.B.P.	GOOD	V.FINE	UNC.
□1862	Chittenden-Spinner*	Red	220.00	325.00	1350.00	6000.00
□1862	Chittenden-Spinner**	Red	220.00	325.00	1350.00	6000.00
□1863	Chittenden-Spinner**	Red	220.00	325.00	1350.00	6000.00

* First Obligation: Similar to 1875–1907 $5 note.
** Second Obligation: Shown above.

TEN DOLLAR NOTES (1869) UNITED STATES NOTES

(Large Size)

Face Design: Portrait of Daniel Webster left, presentation of Indian princess right. (This note is nicknamed "Jackass Note," because the EAGLE between the signatures resembles a donkey when it is held upside down.)

SERIES	SIGNATURES	SEAL	A.B.P.	GOOD	V.FINE	UNC.
□1869	Allison-Spinner	Red	130.00	200.00	900.00	3500.00

TEN DOLLAR NOTES (1875–1880)
UNITED STATES NOTES

(Large Size)

Face Design: Similar to 1869 note.

Back Design: Revised.

SERIES	SIGNATURES	SEAL	A.B.P.	GOOD	V.FINE	UNC.
□1875	Allison-New	Red	170.00	215.00	825.00	4400.00
□Same as above, Series A		Red	170.00	215.00	1125.00	4500.00
□1878	Allison-Gilfillan	Red	170.00	215.00	1050.00	3500.00
□1880	Scofield-Gilfillan	Brown	170.00	215.00	875.00	1850.00
□1880	Bruce-Gilfillan	Brown	125.00	215.00	875.00	2000.00
□1880	Bruce-Wyman	Brown	125.00	215.00	875.00	2000.00
□1880	Bruce-Wyman	Red Plain	125.00	215.00	925.00	2050.00
□1880	Rosecrans-Jordan	Red Plain	125.00	215.00	875.00	2700.00
□1880	Rosecrans-Hyatt	Red Plain	125.00	215.00	875.00	2400.00
□1880	Rosecrans-Hyatt	Red Spikes	125.00	215.00	875.00	2200.00
□1880	Rosecrans-Huston	Red Spikes	125.00	215.00	825.00	2200.00
□1880	Rosecrans-Huston	Brown	170.00	215.00	875.00	2600.00
□1880	Rosecrans-Nebeker	Brown	650.00	2100.00	4500.00	8000.00
□1880	Rosecrans-Nebeker	Red	120.00	1760.00	575.00	1600.00
□1880	Tillman-Morgan	Red	120.00	1760.00	575.00	1600.00

SERIES	SIGNATURES	SEAL	A.B.P.	GOOD	V.FINE	UNC.
□1880	Bruce-Roberts	Red	120.00	160.00	575.00	1600.00
□1880	Lyons-Roberts	Red	120.00	160.00	575.00	1600.00

TEN DOLLAR NOTES (1901) UNITED STATES NOTES
(Large Size)

Face Design: American bison (buffalo) center, portrait of Lewis left, portrait of Clark right.

Back Design: Female allegorical figure in arch.

SERIES	SIGNATURES	SEAL	A.B.P.	GOOD	V.FINE	UNC.
□1901	Lyons-Roberts	Red	210.00	280.00	775.00	2975.00
□1901	Lyons-Treat	Red	210.00	280.00	775.00	2975.00
□1901	Vernon-Treat	Red	210.00	280.00	775.00	2975.00
□1901	Vernon-McClung	Red	210.00	280.00	775.00	2975.00
□1901	Napier-McClung	Red	210.00	280.00	775.00	2975.00
□1901	Parker-Burke	Red	210.00	280.00	775.00	2975.00
□1901	Teehee-Burke	Red	210.00	280.00	775.00	2975.00
□1901	Elliott-White	Red	210.00	280.00	775.00	2975.00
□1901	Speelman-White	Red	210.00	280.00	775.00	2975.00

TEN DOLLAR NOTES (1923) UNITED STATES NOTES
(Large Size)

Face Design: Portrait of President Jackson center, red seal left, red "X" to right.

Back Design

SERIES	SIGNATURES	SEAL	A.B.P.	GOOD	V.FINE	UNC.
□1923	Speelman-White	Red	135.00	200.00	1500.00	5000.00

TEN DOLLAR NOTES (1863–1875)
NATIONAL BANK NOTES
FIRST CHARTER PERIOD (Large Size)

Face Design: Benjamin Franklin and kite left, name of bank and city center. Effigy of Liberty and eagle right.

Back Design: Border green, center black. DeSoto on horseback at Mississippi River.

SERIES	SIGNATURES	SEAL	A.B.P.	GOOD	V.FINE	UNC.
□Original	Chittenden-Spinner	Red	140.00	195.00	950.00	3050.00
□Original	Colby-Spinner	Red	140.00	195.00	950.00	3050.00
□Original	Jeffries-Spinner	Red	400.00	545.00	1450.00	3550.00
□Original	Allison-Spinner	Red	140.00	195.00	950.00	3150.00
□1875	Allison-New	Red	140.00	195.00	950.00	2850.00
□1875	Allison-Wyman	Red	140.00	195.00	1100.00	2950.00
□1875	Allison-Gilfillan	Red	140.00	195.00	1050.00	2750.00
□1875	Scofield-Gilfillan	Red	140.00	195.00	1050.00	2750.00
□1875	Bruce-Gilfillan	Red	140.00	195.00	1050.00	2850.00
□1875	Bruce-Wyman	Red	140.00	195.00	1050.00	2850.00
□1875	Rosecrans-Huston	Red	140.00	195.00	950.00	2850.00
□1875	Rosecrans-Nebeker	Red	140.00	195.00	950.00	2850.00

TEN DOLLAR NOTES (1882) NATIONAL BANK NOTES
SECOND CHARTER PERIOD (Large Size)

First Issue (Brown seal and brown backs)
Face Design: Similar to 1863–1875 note.
Back Design: Similar to 1882 $5 note. Border in brown with green Charter Number.

SERIES	SIGNATURES	SEAL	A.B.P.	GOOD	V.FINE	UNC.
□1882	Bruce-Gilfillan	Brown	55.00	90.00	395.00	1250.00
□1882	Bruce-Wyman	Brown	55.00	90.00	395.00	1250.00
□1882	Bruce-Jordan	Brown	55.00	90.00	395.00	1250.00
□1882	Rosecrans-Jordan	Brown	55.00	90.00	395.00	1250.00
□1882	Rosecrans-Hyatt	Brown	55.00	90.00	395.00	1250.00
□1882	Rosecrans-Huston	Brown	55.00	90.00	395.00	1250.00
□1882	Rosecrans-Nebeker	Brown	55.00	90.00	395.00	1250.00
□1882	Rosecrans-Morgan	Brown	155.00	270.00	790.00	1400.00
□1882	Tillman-Morgan	Brown	55.00	90.00	395.00	1250.00
□1882	Tillman-Roberts	Brown	55.00	90.00	395.00	1250.00

SERIES	SIGNATURES	SEAL	A.B.P.	GOOD	V.FINE	UNC.
□1882	Bruce-Roberts	Brown	55.00	90.00	380.00	1250.00
□1882	Lyons-Roberts	Brown	55.00	90.00	380.00	1250.00
□1882	Lyons-Treat	Brown	55.00	90.00	380.00	1250.00
□1882	Vernon-Treat	Brown	55.00	90.00	380.00	1250.00

Second Issue (Blue seal, green back with date "1882–1908")
Face Design: Similar to 1863–1875 note.
Back Design: Similar to 1882 $5 Second Issue note.
(Large Size)

SERIES	SIGNATURES	SEAL	A.B.P.	GOOD	V.FINE	UNC.
□1882	Rosecrans-Huston	Blue	60.00	90.00	325.00	1000.00
□1882	Rosecrans-Nebeker	Blue	60.00	90.00	325.00	1000.00
□1882	Rosecrans-Morgan	Blue	125.00	215.00	540.00	1350.00
□1882	Tillman-Morgan	Blue	60.00	90.00	325.00	1350.00
□1882	Tillman-Roberts	Blue	60.00	90.00	325.00	1350.00
□1882	Bruce-Roberts	Blue	60.00	90.00	325.00	1350.00
□1882	Lyons-Roberts	Blue	60.00	90.00	325.00	1350.00
□1882	Vernon-Treat	Blue	60.00	90.00	325.00	1350.00
□1882	Vernon-McClung	Blue	60.00	90.00	325.00	1350.00
□1882	Napier-McClung	Blue	60.00	90.00	325.00	1350.00

TEN DOLLAR NOTES (1882) NATIONAL BANK NOTES

(Large Size)

Third Issue (Blue seal, green back with value in block letters)
Face Design: Similar to previous notes. (*see* 1863–1875 note).
Back Design: Similar to 1882 $500 Third Issue note.

SERIES	SIGNATURES	SEAL	A.B.P.	GOOD	V. FINE	UNC.
□1882	Tillman-Roberts	Blue	100.00	150.00	500.00	2200.00
□1882	Lyons-Roberts	Blue	100.00	150.00	500.00	2200.00
□1882	Vernon-Treat	Blue	100.00	150.00	500.00	2200.00
□1882	Napier-McClung	Blue	100.00	150.00	500.00	2000.00

These notes may exist with other signatures, but are very rare.

TEN DOLLAR NOTES (1902) NATIONAL BANK NOTES
THIRD CHARTER PERIOD (Large Size)

First Issue (Red seal and red Charter Numbers)
Face Design: Portrait of President McKinley left, name of bank and city in center.

SERIES	SIGNATURES	SEAL	A.B.P.	GOOD	V.FINE	UNC.
□1902	Lyons-Roberts	Red	80.00	125.00	350.00	1700.00
□1902	Lyons-Treat	Red	80.00	125.00	350.00	1700.00
□1902	Vernon-Treat	Red	80.00	125.00	350.00	1700.00

TEN DOLLAR NOTES (1902) NATIONAL BANK NOTES
THIRD CHARTER PERIOD (Large Size)

Second Issue (Blue seal and numbers, "1902–1908" on the back)
Back Design: Same as 1882 Second Issue note. Date 1902–1908.
Face Design: Same as 1882 Third Issue note.

SERIES	SIGNATURES	SEAL	A.B.P.	GOOD	V.FINE	UNC.
□1902	Lyons-Roberts	Blue	25.00	35.00	100.00	450.00
□1902	Lyons-Treat	Blue	25.00	35.00	100.00	450.00
□1902	Vernon-Treat	Blue	25.00	35.00	100.00	450.00
□1902	Vernon-McClung	Blue	25.00	35.00	100.00	450.00

SERIES	SIGNATURES	SEAL	A.B.P.	GOOD	V.FINE	UNC.
□1902	Napier-McClung	Blue	25.00	35.00	90.00	410.00
□1902	Napier-Thompson	Blue	30.00	45.00	175.00	800.00
□1902	Napier-Burke	Blue	25.00	35.00	100.00	440.00
□1902	Parker-Burke	Blue	25.00	35.00	100.00	440.00
□1902	Teehee-Burke	Blue	25.00	35.00	100.00	440.00

Third Issue (Blue seal and numbers, without date on back.)

SERIES	SIGNATURES	SEAL	A.B.P.	GOOD	V.FINE	UNC.
□1902	Lyons-Roberts	Blue	22.00	32.00	95.00	390.00
□1902	Lyons-Treat	Blue	22.00	32.00	95.00	390.00
□1902	Vernon-Treat	Blue	22.00	32.00	95.00	390.00
□1902	Vernon-McClung	Blue	22.00	32.00	95.00	390.00
□1902	Napier-McClung	Blue	22.00	32.00	95.00	390.00
□1902	Napier-Thompson	Blue	22.00	32.00	105.00	700.00
□1902	Napier-Burke	Blue	22.00	32.00	95.00	390.00
□1902	Parker-Burke	Blue	22.00	32.00	95.00	390.00
□1902	Teehee-Burke	Blue	22.00	32.00	95.00	390.00
□1902	Elliott-Burke	Blue	22.00	32.00	95.00	390.00
□1902	Elliott-White	Blue	22.00	32.00	95.00	390.00
□1902	Speelman-White	Blue	22.00	32.00	95.00	390.00
□1902	Woods-White	Blue	22.00	32.00	95.00	390.00
□1902	Woods-Tate	Blue	22.00	32.00	95.00	390.00
□1902	Jones-Woods	Blue	47.00	94.00	300.00	1155.00

TEN DOLLAR NOTES (1929) NATIONAL BANK NOTES
(Small Size)

Face Design, Type I: Portrait of Hamilton center, name of bank left, brown seal right, Charter Number black.

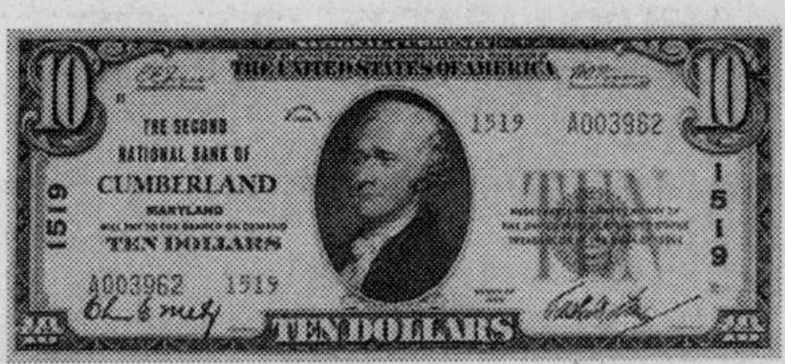

Face Design, Type II: Charter Number added in brown.

Back Design: United States Treasury Building.

SERIES	SIGNATURES	SEAL	A.B.P.	GOOD	V.FINE	UNC.
□1929, Type I	Jones-Woods	Brown	13.00	20.00	50.00	150.00
□1929, Type II	Jones-Woods	Brown	13.00	20.00	50.00	150.00

TEN DOLLAR NOTES (1870-1875)
NATIONAL GOLD BANK NOTES

(Large Size)

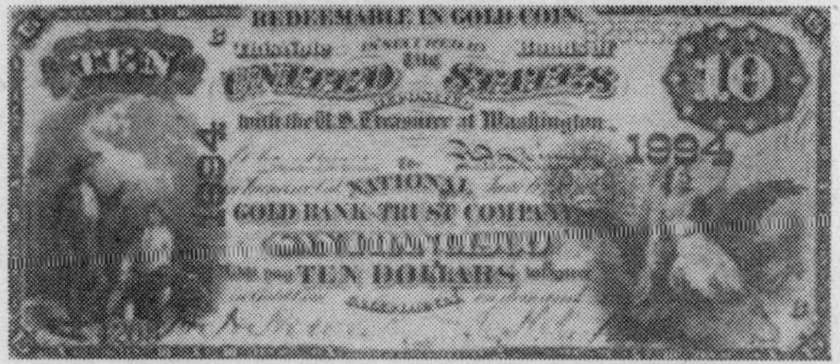

Face Design: Similar to 1863–1875 First Charter Period note.

Back Design: State Seal left, gold coins center, American eagle right.

The following have signatures of Allison-Spinner and a red Treasury Seal.

DATE	BANK	CITY	A.B.P.	GOOD	V. GOOD
□1870	First National Gold Bank	San Francisco	900.00	1100.00	1600.00
□1872	National Gold Bank and Trust Co.	San Francisco	950.00	1150.00	1650.00
□1872	National Gold Bank of D.O. Mills and Co.	Sacramento	1000.00	1900.00	3350.00
□1873	First National Gold Bank	Santa Barbara	1150.00	2000.00	3350.00
□1873	First National Gold Bank	Stockton	1100.00	2200.00	3350.00
□1874	Farmers Nat'l Gold Bank	San Jose	1100.00	2200.00	3350.00
□1874	First National Gold Bank	Petaluma	1100.00	2200.00	6450.00
□1875	First National Gold Bank	Oakland	1100.00	2200.00	7050.00

TEN DOLLAR NOTES (1880) SILVER CERTIFICATES
(Large Size)

Face Design: Portrait of Robert Morris left.

Back Design: Printed in black ink, SILVER in large letters.

SERIES	SIGNATURES	SEAL	A.B.P.	GOOD	V.FINE	UNC.
□1880	Scofield-Gilfillan	Brown	350.00	500.00	2400.00	6200.00
□1880	Bruce-Gilfillan	Brown	350.00	500.00	2400.00	6200.00
□1880	Bruce-Wyman	Brown	350.00	500.00	2400.00	6200.00
□1880	Bruce-Wyman	Red	400.00	500.00	3850.00	8200.00

TEN DOLLAR NOTES (1886) SILVER CERTIFICATES

(Large Size)

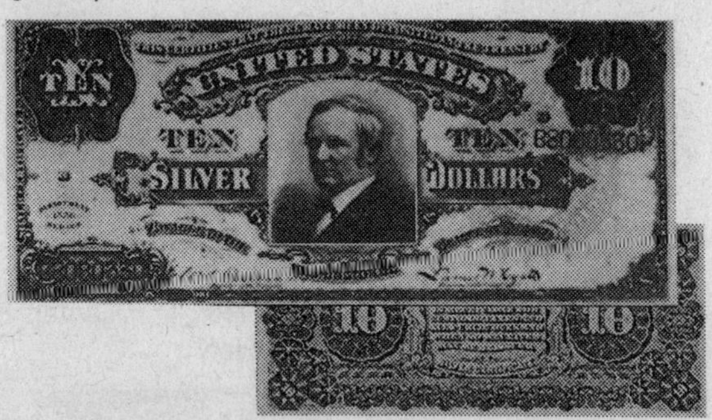

SERIES	SIGNATURES	SEAL	A.B.P.	GOOD	V.FINE	UNC.
□1886	Rosencrans-Jordan	Sm. Red	285.00	480.00	2200.00	7500.00
□1886	Rosecrans-Hyatt	Sm. Red	200.00	325.00	1700.00	6500.00
□1886	Rosecrans-Hyatt	Lg. Red	175.00	325.00	1700.00	6500.00
□1886	Rosecrans-Huston	Lg. Red	195.00	325.00	1700.00	6500.00
□1886	Rosecrans-Huston	Lg. Brown	200.00	325.00	1700.00	6500.00
□1886	Rosecrans-Nebeker	Lg. Brown	195.00	325.00	1700.00	6500.00
□1886	Rosecrans-Nebeker	Sm. Red	335.00	500.00	2400.00	8000.00

TEN DOLLAR NOTES (1891–1908) SILVER CERTIFICATES

(Large Size)

Face Design: Same as 1886 note.

Back Design

SERIES	SIGNATURES	SEAL	A.B.P.	GOOD	V.FINE	UNC.
□1891	Rosecrans-Nebeker	Red	105.00	175.00	850.00	2775.00
□1891	Tillman-Morgan	Red	105.00	150.00	800.00	2775.00
□1891	Bruce-Roberts	Red	105.00	175.00	850.00	2775.00
□1891	Lyons-Roberts	Red	105.00	160.00	830.00	2775.00
□1891	Vernon-Treat	Blue	105.00	160.00	830.00	2775.00
□1891	Vernon-McClung	Blue	105.00	165.00	830.00	2740.00
□1891	Parker-Burke	Blue	105.00	150.00	830.00	2655.00

TEN DOLLAR NOTES (1933) SILVER CERTIFICATES
(Small Size)

Face Design: Portrait of Alexander Hamilton center. Blue seal to left, blue numbers.

Back Design: Green United States Treasury Building.

SERIES	SIGNATURES	SEAL	A.B.P.	GOOD	V.FINE	UNC.
□1933	Julian-Woodin	Blue	1500.00	2000.00	6300.00	15000.00

TEN DOLLAR NOTES (1934) SILVER CERTIFICATES
(Small Size)

Face Design: Blue "10" to left of portrait, Treasury Seal is now to right.
Back Design: Similar to 1933 issue.

TEN DOLLAR NOTES (1934) SILVER CERTIFICATES
(Small Size)

SERIES	SIGNATURES	SEAL	A.B.P.	GOOD	V.FINE	UNC.	★UNC.
□1934	Julian-Morgenthau	Blue	13.00	17.00	30.00	175.00	1500.00
□1934	Julian-Morgenthau*	Yellow	500.00	750.00	5000.00	25000.00	RARE
□1934A	Julian-Morgenthau	Blue	13.00	18.00	30.00	200.00	1800.00
□1934A	Julian-Morgenthau*	Yellow	15.00	25.00	40.00	300.00	1500.00
□1934B	Julian-Vinson	Blue	20.00	31.00	200.00	5000.00	10000.00
□1934C	Julian-Snyder	Blue	13.00	17.00	31.00	150.00	500.00
□1934D	Clark-Snyder	Blue	13.00	17.00	31.00	175.00	2500.00

* Silver Certificates with a yellow seal were a special issue for use in combat areas of North Africa and Europe during World War II.

TEN DOLLAR NOTES (1953) SILVER CERTIFICATES
(Small Size)

Face Design: Gray "10" to left of portrait. Treasury Seal is smaller.
Back Design: Back similar to previous note.

SERIES	SIGNATURES	SEAL	A.B.P.	GOOD	V.FINE	UNC.	★UNC.
□1953	Priest-Humphrey	Blue	13.00	16.00	35.00	200.00	700.00
□1953A	Priest-Anderson	Blue	13.00	19.00	39.00	350.00	1400.00
□1953B	Smith-Dillon	Blue	13.00	18.00	36.00	130.00	NONE

Regarding the 1953 note, there were 720,000 issued. This was the last issue of $10 Silver Certificates. These were not issued with IN GOD WE TRUST on the back. Production ended in 1962.

TEN DOLLAR (1879) REFUNDING CERTIFICATES

Face Design: Portrait of Benjamin Franklin.

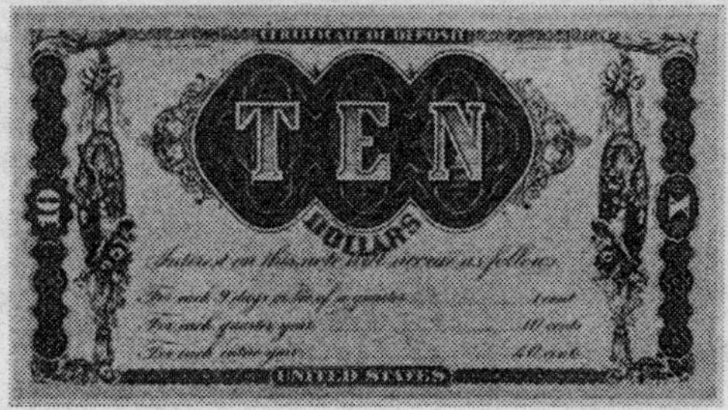

Back Design: Large TEN, ornate cornucopia border.

SERIES	SIGNATURES	SEAL	A.B.P.	GOOD	V.FINE	UNC.
□1879	Scofield-Gilfillan					
	PAY TO ORDER	Red	900.00		VERY RARE	
□1079	Scofield-Gilfillan					
	PAY TO BEARER	Red	700.00	1000.00	2300.00	8300.00

TEN DOLLAR NOTES (1907) GOLD CERTIFICATES
(Large Size)

Face Design: Portrait of Hillegas center, yellow x left, yellow seal right, yellow numbers.

Back Design: The backs are a bright yellow color.

SERIES	SIGNATURES	SEAL	A.B.P.	GOOD	V.FINE	UNC.
□1907	Vernon-Treat	Gold	45.00	65.00	195.00	1025.00
□1907	Vernon-McClung	Gold	45.00	65.00	195.00	950.00
□1907	Napier-McClung (1882)	Gold	45.00	65.00	195.00	850.00
□1907	Napier-McClung (1907)	Gold	45.00	70.00	250.00	1500.00
□1907	Napier-Thompson (1882)	Gold	52.00	88.00	270.00	1350.00
□1907	Napier-Thompson (1907)	Gold	45.00	80.00	300.00	1700.00
□1907	Parker-Burke (1882)	Gold	52.00	65.00	195.00	875.00
□1907	Teehee-Burke	Gold	52.00	65.00	195.00	875.00
□1922	Speelman-White	Gold	52.00	65.00	195.00	750.00

TEN DOLLAR NOTES (1928) GOLD CERTIFICATES
(Small Size)

Face Design: Portrait of Alexander Hamilton center, yellow seal to left, yellow numbers.

Back Design: Printed in green ink.

SERIES	SIGNATURES	SEAL	A.B.P.	GOOD	V.FINE	UNC.
□1928	Woods-Mellon	Gold	19.00	35.00	95.00	600.00

TEN DOLLAR NOTES (1890) TREASURY OR COIN NOTES
(Large Size)

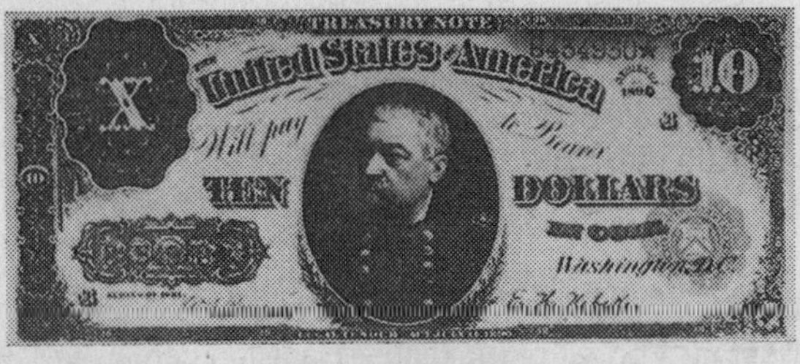

Face Design: Portrait of General Philip Sheridan.

Back Design: Very ornate large TEN.

SERIES	SIGNATURES	SEAL	A.B.P.	GOOD	V.FINE	UNC.
□1890	Rosecrans-Huston	Lg. Brown	230.00	335.00	1600.00	5400.00
□1890	Rosecrans-Nebeker	Lg. Brown	230.00	335.00	1600.00	5400.00
□1890	Rosecrans-Nebeker	Sm. Red	230.00	335.00	1600.00	5400.00

TEN DOLLAR NOTES (1891) TREASURY OR COIN NOTES
(Large Size)

Face Design: Same as 1890 note.
Back Design: Ornate small TEN.

SERIES	SIGNATURES	SEAL	A.B.P.	GOOD	V.FINE	UNC.
□1891	Rosecrans-Nebeker	Sm. Red	135.00	185.00	875.00	3300.00
□1891	Tillman-Morgan	Sm. Red	135.00	185.00	875.00	3300.00
□1891	Bruce-Roberts	Sm. Red	135.00	185.00	875.00	3950.00

TEN DOLLAR NOTES (1914)
FEDERAL RESERVE NOTES

(Large Size)

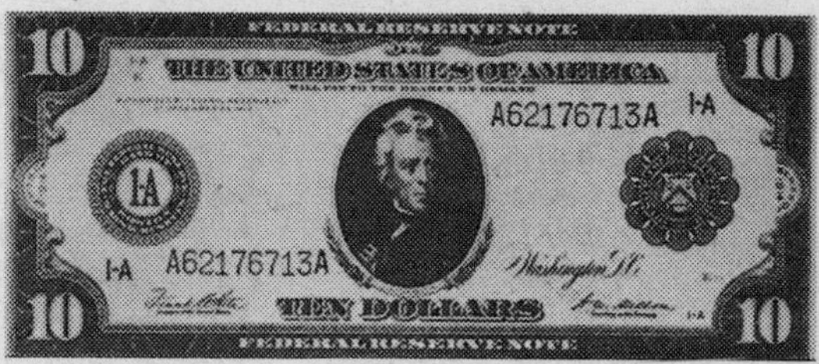

Face Design: Portrait of President Jackson center, Federal Reserve Seal left, Treasury Seal right.

Back Design: Scenes of farming and industry.

The following have signatures of Burke-McAdoo, red seals and red serial numbers.

SERIES	BANK	SEAL	A.B.P.	GOOD	V.FINE	UNC.
□1914	Boston	Red	95.00	150.00	500.00	1850.00
□1914	New York	Red	95.00	150.00	415.00	1650.00
□1914	Philadelphia	Red	95.00	148.00	480.00	1070.00
□1914	Cleveland	Red	95.00	148.00	500.00	1850.00
□1914	Richmond	Red	95.00	148.00	500.00	1850.00
□1914	Atlanta	Red	95.00	148.00	500.00	1850.00
□1914	Chicago	Red	95.00	148.00	475.00	1650.00
□1914	St. Louis	Red	95.00	148.00	480.00	1660.00
□1914	Minneapolis	Red	95.00	148.00	480.00	1750.00
□1914	Kansas City	Red	95.00	148.00	600.00	1850.00
□1914	Dallas	Red	95.00	148.00	480.00	1650.00
□1914	San Francisco	Red	95.00	148.00	500.00	1850.00

TEN DOLLAR NOTES (1914)
FEDERAL RESERVE NOTES

(Large Size)

BANK	SIGNATURES	SEAL	A.B.P.	V.FINE	UNC.
☐Boston	Burke-McAdoo	Blue	26.00	95.00	295.00
☐Boston	Burke-Glass	Blue	26.00	195.00	420.00
☐Boston	Burke-Huston	Blue	26.00	70.00	230.00
☐Boston	White-Mellon	Blue	26.00	70.00	230.00
☐New York	Burke-McAdoo	Blue	26.00	65.00	220.00
☐New York	Burke-Glass	Blue	26.00	65.00	220.00
☐New York	Burke-Huston	Blue	26.00	65.00	220.00
☐New York	White-Mellon	Blue	26.00	65.00	220.00
☐Philadelphia	Burke-McAdoo	Blue	26.00	95.00	280.00
☐Philadelphia	Burke-Glass	Blue	26.00	95.00	280.00
☐Philadelphia	Burke-Huston	Blue	26.00	70.00	230.00
☐Philadelphia	White-Mellon	Blue	26.00	70.00	230.00
☐Cleveland	Burke-McAdoo	Blue	26.00	85.00	270.00
☐Cleveland	Burke-Glass	Blue	26.00	195.00	395.00
☐Cleveland	Burke-Huston	Blue	26.00	65.00	220.00
☐Cleveland	White-Mellon	Blue	26.00	65.00	220.00
☐Richmond	Burke-McAdoo	Blue	26.00	110.00	330.00
☐Richmond	Burke-Glass	Blue	26.00	110.00	330.00
☐Richmond	Burke-Huston	Blue	26.00	70.00	230.00
☐Richmond	White-Mellon	Blue	26.00	70.00	230.00
☐Atlanta	Burke-McAdoo	Blue	26.00	110.00	330.00
☐Atlanta	Burke-Glass	Blue	26.00	265.00	445.00
☐Atlanta	Burke-Huston	Blue	26.00	95.00	295.00
☐Atlanta	White-Mellon	Blue	26.00	70.00	230.00
☐Chicago	Burke-McAdoo	Blue	26.00	65.00	225.00
☐Chicago	Burke-Glass	Blue	26.00	65.00	225.00
☐Chicago	Burke-Huston	Blue	26.00	65.00	225.00
☐Chicago	White-Mellon	Blue	26.00	65.00	225.00
☐St. Louis	Burke-McAdoo	Blue	26.00	67.00	225.00
☐St. Louis	Burke-Glass	Blue	26.00	195.00	370.00
☐St. Louis	Burke-Huston	Blue	26.00	65.00	220.00
☐St. Louis	White-Mellon	Blue	26.00	65.00	220.00
☐Minneapolis	Burke-McAdoo	Blue	26.00	95.00	295.00
☐Minneapolis	Burke-Glass	Blue	26.00	67.00	225.00
☐Minneapolis	Burke-Huston	Blue	26.00	67.00	225.00
☐Minneapolis	White-Mellon	Blue	26.00	65.00	220.00
☐Kansas City	Burke-McAdoo	Blue	26.00	67.00	225.00
☐Kansas City	Burke-Glass	Blue	26.00	127.00	340.00

BANK	SIGNATURES	SEAL	A.B.P.	V.FINE	UNC.
☐Kansas City	Burke-Huston	Blue	26.00	67.00	225.00
☐Kansas City	White-Mellon	Blue	26.00	67.00	225.00
☐Dallas	Burke-McAdoo	Blue	26.00	67.00	230.00
☐Dallas	Burke-Glass	Blue	26.00	320.00	600.00
☐Dallas	Burke-Huston	Blue	26.00	95.00	330.00
☐Dallas	White-Mellon	Blue	26.00	110.00	360.00
☐San Francisco	Burke-McAdoo	Blue	26.00	270.00	510.00
☐San Francisco	Burke-Glass	Blue	26.00	220.00	430.00
☐San Francisco	Burke-Huston	Blue	26.00	270.00	510.00
☐San Francisco	White Mellon	Blue	26.00	67.00	225.00

TEN DOLLAR NOTES (1928–1928A)
FEDERAL RESERVE NOTES

(Small Size)

Face Design: Portrait of Alexander Hamilton center, black Federal Reserve Seal left, with number over green Treasury Seal to the right.

Back Design: United States Treasury Building.

SERIES OF 1928, SIGNATURES OF TATE-MELLON, GREEN SEAL

BANK	A.B.P.	V.FINE	UNC.	★UNC.	BANK	A.B.P.	V.FINE	UNC.	★UNC.
☐ Boston	15.00	45.00	350.00	1500.00	☐ Chicago	18.00	40.00	225.00	1500.00
☐ New York	15.00	35.00	220.00	1200.00	☐ St. Louis	18.00	55.00	200.00	1200.00
☐ Philadelphia	15.00	40.00	220.00	1200.00	☐ Minneapolis	18.00	85.00	400.00	2500.00
☐ Cleveland	15.00	40.00	200.00	1200.00	☐ Kansas City	18.00	50.00	250.00	1500.00

BANK	A.B.P.	V.FINE	UNC.	★UNC.	BANK	A.B.P.	V.FINE	UNC.	★UNC.
☐ Richmond	34.00	70.00	350.00	2000.00	☐ Dallas	32.00	70.00	300.00	5000.00
☐ Atlanta	34.00	70.00	250.00	2000.00	☐ San Francisco	37.00	50.00	275.00	4500.00

SERIES OF 1928A, SIGNATURES OF WOODS-MELLON, GREEN SEAL

BANK	A.B.P.	V.FINE	UNC.	★UNC.	BANK	A.B.P.	V.FINE	UNC.	★UNC.
☐ Boston	55.00	85.00	550.00	1500.00	☐ Chicago	50.00	100.00	275.00	1100.00
☐ New York	55.00	85.00	350.00	1100.00	☐ St. Louis	50.00	100.00	250.00	1100.00
☐ Philadelphia	55.00	85.00	350.00	1600.00	☐ Minneapolis	100.00	170.00	2000.00	5000.00
☐ Cleveland	55.00	85.00	275.00	1100.00	☐ Kansas City	75.00	130.00	350.00	5000.00
☐ Richmond	80.00	130.00	700.00	2000.00	☐ Dallas	75.00	130.00	600.00	5000.00
☐ Atlanta	55.00	85.00	400.00	1600.00	☐ San Francisco	75.00	130.00	425.00	2000.00

TEN DOLLAR NOTES (1928B-1928C)
FEDERAL RESERVE NOTES

(Small Size)

Face Design: Alexander Hamilton; black Federal Reserve Seal left, has letter instead of number.
Back Design: Same as 1928–1928A note.

SERIES OF 1928B, SIGNATURES OF WOODS-MELLON, GREEN SEAL

BANK	A.B.P.	V.FINE	UNC.	★UNC.	BANK	A.B.P.	V.FINE	UNC.	★UNC.
☐ Boston	17.00	36.00	130.00	835.00	☐ Chicago	17.00	30.00	125.00	835.00
☐ New York	14.00	26.00	115.00	835.00	☐ St. Louis	17.00	30.00	125.00	835.00
☐ Philadelphia	17.00	36.00	140.00	835.00	☐ Minneapolis	27.00	50.00	165.00	835.00
☐ Cleveland	17.00	36.00	145.00	835.00	☐ Kansas City	17.00	30.00	120.00	835.00
☐ Richmond	22.00	40.00	150.00	835.00	☐ Dallas	27.00	50.00	175.00	835.00
☐ Atlanta	24.00	40.00	165.00	835.00	☐ San Francisco	24.00	45.00	165.00	835.00

SERIES OF 1928C, SIGNATURES OF WOOD-MILLS, GREEN SEAL

BANK	A.B.P.	V.FINE	UNC.	★UNC.
☐New York	45.00	75.00	400.00	—
☐Cleveland	85.00	500.00	2000.00	15000.00
☐Richmond	260.00	2500.00	10000.00	—
☐Chicago	50.00	85.00	425.00	—

TEN DOLLAR NOTES (1934)
FEDERAL RESERVE NOTES

(Small Size)

SERIES OF 1934,
SIGNATURES OF JULIAN-MORGENTHAU, GREEN SEAL

BANK	A.B.P.	V.FINE	UNC.	★UNC.	BANK	A.B.P.	V.FINE	UNC.	★UNC.
☐ Boston	13.00	16.00	65.00	475.00	☐ Chicago	13.00	21.00	80.00	375.00
☐ New York	13.00	21.00	70.00	375.00	☐ St. Louis	13.00	21.00	85.00	475.00
☐ Philadelphia	13.00	21.00	85.00	475.00	☐ Minneapolis	13.00	21.00	85.00	475.00
☐ Cleveland	13.00	21.00	85.00	475.00	☐ Kansas City	13.00	21.00	85.00	475.00
☐ Richmond	13.00	21.00	85.00	475.00	☐ Dallas	13.00	21.00	85.00	475.00
☐ Atlanta	13.00	21.00	85.00	475.00	☐ San Francisco	13.00	21.00	85.00	475.00

The green Treasury Seal on this note is known in a light and dark color. The light seal is worth about 10–20 percent more in most cases. REDEEMABLE IN GOLD removed from obligation over Federal Reserve Seal.

TEN DOLLAR NOTES (1934)
FEDERAL RESERVE NOTES

(Small Size)

SERIES OF 1934A,
SIGNATURES OF JULIAN-MORGENTHAU, GREEN SEAL

BANK	A.B.P.	V.FINE	UNC.	★UNC.	BANK	A.B.P.	V.FINE	UNC.	★UNC.
☐ Boston	12.00	16.00	55.00	325.00	☐ Chicago	12.00	16.50	55.00	325.00
☐ New York	12.00	16.00	55.00	325.00	☐ St. Louis	12.00	16.50	55.00	325.00
☐ Philadelphia	12.00	16.00	55.00	325.00	☐ Minneapolis	12.00	16.50	75.00	325.00
☐ Cleveland	12.00	16.00	55.00	325.00	☐ Kansas City	12.00	16.50	62.00	325.00
☐ Richmond	12.00	16.00	55.00	325.00	☐ Dallas	12.00	16.50	62.00	375.00
☐ Atlanta	12.00	16.00	55.00	345.00	☐ San Francisco*	12.00	16.50	52.00	375.00

* San Francisco, 1934A, with brown seal and overprinted HAWAII on face and back. Special issue for use in combat areas during World War II. Value in V. FINE $100, value in UNC. $1000. ★UNC $10000.00

SERIES OF 1934B,
SIGNATURES OF JULIAN-VINSON, GREEN SEAL

BANK	A.B.P.	V.FINE	UNC.	★UNC.	BANK	A.B.P.	V.FINE	UNC.	★UNC.
☐ Boston	12.00	20.00	100.00	575.00	☐ Chicago	12.00	20.00	50.00	575.00
☐ New York	12.00	20.00	60.00	575.00	☐ St. Louis	12.00	20.00	60.00	575.00
☐ Philadelphia	12.00	20.00	60.00	575.00	☐ Minneapolis	12.00	20.00	125.00	2000.00
☐ Cleveland	12.00	20.00	100.00	575.00	☐ Kansas City	12.00	20.00	60.00	575.00
☐ Richmond	12.00	20.00	70.00	575.00	☐ Dallas	12.00	20.00	90.00	1500.00
☐ Atlanta	12.00	20.00	70.00	575.00	☐ San Francisco	12.00	20.00	70.00	575.00

SERIES OF 1934C, SIGNATURES OF JULIAN-SNYDER, GREEN SEAL

BANK	A.B.P.	V.FINE	UNC.	★UNC.	BANK	A.B.P.	V.FINE	UNC.	★UNC.
☐ Boston	12.00	20.00	60.00	450.00	☐ Chicago	12.00	20.00	60.00	400.00
☐ New York	12.00	20.00	60.00	425.00	☐ St. Louis	12.00	20.00	60.00	450.00
☐ Philadelphia	12.00	20.00	60.00	450.00	☐ Minneapolis	12.00	20.00	60.00	1000.00
☐ Cleveland	12.00	20.00	60.00	450.00	☐ Kansas City	12.00	20.00	60.00	450.00
☐ Richmond	12.00	20.00	60.00	450.00	☐ Dallas	12.00	20.00	60.00	500.00
☐ Atlanta	12.00	20.00	60.00	450.00	☐ San Francisco	12.00	20.00	60.00	450.00

SERIES OF 1934D, SIGNATURES OF CLARK-SNYDER, GREEN SEAL

BANK	A.B.P.	V.FINE	UNC.	★UNC.	BANK	A.B.P.	V.FINE	UNC.	★UNC.
☐ Boston	12.00	20.00	55.00	500.00	☐ Chicago	12.00	20.00	55.00	500.00
☐ New York	12.00	20.00	55.00	500.00	☐ St. Louis	12.00	20.00	90.00	625.00
☐ Philadelphia	12.00	20.00	55.00	500.00	☐ Minneapolis	12.00	20.00	90.00	750.00
☐ Cleveland	12.00	20.00	55.00	500.00	☐ Kansas City	12.00	20.00	90.00	750.00
☐ Richmond	12.00	20.00	55.00	900.00	☐ Dallas	12.00	20.00	90.00	1000.00
☐ Atlanta	12.00	20.00	55.00	500.00	☐ San Francisco	12.00	20.00	90.00	1000.00

TEN DOLLAR NOTES (1950)
FEDERAL RESERVE NOTES

SERIES OF 1950, SIGNATURES OF CLARK-SNYDER, GREEN SEAL

BANK	A.B.P.	V.FINE	UNC.	★UNC.	BANK	A.B.P.	V.FINE	UNC.	★UNC.
☐ Boston	12.00	30.00	85.00	500.00	☐ Chicago	12.00	30.00	85.00	500.00
☐ New York	12.00	30.00	85.00	500.00	☐ St. Louis	12.00	30.00	85.00	500.00
☐ Philadelphia	12.00	30.00	85.00	500.00	☐ Minneapolis	12.00	30.00	85.00	500.00
☐ Cleveland	12.00	30.00	85.00	500.00	☐ Kansas City	12.00	35.00	85.00	500.00
☐ Richmond	12.00	30.00	85.00	500.00	☐ Dallas	12.00	30.00	85.00	500.00
☐ Atlanta	12.00	30.00	85.00	500.00	☐ San Francisco	12.00	30.00	85.00	500.00

(Small Size)

SERIES OF 1950A, SIGNATURES OF PRIEST-HUMPHERY, GREEN SEAL

BANK	A.B.P.	V.FINE	UNC.	★UNC.	BANK	A.B.P.	V.FINE	UNC.	★UNC.
☐ Boston	12.00	28.00	65.00	225.00	☐ Chicago	12.00	28.00	65.00	325.00
☐ New York	12.00	28.00	65.00	225.00	☐ St. Louis	12.00	28.00	65.00	325.00
☐ Philadelphia	12.00	28.00	65.00	325.00	☐ Minneapolis	12.00	30.00	125.00	500.00
☐ Cleveland	12.00	28.00	65.00	325.00	☐ Kansas City	12.00	30.00	65.00	400.00
☐ Richmond	12.00	28.00	65.00	500.00	☐ Dallas	12.00	30.00	65.00	300.00
☐ Atlanta	12.00	28.00	65.00	325.00	☐ San Francisco	12.00	28.00	65.00	225.00

SERIES OF 1950B, SIGNATURES OF PRIEST-ANDERSON, GREEN SEAL

BANK	A.B.P.	V.FINE	UNC.	★UNC.	BANK	A.B.P.	V.FINE	UNC.	★UNC.
☐ Boston	12.00	25.00	50.00	150.00	☐ Chicago	12.00	25.00	50.00	150.00
☐ New York	12.00	25.00	50.00	150.00	☐ St. Louis	12.00	25.00	50.00	150.00
☐ Philadelphia	12.00	25.00	50.00	150.00	☐ Minneapolis	12.00	28.00	50.00	400.00
☐ Cleveland	12.00	25.00	50.00	150.00	☐ Kansas City	12.00	28.00	50.00	150.00
☐ Richmond	12.00	25.00	50.00	150.00	☐ Dallas	12.00	28.00	50.00	450.00
☐ Atlanta	12.00	25.00	50.00	150.00	☐ San Francisco	12.00	25.00	50.00	150.00

SERIES OF 1950C, SIGNATURES OF SMITH-DILLON, GREEN SEAL

BANK	A.B.P.	V.FINE	UNC.	★UNC.	BANK	A.B.P.	V.FINE	UNC.	★UNC.
☐ Boston	12.00	25.00	55.00	350.00	☐ Chicago	12.00	25.00	55.00	350.00
☐ New York	12.00	25.00	55.00	350.00	☐ St. Louis	12.00	25.00	65.00	350.00
☐ Philadelphia	12.00	25.00	55.00	350.00	☐ Minneapolis	15.00	30.00	95.00	350.00
☐ Cleveland	12.00	25.00	55.00	350.00	☐ Kansas City	15.00	30.00	95.00	350.00
☐ Richmond	12.00	25.00	55.00	350.00	☐ Dallas	15.00	30.00	85.00	350.00
☐ Atlanta	12.00	25.00	55.00	350.00	☐ San Francisco	12.00	25.00	85.00	350.00

SERIES OF 1950D, SIGNATURES OF GRANAHAN-DILLON, GREEN SEAL

BANK	A.B.P.	V.FINE	UNC.	★UNC.	BANK	A.B.P.	V.FINE	UNC.	★UNC.
☐ Boston	12.00	25.00	60.00	250.00	☐ Chicago	12.00	25.00	60.00	250.00
☐ New York	12.00	25.00	60.00	250.00	☐ St. Louis	12.00	25.00	60.00	250.00
☐ Philadelphia	12.00	25.00	60.00	250.00	☐ Minneapolis	15.00	30.00	60.00	250.00
☐ Cleveland	12.00	25.00	60.00	250.00	☐ Kansas City	15.00	30.00	60.00	250.00
☐ Richmond	12.00	25.00	60.00	250.00	☐ Dallas	15.00	30.00	60.00	250.00
☐ Atlanta	12.00	25.00	60.00	250.00	☐ San Francisco	12.00	25.00	60.00	250.00

SERIES OF 1950E, SIGNATURES OF GRANAHAN-FOWLER, GREEN SEAL

BANK	A.B.P.	V.FINE	UNC.	★UNC.	BANK	A.B.P.	V.FINE	UNC.	★UNC.
☐ New York	14.00	28.00	100.00	350.00	☐ Chicago	14.00	28.00	100.00	300.00
					☐ San Francisco	14.00	28.00	140.00	500.00

TEN DOLLAR NOTES (1963)
FEDERAL RESERVE NOTES
(IN GOD WE TRUST IS ADDED ON BACK)

SERIES OF 1963, SIGNATURES OF GRANAHAN-DILLON, GREEN SEAL

BANK	A.B.P.	V.FINE	UNC.	★UNC.	BANK	A.B.P.	V.FINE	UNC.	★UNC.
☐ Boston	—	12.00	50.00	100.00	☐ Chicago	—	12.00	50.00	100.00
☐ New York	—	12.00	50.00	100.00	☐ St. Louis	—	12.00	50.00	100.00
☐ Philadelphia	—	12.00	50.00	100.00	☐ Minneapolis	—	12.00	50.00	100.00
☐ Cleveland	—	12.00	50.00	100.00	☐ Kansas City	—	12.00	50.00	100.00
☐ Richmond	—	12.00	50.00	100.00	☐ Dallas	—	12.00	50.00	100.00
☐ Atlanta	—	12.00	50.00	100.00	☐ San Francisco	—	12.00	50.00	100.00

SERIES OF 1963A, SIGNATURES OF GRANAHAN-FOWLER, GREEN SEAL

BANK	A.B.P.	V.FINE	UNC.	★UNC.	BANK	A.B.P.	V.FINE	UNC.	★UNC.
☐ Boston	—	12.00	40.00	90.00	☐ Chicago	—	12.00	40.00	90.00
☐ New York	—	12.00	40.00	90.00	☐ St. Louis	—	12.00	40.00	90.00
☐ Philadelphia	—	12.00	40.00	90.00	☐ Minneapolis	—	12.00	40.00	90.00
☐ Cleveland	—	12.00	40.00	90.00	☐ Kansas City	—	12.00	40.00	90.00
☐ Richmond	—	12.00	40.00	90.00	☐ Dallas	—	12.00	40.00	90.00
☐ Atlanta	—	12.00	40.00	90.00	☐ San Francisco	—	12.00	40.00	90.00

TEN DOLLAR NOTES (1969)
FEDERAL RESERVE NOTES
(WORDING IN GREEN TREASURY SEAL IS CHANGED FROM LATIN TO ENGLISH)

SERIES OF 1969, SIGNATURES OF ELSTON-KENNEDY, GREEN SEAL

BANK	A.B.P.	V.FINE	UNC.	★UNC.	BANK	A.B.P.	V.FINE	UNC.	★UNC.
☐ Boston	—	12.00	37.00	80.00	☐ Chicago	—	12.00	37.00	80.00
☐ New York	—	12.00	37.00	80.00	☐ St. Louis	—	12.00	37.00	80.00
☐ Philadelphia	—	12.00	37.00	80.00	☐ Minneapolis	—	12.00	37.00	80.00
☐ Cleveland	—	12.00	37.00	80.00	☐ Kansas City	—	12.00	37.00	80.00
☐ Richmond	—	12.00	37.00	80.00	☐ Dallas	—	12.00	37.00	80.00
☐ Atlanta	—	12.00	37.00	80.00	☐ San Francisco	—	12.00	37.00	80.00

SERIES OF 1969A, SIGNATURES OF KABIS-CONNALLY, GREEN SEAL

BANK	A.B.P.	V.FINE	UNC.	★UNC.	BANK	A.B.P.	V.FINE	UNC.	★UNC.
☐ Boston	—	12.00	35.00	70.00	☐ Chicago	—	12.00	35.00	70.00
☐ New York	—	12.00	35.00	70.00	☐ St. Louis	—	12.00	35.00	70.00
☐ Philadelphia	—	12.00	35.00	70.00	☐ Minneapolis	—	15.00	35.00	70.00
☐ Cleveland	—	12.00	35.00	70.00	☐ Kansas City	—	12.00	35.00	70.00
☐ Richmond	—	12.00	35.00	70.00	☐ Dallas	—	12.00	35.00	70.00
☐ Atlanta	—	12.00	35.00	70.00	☐ San Francisco	—	12.00	35.00	70.00

SERIES OF 1969B, SIGNATURES OF BANUELOS-CONNALLY, GREEN SEAL

BANK	A.B.P.	V.FINE	UNC.	★UNC.	BANK	A.B.P.	V.FINE	UNC.	★UNC.
☐ Boston	—	25.00	160.00	—	☐ Chicago	—	25.00	160.00	250.00
☐ New York	—	25.00	160.00	300.00	☐ St. Louis	—	25.00	160.00	250.00
☐ Philadelphia	—	25.00	160.00	—	☐ Minneapolis	—	25.00	160.00	—
☐ Cleveland	—	25.00	160.00	—	☐ Kansas City	—	25.00	160.00	300.00
☐ Richmond	—	25.00	160.00	350.00	☐ Dallas	—	25.00	160.00	—
☐ Atlanta	—	25.00	160.00	300.00	☐ San Francisco	—	25.00	160.00	300.00

SERIES OF 1969C, SIGNATURES OF BANUELOS-SHULTZ, GREEN SEAL

BANK	A.B.P.	V.FINE	UNC.	★UNC.	BANK	A.B.P.	V.FINE	UNC.	★UNC.
☐ Boston	—	—	40.00	80.00	☐ Chicago	—	—	40.00	80.00
☐ New York	—	—	40.00	80.00	☐ St. Louis	—	—	40.00	80.00
☐ Philadelphia	—	—	40.00	80.00	☐ Minneapolis	—	—	40.00	80.00
☐ Cleveland	—	—	40.00	80.00	☐ Kansas City	—	—	40.00	80.00
☐ Richmond	—	—	40.00	80.00	☐ Dallas	—	—	40.00	80.00
☐ Atlanta	—	—	40.00	80.00	☐ San Francisco	—	—	40.00	80.00

TEN DOLLAR NOTES (1974)
FEDERAL RESERVE NOTES

SERIES OF 1974, SIGNATURES OF NEFF-SIMON, GREEN SEAL

BANK	A.B.P.	V.FINE	UNC.	★UNC.	BANK	A.B.P.	V.FINE	UNC.	★UNC.
☐ Boston	—	—	35.00	70.00	☐ Chicago	—	—	35.00	70.00
☐ New York	—	—	35.00	70.00	☐ St. Louis	—	—	35.00	70.00
☐ Philadelphia	—	—	35.00	70.00	☐ Minneapolis	—	—	35.00	70.00
☐ Cleveland	—	—	35.00	70.00	☐ Kansas City	—	—	35.00	70.00
☐ Richmond	—	—	35.00	70.00	☐ Dallas	—	—	35.00	70.00
☐ Atlanta	—	—	35.00	70.00	☐ San Francisco	—	—	35.00	70.00

TEN DOLLAR NOTES (1977)
FEDERAL RESERVE NOTES

SERIES OF 1977, SIGNATURES OF MORTON-BLUMENTHAL, GREEN SEAL

BANK	A.B.P.	V.FINE	UNC.	★UNC.	BANK	A.B.P.	V.FINE	UNC.	★UNC.
☐ Boston	—	—	35.00	60.00	☐ Chicago	—	—	35.00	60.00
☐ New York	—	—	35.00	60.00	☐ St. Louis	—	—	35.00	60.00
☐ Philadelphia	—	—	35.00	60.00	☐ Minneapolis	—	—	35.00	90.00
☐ Cleveland	—	—	35.00	60.00	☐ Kansas City	—	—	35.00	60.00
☐ Richmond	—	—	35.00	60.00	☐ Dallas	—	—	35.00	60.00
☐ Atlanta	—	—	35.00	60.00	☐ San Francisco	—	—	35.00	60.00

TEN DOLLAR NOTES (1981)
FEDERAL RESERVE NOTES

SERIES OF 1981, SIGNATURES OF BUCHANAN-REGAN, GREEN SEAL

★Notes not issued for all banks

BANK	A.B.P.	V.FINE	UNC.	★UNC.	BANK	A.B.P.	V.FINE	UNC.	★UNC.
☐ Boston	—	—	35.00	60.00	☐ Chicago	—	—	35.00	60.00
☐ New York	—	—	35.00	60.00	☐ St. Louis	—	—	35.00	—
☐ Philadelphia	—	—	35.00	60.00	☐ Minneapolis	—	—	35.00	60.00
☐ Cleveland	—	—	35.00	60.00	☐ Kansas City	—	—	35.00	—
☐ Richmond	—	—	35.00	60.00	☐ Dallas	—	—	35.00	—
☐ Atlanta	—	—	35.00	60.00	☐ San Francisco	—	—	35.00	60.00

SERIES OF 1981A, SIGNATURES OF ORTEGA-REGAN, GREEN SEAL

★Notes not issued for all banks

BANK	A.B.P.	V.FINE	UNC.	★UNC.	BANK	A.B.P.	V.FINE	UNC.	★UNC.
☐ Boston	—	—	35.00	—	☐ Chicago	—	—	35.00	—
☐ New York	—	—	35.00	100.00	☐ St. Louis	—	—	35.00	—
☐ Philadelphia	—	—	35.00	—	☐ Minneapolis	—	—	35.00	—
☐ Cleveland	—	—	35.00	—	☐ Kansas City	—	—	35.00	—
☐ Richmond	—	—	35.00	—	☐ Dallas	—	—	35.00	—
☐ Atlanta	—	—	35.00	80.00	☐ San Francisco	—	—	35.00	—

TEN DOLLAR NOTES (1985)
FEDERAL RESERVE NOTES

SERIES OF 1985, SIGNATURES OF ORTEGA-BAKER, GREEN SEAL

★Notes not issued for all banks

BANK	A.B.P.	V.FINE	UNC.	★UNC.	BANK	A.B.P.	V.FINE	UNC.	★UNC.
☐ Boston	—	—	35.00	60.00	☐ Chicago	—	—	35.00	—
☐ New York	—	—	35.00	60.00	☐ St. Louis	—	—	35.00	60.00
☐ Philadelphia	—	—	35.00	—	☐ Minneapolis	—	—	35.00	—
☐ Cleveland	—	—	35.00	60.00	☐ Kansas City	—	—	35.00	—
☐ Richmond	—	—	35.00	—	☐ Dallas	—	—	35.00	60.00
☐ Atlanta	—	—	35.00	60.00	☐ San Francisco	—	—	35.00	60.00

TEN DOLLAR NOTES (1988)
FEDERAL RESERVE NOTES

SERIES OF 1988A, SIGNATURES OF VILLALPANDO-BRADY, GREEN SEAL

★Notes not issued for all banks

BANK	A.B.P.	V.FINE	UNC.	★UNC.	BANK	A.B.P.	V.FINE	UNC.	★UNC.
☐ Boston	—	—	35.00	100.00	☐ Chicago	—	—	35.00	—
☐ New York	—	—	35.00	100.00	☐ St. Louis	—	—	35.00	—
☐ Philadelphia	—	—	35.00	—	☐ Minneapolis	—	—	35.00	—
☐ Cleveland	—	—	35.00	100.00	☐ Kansas City	—	—	35.00	—
☐ Richmond	—	—	35.00	—	☐ Dallas	—	—	35.00	—
☐ Atlanta	—	—	35.00	—	☐ San Francisco	—	—	35.00	100.00

TEN DOLLAR NOTES (1990)
FEDERAL RESERVE NOTES
SERIES OF 1990, SIGNATURES OF VILLALPANDO-BRADY, GREEN SEAL

★Notes not issued for all banks

BANK	A.B.P.	V.FINE	UNC.	★UNC.	BANK	A.B.P.	V.FINE	UNC.	★UNC.
□ Boston	—	—	20.00	—	□Chicago	—	—	20.00	35.00
□ New York	—	—	20.00	35.00	□St. Louis	—	—	20.00	35.00
□ Philadelphia	—	—	20.00	35.00	□Minneapolis	—	—	20.00	—
□ Cleveland	—	—	20.00	—	□Kansas City	—	—	20.00	—
□ Richmond	—	—	20.00	—	□Dallas	—	—	20.00	—
□ Atlanta	—	—	20.00	—	□San Francisco	—	—	20.00	—

TEN DOLLAR NOTES (1993)
FEDERAL RESERVE NOTES
SERIES OF 1993, SIGNATURES OF WITHROW-BENTSEN, GREEN SEAL

★Notes not issued for all banks

BANK	A.B.P.	V.FINE	UNC.	★UNC.	BANK	A.B.P.	V.FINE	UNC.	★UNC.
□ Boston	—	—	20.00	—	□Chicago	—	—	20.00	35.00
□ New York	—	—	20.00	35.00	□St. Louis	—	—	20.00	—
□ Philadelphia	—	—	20.00	35.00					
□ Cleveland	—	—	20.00	—	□Kansas City	—	—	20.00	—
□ Atlanta	—	—	20.00	—	□San Francisco	—	—	20.00	—

TEN DOLLAR NOTES (1995)
FEDERAL RESERVE NOTES
SERIES OF 1995, SIGNATURES OF WITHROW-RUBIN, GREEN SEAL

★Notes not issued for all banks

BANK	A.B.P.	V.FINE	UNC.	★UNC.	BANK	A.B.P.	V.FINE	UNC.	★UNC.
□ Boston	—	15.00	20.00	—	□Chicago	—	—	20.00	35.00
□ New York	—	15.00	20.00	—	□St. Louis	—	—	20.00	35.00
□ Philadelphia	—	15.00	20.00	—	□Minneapolis	—	—	20.00	—
□ Cleveland	—	15.00	20.00	35.00	□Kansas City	—	—	20.00	—
□ Richmond		15.00	20.00	35.00	□Dallas	—	—	20.00	—
□ Atlanta	—	—	20.00	50.00	□San Francisco	—	—	20.00	35.00

TEN DOLLAR NOTES (1915–1918)
FEDERAL RESERVE BANK NOTES

(Large Size)

Face Design: Portrait of President Jackson to left, bank and city in center, blue seal to the right.

Back Design: Similar to 1914 note.

BANK	SERIES	GOV'T SIGNATURES	BANK SIGNATURES	A.B.P.	GOOD	V.FINE	UNC.
☐New York	1918	Teehee-Burke	Hendricks-Strong	300.00	545.00	1300.00	3500.00
☐Atlanta	1915	Teehee-Burke	Bell-Wellborn	535.00	845.00	2500.00	5200.00
☐Atlanta	1918	Elliott-Burke	Bell-Wellborn	300.00	545.00	1300.00	3500.00
☐Chicago	1915	Teehee-Burke	McLallen-McDougal	300.00	545.00	1300.00	3500.00
☐Chicago	1918	Teehee-Burke	McCloud-McDougal	300.00	545.00	1300.00	3600.00
☐St. Louis	1918	Teehee-Burke	Attebery-Wells	300.00	545.00	1300.00	3600.00
☐Kansas City	1915	Teehee-Burke	Anderson-Miller	300.00	545.00	7300.00	3600.00

BANK	SERIES	GOV'T SIGNATURES	BANK SIGNATURES	A.B.P.	GOOD	V.FINE	UNC.
☐Kansas City	1915	Teehee-Burke	Cross-Miller	110.00	555.00	1275.00	3500.00
☐Kansas City	1915	Teehee-Burke	Helm-Miller	255.00	4300.00	2475.00	4600.00
☐Dallas	1915	Teehee-Burke	Hoopes-Van Zandt	110.00	1950.00	1275.00	3600.00
☐Dallas	1915	Teehee-Burke	Gilbert-Van Zandt	255.00	855.00	2500.00	5100.00
☐Dallas	1918	Teehee-Burke	Talley-Van Zandt	155.00	650.00	2225.00	4200.00

TEN DOLLAR NOTES (1929)
FEDERAL RESERVE BANK NOTES

(Small Size)

Face Design: Portrait of Alexander Hamilton.

Back Design: Same as all Small Size $10 notes.

SIGNATURES OF JONES-WOODS, BROWN SEAL

BANK	SEAL	A.B.P.	GOOD	V.FINE	UNC.	★UNC.
☐Boston	Brown	10.00	20.00	45.00	250.00	8000.00
☐New York	Brown	10.00	20.00	45.00	175.00	2500.00
☐Philadelphia	Brown	10.00	20.00	45.00	250.00	3500.00
☐Cleveland	Brown	10.00	20.00	45.00	250.00	3500.00

BANK	SEAL	A.B.P.	GOOD	V.FINE	UNC.	★UNC.
☐Richmond	Brown	12.00	20.00	45.00	450.00	3500.00
☐Atlanta	Brown	12.00	20.00	45.00	375.00	3800.00
☐Chicago	Brown	12.00	20.00	45.00	400.00	3500.00
☐St. Louis	Brown	12.00	20.00	45.00	325.00	2800.00
☐Minneapolis	Brown	12.00	20.00	45.00	325.00	3000.00
☐Kansas City	Brown	12.00	20.00	45.00	325.00	3000.00
☐Dallas	Brown	200.00	400.00	850.00	2500.00	6000.00
☐San Francisco	Brown	12.00	20.00	45.00	1500.00	4000.00

TWENTY DOLLAR NOTES

ORDER OF ISSUE

TWENTY DOLLAR NOTES (1861) DEMAND NOTES
(Large Size)

Face Design: Liberty with sword and shield.

Back Design: Intricate design of numerals, "20." Demand Notes have no Treasury Seal.

SERIES	PAYABLE AT	A.B.P.	GOOD	V.GOOD
☐1861	Boston (I)	RARE	RARE	RARE
☐1861	New York (I)	6200.00	9300.00	20,000.00
☐1861	Philadelphia (I)	6200.00	9300.00	20,000.00
☐1861	Cincinnati (I)	RARE	RARE	RARE
☐1861	St. Louis (I)	(Unknown in any collection)		
☐1861	Boston (II)	RARE	RARE	RARE
☐1861	New York (II)	6200.00	9300.00	20,000.00
☐1861	Philadelphia (II)	6200.00	9300.00	20,000.00
☐1861	Cincinnati (II)	RARE	RARE	RARE
☐1861	St. Louis (II)	(Unknown in any collection)		

Counterfeits exist. Use caution in buying.

TWENTY DOLLAR NOTES (1862–1863)
UNITED STATES NOTES
(ALSO KNOWN AS LEGAL TENDER NOTES)

(Large Size)

Face Design: Liberty with sword and shield.

Back Design: Second obligation. This note was also issued with first obligation on the back.

SERIES	SIGNATURES	SEAL	A.B.P.	GOOD	V.FINE	UNC.
□1862	Chittenden-Spinner*	Red	500.00	700.00	2400.00	7800.00
□1862	Chittenden-Spinner**	Red	500.00	700.00	2400.00	7800.00
□1863	Chittenden-Spinner**	Red	500.00	700.00	2400.00	7800.00

* First Obligation: Similar to 1875–1907 $5 note.
** Second Obligation: Shown above.

TWENTY DOLLAR NOTES (1869)
UNITED STATES NOTES
(ALSO KNOWN AS LEGAL TENDER NOTES)

(Large Size)

SERIES	SIGNATURES	SEAL	A.B.P.	GOOD	V.FINE	UNC.
☐1869	Allison-Spinner	Red	375.00	525.00	2400.00	8000.00
	Series Back Design: Revised					
☐1875	Allison-New	Red	240.00	375.00	1325.00	4600.00
☐1878	Allison-Gilfillan	Red	225.00	310.00	975.00	3100.00
☐1878	Watermark Paper		275.00	510.00	1875.00	4800.00
☐1880	Scofield-Gilfillan	Lg. Brown	590.00	885.00	3250.00	14000.00
☐1880	Bruce-Gilfillan	Lg. Brown	190.00	395.00	2650.00	4900.00
☐1880	Bruce-Wyman	Lg. Brown	150.00	385.00	2175.00	4200.00
☐1880	Bruce-Wyman	Lg. Red	565.00	820.00	2250.00	13500.00
☐1880	Rosecrans-Jordan	Lg. Red	150.00	275.00	975.00	4000.00
☐1880	Rosecrans-Hyatt	Red Plain	140.00	265.00	1000.00	3600.00
☐1880	Rosecrans-Hyatt	Red Spikes	110.00	165.00	850.00	2500.00
☐1880	Rosecrans-Huston	Lg. Red	110.00	165.00	875.00	2600.00
☐1880	Rosecrans-Huston	Lg. Brown	110.00	165.00	900.00	2700.00
☐1880	Rosecrans-Nebeker	Lg. Brown	110.00	165.00	2375.00	13500.00
☐1800	Rosecrans-Nebeker	Sm. Red	110.00	155.00	575.00	2500.00
☐1880	Tillman-Morgan	Sm. Red	110.00	155.00	575.00	2000.00
☐1880	Bruce-Roberts	Sm. Red	110.00	155.00	575.00	2000.00
☐1880	Lyons-Roberts	Sm. Red	110.00	155.00	675.00	2150.00
☐1880	Vernon-Treat	Sm. Red	110.00	155.00	725.00	2250.00
☐1880	Vernon-McClung	Sm. Red	110.00	155.00	675.00	2150.00
☐1880	Teehee-Burke	Sm. Red	110.00	150.00	650.00	2025.00
☐1880	Elliott-White	Sm. Red	110.00	100.00	575.00	1450.00

TWENTY DOLLAR NOTES (1863–1875)
NATIONAL BANK NOTES
FIRST CHARTER PERIOD (Large Size)

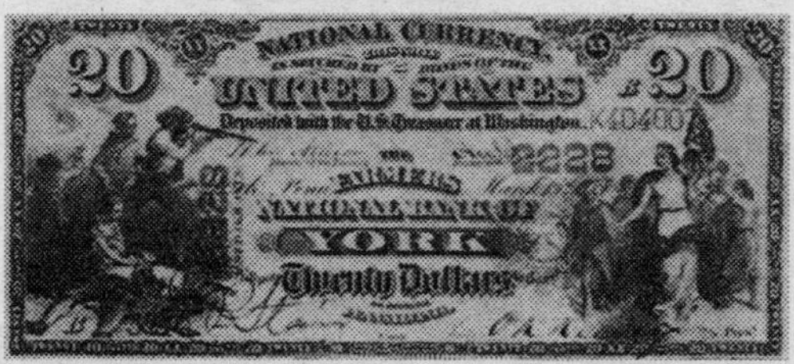

Face Design: Battle of Lexington left, name of bank in center. Columbia with flag right.

Back Design: Green border, black center picture of baptism of Pocahontas.

SERIES	SIGNATURES	SEAL	A.B.P.	GOOD	V.FINE	UNC.
☐Original	Chittenden-Spinner	Red	300.00	425.00	1800.00	5900.00
☐Original	Colby-Spinner	Red	300.00	425.00	1800.00	5800.00
☐Original	Jeffries-Spinner	Red	300.00	675.00	2750.00	8100.00
☐Original	Allison-Spinner	Red	300.00	425.00	1800.00	5800.00
☐1875	Allison-New	Red	300.00	425.00	1800.00	5800.00
☐1875	Allison-Wyman	Red	300.00	425.00	1800.00	5800.00
☐1875	Allison-Gilfillan	Red	300.00	425.00	1800.00	5800.00
☐1875	Scofield-Gilfillan	Red	300.00	425.00	1800.00	5800.00
☐1875	Bruce-Gilfillan	Red	300.00	425.00	1800.00	5800.00
☐1875	Bruce-Wyman	Red	300.00	425.00	1800.00	5800.00
☐1875	Rosecrans-Huston	Red	300.00	425.00	1800.00	5800.00
☐1875	Rosecrans-Nebeker	Red	300.00	525.00	2000.00	6750.00
☐1875	Tillman-Morgan	Red	300.00	525.00	2000.00	6750.00

TWENTY DOLLAR NOTES (1882)
NATIONAL BANK NOTES

SECOND CHARTER PERIOD (Large Size)

First Issue (Brown seal and brown backs.)
Face Design: Similar to First Charter Period note.
Back Design: Similar to 1882 $5 note. Border is brown, green Charter Number in center.

SERIES	SIGNATURES	SEAL	A.B.P.	GOOD	V.FINE	UNC.
□1882	Bruce-Gilfillan	Brown	75.00	125.00	525.00	1500.00
□1882	Bruce-Wyman	Brown	75.00	125.00	525.00	1500.00
□1882	Bruce-Jordan	Brown	75.00	125.00	525.00	1500.00
□1882	Rosecrans-Jordan	Brown	75.00	125.00	525.00	1500.00
□1882	Rosecrans-Hyatt	Brown	75.00	125.00	525.00	1500.00
□1882	Rosecrans-Huston	Brown	75.00	125.00	525.00	1500.00
□1882	Rosecrans-Nebeker	Brown	75.00	125.00	525.00	1500.00
□1882	Rosecrans-Morgan	Brown	145.00	315.00	895.00	2400.00
□1882	Tillman-Morgan	Brown	75.00	125.00	525.00	1500.00
□1882	Tillman-Roberts	Brown	75.00	125.00	525.00	1500.00
□1882	Bruce-Roberts	Brown	75.00	125.00	525.00	1500.00
□1882	Lyons-Roberts	Brown	75.00	125.00	525.00	1500.00
□1882	Lyons-Treat	Brown	75.00	125.00	525.00	1500.00
□1882	Vernon-Treat	Brown	75.00	125.00	525.00	1500.00

SECOND CHARTER PERIOD, Second Issue

Face Design: Similar to First Charter Period note.
Back Design: Similar to 1882 $5.00 Second Issue note.

SERIES	SIGNATURES	SEAL	A.B.P.	GOOD	V.FINE	UNC.
□1882	Rosecrans-Huston	Blue	65.00	115.00	450.00	1275.00
□1882	Rosecrans-Nebeker	Blue	65.00	115.00	450.00	1275.00
□1882	Rosecrans-Morgan	Blue	130.00	330.00	950.00	1925.00
□1882	Tillman-Morgan	Blue	65.00	115.00	450.00	1275.00
□1882	Tillman-Roberts	Blue	65.00	115.00	450.00	1275.00
□1882	Bruce-Roberts	Blue	65.00	115.00	450.00	1275.00
□1882	Lyons-Roberts	Blue	65.00	115.00	450.00	1275.00
□1882	Vernon-Treat	Blue	65.00	115.00	450.00	1275.00
□1882	Napier-McClung	Blue	65.00	115.00	450.00	1275.00

SECOND CHARTER PERIOD, Third Issue. Large Size

Face Design: Similar to First Charter Period note with blue seal.
Back Design: Similar to 1882 Third Issue note, green back, value in block letters.

SERIES	SIGNATURES	SEAL	A.B.P.	GOOD	V.FINE	UNC.
□1882	Tillman-Morgan	Blue	90.00	130.00	550.00	2250.00
□1882	Lyons-Roberts	Blue	63.00	255.00	750.00	2575.00
□1882	Lyons-Treat	Blue	100.00	155.00	550.00	2575 00
□1882	Vernon-Treat	Blue	100.00	155.00	550.00	2250.00
□1882	Napier-McClung	Blue	100.00	155.00	550.00	2250.00
□1882	Teehee-Burke	Blue	100.00	155.00	675.00	2675.00

TWENTY DOLLAR NOTES (1902)
NATIONAL BANK NOTES
THIRD CHARTER PERIOD, First Issue (Large Size)

Face Design: Portrait of McCulloch left, name of bank center, Treasury Seal right.

SERIES	SIGNATURES	SEAL	A.B.P.	GOOD	V.FINE	UNC.
□1902	Lyons-Roberts	Red	135.00	200.00	450.00	1400.00
□1902	Lyons-Treat	Red	135.00	200.00	450.00	1400.00
□1902	Vernon-Treat	Red	135.00	200.00	450.00	1400.00

Second Issue (Date "1902–1908" added on back, Treasury Seal and serial numbers blue)

SERIES	SIGNATURES	SEAL	A.B.P.	GOOD	V.FINE	UNC.
□1902	Lyons-Roberts	Blue	32.00	50.00	135.00	475.00
□1902	Lyons-Treat	Blue	32.00	50.00	135.00	475.00
□1902	Vernon-Treat	Blue	32.00	50.00	135.00	475.00
□1902	Vernon-McClung	Blue	32.00	50.00	135.00	475.00
□1902	Napier-McClung	Blue	32.00	50.00	135.00	475.00
□1902	Napier-Thompson	Blue	32.00	50.00	135.00	670.00
□1902	Napier-Burke	Blue	32.00	50.00	135.00	475.00
□1902	Parker-Burke	Blue	32.00	50.00	135.00	475.00

Third Issue (Date "1902–1908" removed from back, seal and serial numbers blue)

SERIES	SIGNATURES	SEAL	A.B.P.	GOOD	V.FINE	UNC.
□1902	Lyons-Roberts	Blue	32.00	45.00	100.00	435.00
□1902	Lyons-Treat	Blue	32.00	45.00	100.00	435.00
□1902	Vernon-Treat	Blue	32.00	45.00	100.00	435.00
□1902	Vernon-McClung	Blue	32.00	45.00	100.00	435.00

SERIES	SIGNATURES	SEAL	A.B.P.	GOOD	V.FINE	UNC.
□1902	Napier-McClung	Blue	32.00	45.00	120.00	435.00
□1902	Napier-Thompson	Blue	32.00	63.00	125.00	435.00
□1902	Napier-Burke	Blue	32.00	45.00	100.00	435.00
□1902	Parker-Burke	Blue	32.00	45.00	100.00	435.00
□1902	Teehee-Burke	Blue	32.00	45.00	100.00	435.00
□1902	Elliott-Burke	Blue	32.00	45.00	100.00	435.00
□1902	Elliott-White	Blue	32.00	45.00	100.00	435.00
□1902	Speelman-White	Blue	32.00	45.00	100.00	435.00
□1902	Woods-White	Blue	32.00	45.00	100.00	405.00
□1902	Woods-Tate	Blue	32.00	55.00	200.00	580.00
□1902	Jones-Woods	Blue	39.00	615.00	1165.00	5275.00

TWENTY DOLLAR NOTES (1929)
NATIONAL BANK NOTES

(Small Size)

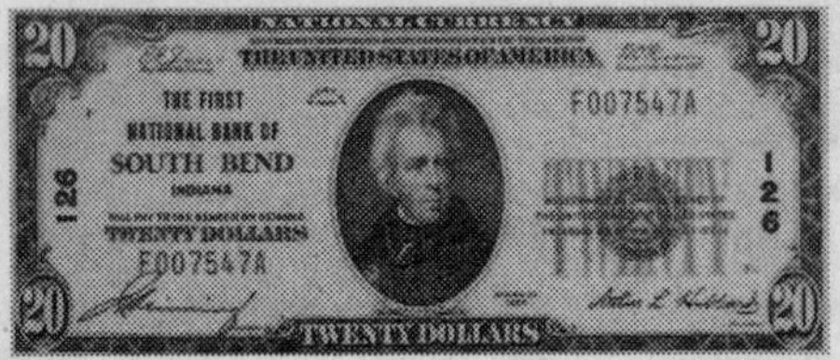

Face Design, Type I: Portrait of President Jackson in center, name of bank to left, brown seal right. Charter number in black.

Face Design, Type II.

Back Design: The White House, similar to all $20 Small Notes.

SERIES	SIGNATURES	SEAL	A.B.P.	GOOD	V.FINE	UNC.
□1929, Type I	Jones-Woods	Brown	24.00	30.00	55.00	150.00
□1929, Type II	Jones-Woods	Brown	24.00	30.00	55.00	165.00

TWENTY DOLLAR NOTES (1880)
SILVER CERTIFICATES

(Large Size)

Face Dosign: Portrait of Stephen Decatur right. TWENTY SILVER DOLLARS in center.

Back Design: SILVER in large block letters.

SERIES	SIGNATURES	SEAL	A.B.P.	GOOD	V.FINE	UNC.
□1880	Scofield-Gilfillan	Brown	700.00	1200.00	5500.00	23000.00
□1880	Bruce-Gilfillan	Brown	700.00	1200.00	5500.00	23000.00
□1880	Bruce-Wyman	Brown	700.00	1200.00	5500.00	23000.00
□1880	Bruce-Wyman	Sm. Red	900.00	1700.00	6000.00	26500.00

This note was also issued in the Series of 1878. They are very rare.

TWENTY DOLLAR NOTES (1886)
SILVER CERTIFICATES

(Large Size)

Face Design: Portrait of Daniel Manning center, Agriculture left, Industry right.

Back Design: Double-diamond design center.

SERIES	SIGNATURES	SEAL	A.B.P.	GOOD	V.FINE	UNC.
□1886	Rosecrans-Hyatt	Lg. Red	950.00	1300.00	5300.00	25000.00
□1886	Rosecrans-Huston	Lg. Brown	950.00	1300.00	5300.00	22500.00
□1886	Rosecrans-Nebeker	Lg. Brown	950.00	1300.00	5300.00	22500.00
□1886	Rosecrans-Nebeker	Sm. Red	950.00	1300.00	5750.00	95000.00

TWENTY DOLLAR NOTES (1891)
SILVER CERTIFICATES
(NOT ISSUED IN SMALL SIZE NOTES)

(Large Size)

Face Design: Same as 1886 note.

Back Design: Revised.

SERIES	SIGNATURES	SEAL	A.B.P.	GOOD	V.FINE	UNC.
□1891	Rosecrans-Nebeker	Red	160.00	210.00	1675.00	4800.00
□1891	Tillman-Morgan	Red	160.00	210.00	1675.00	4800.00
□1891	Bruce-Roberts	Red	160.00	210.00	1675.00	4800.00
□1891	Lyons-Roberts	Red	160.00	210.00	1675.00	4800.00
□1891	Parker-Burke	Blue	160.00	210.00	1675.00	4800.00
□1891	Teehee-Burke	Blue	160.00	210.00	1675.00	4800.00

TWENTY DOLLAR NOTES (1882) GOLD CERTIFICATES
(Large Size)

Face Design: Portrait of President Garfield right, TWENTY DOLLARS IN GOLD COIN center.

Back Design: Large “20” left, eagle and arrows center, bright orange color.

SERIES	SIGNATURES	SEAL	A.B.P.	GOOD	V.FINE	UNC.
□1882*	Bruce-Gilfillan	Brown	3400.00	5200.00	18500.00	32500.00
□1882	Bruce-Gilfillan	Brown	2700.00	4200.00	12000.00	32000.00
□1882	Bruce-Wyman	Brown	1400.00	2000.00	12000.00	44000.00
□1882	Rosecrans-Huston	Brown	1700.00	2650.00	12500.00	35000.00
□1882	Lyons-Roberts	Red	110.00	225.00	1100.00	5200.00

*This note has a countersigned signature.

TWENTY DOLLAR NOTES (1905) GOLD CERTIFICATES
(Large Size)

Face Design: Portrait of President Washington center, "XX" left, Treasury Seal right.

Back Design: Eagle and shield center, printed in bright orange color.

SERIES	SIGNATURES	SEAL	A.B.P.	GOOD	V.FINE	UNC.
□1905	Lyons-Roberts	Red	310.00	400.00	2400.00	9500.00
□1905	Lyons-Treat	Red	310.00	400.00	2400.00	9400.00
□1906	Vernon-Treat	Gold	80.00	125.00	380.00	1300.00
□1906	Vernon-McClung	Gold	80.00	125.00	380.00	1300.00
□1906	Napier-McClung	Gold	80.00	125.00	380.00	1300.00
□1906	Napier-Thompson	Gold	95.00	150.00	640.00	1950.00
□1906	Parker-Burke	Gold	80.00	125.00	380.00	1300.00
□1906	Tehee-Burke	Gold	80.00	125.00	380.00	1300.00
□1922	Speelman-White	Gold	80.00	125.00	380.00	1275.00

TWENTY DOLLAR NOTES (1928) GOLD CERTIFICATES
(Small Size)

Face Design: Portrait of President Jackson center, gold seal left, gold serial numbers.

Back Design: The White House, printed green, similar to all Small Size $20 Notes.

SERIES	SIGNATURES	SEAL	A.B.P.	V.FINE	UNC.
□1928	Woods-Mellon	Gold	40.00	120.00	750.00

TWENTY DOLLAR NOTES (1890) TREASURY NOTES
(Large Size)

Face Design: Portrait of John Marshall, Supreme Court Chief Justice, left, "20" center.

Back Design

SERIES	SIGNATURES	SEAL	A.B.P.	GOOD	V.FINE	UNC.
□1890	Rosecrans-Huston	Brown	900.00	1250.00	6500.00	16000.00
□1890	Rosecrans-Nebeker	Brown	900.00	1250.00	6500.00	16000.00
□1890	Rosecrans-Nebeker	Red	900.00	1250.00	6500.00	16000.00

(Large Size)

Back Design

Face Design: Same as previous note.

SERIES	SIGNATURES	SEAL	A.B.P.	GOOD	V.FINE	UNC.
□1891	Tillman-Morgan	Red	750.00	1130.00	5300.00	13,500.00
□1891	Bruce-Roberts	Red	750.00	1130.00	5300.00	13,500.00

TWENTY DOLLAR NOTES (1914)
FEDERAL RESERVE NOTES

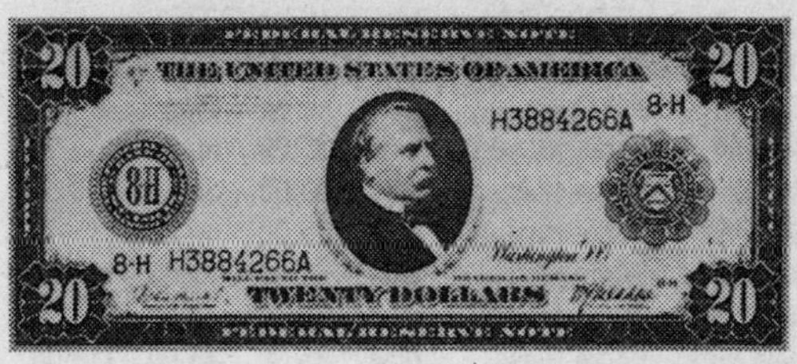

(Large Size)

Face Design: Portrait of President Cleveland center, Federal Reserve Seal left, Treasury Seal right.

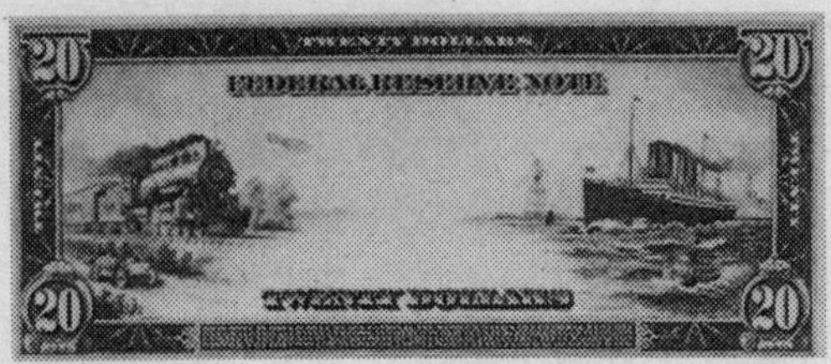

Back Design: Scenes of transportation. Locomotive left, steamship right
(Small Size)

SERIES OF 1914, SIGNATURES OF BURKE-McADOO, RED TREASURY SEAL

BANK	A.B.P.	V.FINE	UNC.	BANK	A.B.P.	V.FINE	UNC.
☐ Boston	60.00	450.00	1600.00	☐ Chicago	125.00	600.00	2700.00
☐ New York	60.00	450.00	1600.00	☐ St. Louis	125.00	600.00	2700.00
☐ Philadelphia	60.00	450.00	1600.00	☐ Minneapolis	125.00	600.00	2900.00
☐ Cleveland	60.00	450.00	1600.00	☐ Kansas City	125.00	600.00	2850.00
☐ Richmond	60.00	600.00	1900.00	☐ Dallas	125.00	600.00	2600.00
☐ Atlanta	60.00	800.00	2100.00	☐ San Francisco	125.00	750.00	2900.00

SERIES OF 1914, BLUE TREASURY SEAL AND BLUE SERIAL NUMBERS

(Small Size)
This note was issued with signatures of Burke-McAdoo, Burke-Glass, Burke-Huston, and White-Mellon.

TWENTY DOLLAR NOTES (1914)
FEDERAL RESERVE NOTES
1914, BLUE TREASURY SEAL AND BLUE NUMBERS

DATE	CITY	SIGNATURES	SEAL	A.B.P.	GOOD	V.FINE	UNC.
1914	Boston	Burke-McAdoo	Blue	35.00	50.00	155.00	400.00
1914	Boston	Burke-Glass	Blue	35.00	55.00	200.00	450.00
1914	Boston	Burke-Huston	Blue	35.00	45.00	115.00	300.00
1914	Boston	White-Mellon	Blue	35.00	45.00	115.00	300.00
1914	New York	Burke-McAdoo	Blue	35.00	45.00	115.00	300.00
1914	New York	Burke-Glass	Blue	35.00	45.00	115.00	300.00
1914	New York	Burke-Huston	Blue	35.00	45.00	115.00	300.00
1914	New York	White-Mellon	Blue	35.00	45.00	115.00	300.00
1914	Phila.	Burke-McAdoo	Blue	35.00	47.00	135.00	350.00
1914	Phila.	Burke-Glass	Blue	35.00	50.00	200.00	475.00
1914	Phila.	Burke-Huston	Blue	35.00	45.00	115.00	300.00
1914	Phila.	White-Mellon	Blue	35.00	45.00	115.00	300.00
1914	Cleveland	Burke-McAdoo	Blue	35.00	45.00	150.00	400.00

DATE	CITY	SIGNATURES	SEAL	A.B.P.	GOOD	V.FINE	UNC.
1914	Cleveland	Burke-Glass	Blue	35.00	50.00	200.00	475.00
1914	Cleveland	Burke-Huston	Blue	35.00	45.00	125.00	350.00
1914	Cleveland	White-Mellon	Blue	35.00	45.00	125.00	300.00
1914	Richmond	Burke-McAdoo	Blue	35.00	55.00	180.00	520.00
1914	Richmond	Burke-Glass	Blue	35.00	55.00	180.00	500.00
1914	Richmond	Burke-Huston	Blue	35.00	52.00	150.00	420.00
1914	Richmond	White-Mellon	Blue	35.00	50.00	150.00	385.00
1914	Atlanta	Burke-McAdoo	Blue	35.00	45.00	120.00	300.00
1914	Atlanta	Burke-Glass	Blue	90.00	170.00	1060.00	1600.00
1914	Atlanta	Burke-Huston	Blue	35.00	45.00	150.00	350.00
1914	Atlanta	White-Mellon	Blue	35.00	55.00	200.00	400.00
1914	Chicago	Burke-McAdoo	Blue	35.00	45.00	105.00	300.00
1914	Chicago	Burke-Glass	Blue	35.00	45.00	105.00	300.00
1914	Chicago	Burke-Huston	Blue	35.00	45.00	105.00	300.00
1914	Chicago	White-Mellon	Blue	35.00	45.00	105.00	300.00
1914	St. Louis	Burke-McAdoo	Blue	35.00	45.00	105.00	300.00
1914	St. Louis	Burke-Glass	Blue	35.00	55.00	200.00	475.00
1914	St. Louis	Burke-Huston	Blue	35.00	45.00	110.00	300.00
1914	St. Louis	White-Mellon	Blue	35.00	50.00	150.00	400.00
1914	Minneapolis	Burke-McAdoo	Blue	35.00	45.00	125.00	350.00
1914	Minneapolis	Burke-Glass	Blue	44.00	70.00	550.00	1220.00
1914	Minneapolis	Burke-Huston	Blue	35.00	45.00	125.00	350.00
1914	Minneapolis	White-Mellon	Blue	35.00	45.00	110.00	300.00
1914	Kansas City	Burke-McAdoo	Blue	35.00	45.00	150.00	410.00
1914	Kansas City	Burke-Glass	Blue	89.00	170.00	1050.00	1665.00
1914	Kansas City	Burke-Huston	Blue	35.00	45.00	125.00	350.00
1914	Kansas City	White-Mellon	Blue	39.00	55.00	200.00	475.00
1914	Dallas	Burke-McAdoo	Blue	35.00	45.00	125.00	350.00
1914	Dallas	Burke-Glass	Blue	35.00	55.00	200.00	550.00
1914	Dallas	Burke-Huston	Blue	35.00	45.00	130.00	360.00
1914	Dallas	White-Mellon	Blue	35.00	45.00	130.00	375.00
1914	San Fran.	Burke-McAdoo	Blue	35.00	45.00	130.00	375.00
1914	San Fran.	Burke-Glass	Blue	35.00	45.00	150.00	400.00
1914	San Fran.	Burke-Huston	Blue	35.00	45.00	150.00	385.00
1914	San Fran.	White-Mellon	Blue	35.00	45.00	110.00	400.00

TWENTY DOLLAR NOTES (1928)
FEDERAL RESERVE NOTES

(Small Size)

Face Design: Portrait of President Jackson center, black Federal Reserve Seal with numeral for district in center. City of issuing bank in Seal circle. Green Treasury Seal right.

Back Design: Picture of the White House, similar to all Small Size $20 Notes.

(Small Size)

SERIES OF 1928, SIGNATURES OF TATE-MELLON, GREEN SEAL

BANK	A.B.P.	V.FINE	UNC.	★UNC.	BANK	A.B.P.	V.FINE	UNC.	★UNC.
☐ Boston	31.00	54.00	275.00	2200.00	☐ Chicago	31.00	44.00	225.00	1800.00
☐ New York	31.00	44.00	250.00	1500.00	☐ St. Louis	31.00	54.00	250.00	2200.00
☐ Philadelphia	31.00	54.00	350.00	2000.00	☐ Minneapolis	31.00	54.00	400.00	2200.00
☐ Cleveland	31.00	74.00	325.00	1800.00	☐ Kansas City	31.00	64.00	250.00	1800.00
☐ Richmond	31.00	74.00	350.00	3000.00	☐ Dallas	31.00	64.00	400.00	7500.00
☐ Atlanta	31.00	64.00	400.00	3000.00	☐ San Francisco	31.00	54.00	350.00	2000.00

(Small Size)

SERIES OF 1928A, SIGNATURES OF WOODS-MELLON, GREEN SEAL

CITY	A.B.P.	V.FINE	UNC.	★UNC.	CITY	A.B.P.	V.FINE	UNC.	★UNC.
☐ Boston	33.00	62.00	400.00	4250.00	☐ Chicago	33.00	62.00	250.00	4250.00
☐ New York	33.00	62.00	300.00	4250.00	☐ St. Louis	33.00	72.00	450.00	4250.00
☐ Philadelphia	33.00	67.00	300.00	4250.00	☐ Minneapolis	NOT ISSUED			
☐ Cleveland	33.00	72.00	300.00	4250.00	☐ Kansas City	45.00	82.00	800.00	4250.00
☐ Richmond	25.00	52.00	300.00	4250.00	☐ Dallas	25.00	62.00	300.00	4250.00
☐ Atlanta	33.00	62.00	300.00	4250.00	☐ San Francisco	NOT ISSUED			

TWENTY DOLLAR NOTES (1928)
FEDERAL RESERVE NOTES

(Small Size)

SERIES OF 1928B, SIGNATURES OF WOODS-MELLON, GREEN SEAL

The face and back design are similar to previous note. Numeral in Federal Reserve Seal is now changed to a letter.

BANK	A.B.P.	V.FINE	UNC.	★UNC.	BANK	A.B.P.	V.FINE	UNC.	★UNC.
☐ Boston	23.00	42.00	200.00	1000.00	☐ Chicago	21.00	37.00	200.00	1000.00
☐ New York	23.00	42.00	200.00	1000.00	☐ St. Louis	21.00	52.00	200.00	1000.00
☐ Philadelphia	23.00	42.00	200.00	1000.00	☐ Minneapolis	21.00	52.00	200.00	1500.00
☐ Cleveland	23.00	32.00	200.00	1000.00	☐ Kansas City	21.00	37.00	200.00	1000.00
☐ Richmond	23.00	37.00	200.00	1000.00	☐ Dallas	21.00	67.00	200.00	1000.00
☐ Atlanta	23.00	22.00	200.00	1000.00	☐ San Francisco	21.00	37.00	200.00	1000.00

SERIES OF 1928C, SIGNATURES OF WOODS-MILLS, GREEN SEAL

Only two banks issued this note.

BANK	A.B.P.	V.FINE	UNC.	★UNC.	BANK	A.B.P.	V.FINE	UNC.	★UNC.
☐ Chicago	100.00	700.00	2000.00	NONE	☐ San Francisco	100.00	1000.00	4500.00	NONE

TWENTY DOLLAR NOTES (1934)
FEDERAL RESERVE NOTES

(Small Size)

SIGNATURES OF JULIAN-MORGENTHAU, GREEN SEAL

Face and back design are similar to previous note. "Redeemable in Gold" removed from obligation over Federal Reserve Seal.

BANK	A.B.P.	V.FINE	UNC.	★UNC.	BANK	A.B.P.	V.FINE	UNC.	★UNC.
☐ Boston	22.00	27.00	85.00	600.00	☐ St. Louis	22.00	27.00	85.00	600.00
☐ New York	22.00	27.00	85.00	600.00	☐ Minneapolis	22.00	27.00	120.00	600.00
☐ Philadelphia	22.00	27.00	85.00	600.00	☐ Kansas City	22.00	27.00	105.00	600.00
☐ Cleveland	22.00	27.00	85.00	600.00	☐ Dallas	22.00	27.00	110.00	600.00
☐ Richmond	22.00	27.00	90.00	600.00	☐ San Francisco	22.00	27.00	90.00	600.00
☐ Atlanta	22.00	27.00	90.00	600.00	☐ San Francisco*				
☐ Chicago	22.00	27.00	85.00	600.00	(HAWAII)	36.00	175.00	2500.00	12000.00

* The San Francisco Federal Reserve Note with brown seal and brown serial numbers, and overprinted HAWAII on face and back, was a special issue for the armed forces in the Pacific area during World War II.

TWENTY DOLLAR NOTES (1934A)
FEDERAL RESERVE NOTES

(Small Size)

SERIES OF 1934A, SIGNATURES OF JULIAN-MORGENTHAU

BANK	A.B.P.	V.FINE	UNC.	★UNC.	BANK	A.B.P.	V.FINE	UNC.	★UNC.
☐ Boston	22.00	30.00	65.00	500.00	☐ St. Louis	22.00	35.00	65.00	500.00
☐ New York	22.00	30.00	75.00	500.00	☐ Minneapolis	31.00	50.00	110.00	500.00
☐ Philadelphia	22.00	30.00	75.00	500.00	☐ Kansas City	22.00	37.00	75.00	500.00
☐ Cleveland	22.00	30.00	70.00	500.00	☐ Dallas	22.00	37.00	75.00	500.00
☐ Richmond	22.00	30.00	90.00	500.00	☐ San Francisco	22.00	32.00	75.00	500.00
☐ Atlanta	22.00	30.00	70.00	500.00	☐ San Francisco*				
☐ Chicago	22.00	30.00	85.00	500.00	(HAWAII)	28.00	75.00	1250.00	10000.00

* The San Francisco Federal Reserve Note with brown seal and brown serial numbers, and overprinted HAWAII on face and back, was a special issue for the armed forces in the Pacific area during World War II.

(Small Size)

SERIES OF 1934B,
SIGNATURES OF JULIAN-VINSON, GREEN SEAL

BANK	A.B.P.	V.FINE	UNC.	★UNC.	BANK	A.B.P.	V.FINE	UNC.	★UNC.
☐ Boston	21.00	30.00	110.00	950.00	☐ Chicago	21.00	30.00	110.00	950.00
☐ New York	21.00	30.00	110.00	950.00	☐ St. Louis	21.00	30.00	110.00	950.00
☐ Philadelphia	21.00	30.00	110.00	950.00	☐ Minneapolis	21.00	30.00	110.00	950.00
☐ Cleveland	21.00	30.00	110.00	950.00	☐ Kansas City	21.00	30.00	110.00	950.00
☐ Richmond	21.00	30.00	110.00	950.00	☐ Dallas	21.00	30.00	110.00	950.00
☐ Atlanta	21.00	30.00	110.00	950.00	☐ San Francisco	21.00	30.00	110.00	950.00

SERIES OF 1934C, SIGNATURES OF JULIAN-SNYDER, GREEN SEAL

Back Design: This has been modified with this series, with or without balcony added to the White House.

BANK	A.B.P.	V.FINE	UNC.	★UNC.	BANK	A.B.P.	V.FINE	UNC.	★UNC.
☐ Boston	22.00	29.00	100.00	600.00	☐ Chicago	22.00	30.00	100.00	600.00
☐ New York	22.00	29.00	100.00	600.00	☐ St. Louis	22.00	30.00	100.00	600.00
☐ Philadelphia	22.00	29.00	100.00	600.00	☐ Minneapolis	22.00	30.00	100.00	600.00
☐ Cleveland	22.00	29.00	100.00	600.00	☐ Kansas City	22.00	30.00	100.00	600.00
☐ Richmond	22.00	29.00	100.00	600.00	☐ Dallas	22.00	30.00	100.00	600.00
☐ Atlanta	22.00	29.00	100.00	600.00	☐ San Francisco	22.00	30.00	100.00	600.00

SERIES OF 1934D, SIGNATURES OF CLARK-SNYDER, GREEN SEAL

BANK	A.B.P.	V.FINE	UNC.	★UNC.	BANK	A.B.P.	V.FINE	UNC.	★UNC.
☐ Boston	22.00	28.00	70.00	800.00	☐ Chicago	22.00	30.00	70.00	800.00
☐ New York	22.00	28.00	70.00	800.00	☐ St. Louis	22.00	30.00	70.00	800.00
☐ Philadelphia	22.00	28.00	70.00	800.00	☐ Minneapolis	22.00	30.00	70.00	800.00
☐ Cleveland	22.00	28.00	70.00	800.00	☐ Kansas City	22.00	30.00	70.00	800.00
☐ Richmond	22.00	28.00	70.00	800.00	☐ Dallas	22.00	30.00	70.00	800.00
☐ Atlanta	22.00	28.00	70.00	800.00	☐ San Francisco	22.00	30.00	70.00	800.00

TWENTY DOLLAR NOTES (1950)
FEDERAL RESERVE NOTES

(Small Size)

SERIES OF 1950, SIGNATURES OF CLARK-SNYDER, GREEN SEAL

The black Federal Seal and green Treasury Seal are slightly smaller.

BANK	A.B.P.	V.FINE	UNC.	★UNC.	BANK	A.B.P.	V.FINE	UNC.	★UNC.
☐ Boston	22.00	30.00	100.00	500.00	☐ Chicago	22.00	30.00	100.00	500.00
☐ New York	22.00	30.00	100.00	500.00	☐ St. Louis	22.00	30.00	100.00	500.00
☐ Philadelphia	22.00	30.00	100.00	500.00	☐ Minneapolis	22.00	30.00	100.00	500.00
☐ Cleveland	22.00	30.00	100.00	500.00	☐ Kansas City	22.00	30.00	100.00	500.00

BANK	A.B.P.	V.FINE	UNC.	★UNC.	BANK	A.B.P.	V.FINE	UNC.	★UNC.
☐ Richmond	22.00	30.00	100.00	500.00	☐ Dallas	26.00	30.00	100.00	500.00
☐ Atlanta	22.00	30.00	100.00	500.00	☐ San Francisco	26.00	30.00	100.00	500.00

SERIES OF 1950A, SIGNATURES OF PRIEST-HUMPHERY, GREEN SEAL

BANK	A.B.P.	V.FINE	UNC.	★UNC.	BANK	A.B.P.	V.FINE	UNC.	★UNC.
☐ Boston	21.00	25.00	85.00	350.00	☐ Chicago	21.00	25.00	85.00	350.00
☐ New York	21.00	25.00	85.00	350.00	☐ St. Louis	21.00	25.00	85.00	350.00
☐ Philadelphia	21.00	25.00	85.00	350.00	☐ Minneapolis	21.00	27.00	05.00	050.00
☐ Cleveland	21.00	25.00	85.00	350.00	☐ Kansas City	21.00	25.00	85.00	350.00
☐ Richmond	21.00	25.00	85.00	350.00	☐ Dallas	21.00	25.00	85.00	350.00
☐ Atlanta	21.00	25.00	85.00	350.00	☐ San Francisco	21.00	25.00	85.00	350.00

SERIES OF 1950B, SIGNATURES OF PRIEST-ANDERSON, GREEN SEAL

BANK	A.B.P.	V.FINE	UNC.	★UNC.	BANK	A.B.P.	V.FINE	UNC.	★UNC.
☐ Boston	21.00	25.00	65.00	300.00	☐ Chicago	21.00	25.00	65.00	300.00
☐ New York	21.00	25.00	65.00	300.00	☐ St. Louis	21.00	25.00	65.00	300.00
☐ Philadelphia	21.00	25.00	65.00	300.00	☐ Minneapolis	21.00	25.00	65.00	300.00
☐ Cleveland	21.00	25.00	65.00	300.00	☐ Kansas City	21.00	25.00	65.00	300.00
☐ Richmond	21.00	25.00	65.00	300.00	☐ Dallas	21.00	25.00	65.00	300.00
☐ Atlanta	21.00	25.00	65.00	300.00	☐ San Francisco	21.00	25.00	65.00	300.00

SERIES OF 1950C, SIGNATURES OF SMITH-DILLON, GREEN SEAL

BANK	A.B.P.	V.FINE	UNC.	★UNC.	BANK	A.B.P.	V.FINE	UNC.	★UNC.
☐ Boston	21.00	24.00	70.00	400.00	☐ Chicago	21.00	24.00	70.00	400.00
☐ New York	21.00	24.00	70.00	400.00	☐ St. Louis	21.00	24.00	70.00	400.00
☐ Philadelphia	21.00	24.00	70.00	400.00	☐ Minneapolis	21.00	24.00	70.00	400.00
☐ Cleveland	21.00	24.00	70.00	400.00	☐ Kansas City	21.00	24.00	70.00	400.00
☐ Richmond	21.00	24.00	70.00	400.00	☐ Dallas	21.00	24.00	70.00	400.00
☐ Atlanta	21.00	24.00	70.00	400.00	☐ San Francisco	21.00	24.00	70.00	400.00

SERIES OF 1950D, SIGNATURES OF GRANAHAN-DILLON, GREEN SEAL

BANK	A.B.P.	V.FINE	UNC.	★UNC.	BANK	A.B.P.	V.FINE	UNC.	★UNC.
☐ Boston	21.00	24.00	75.00	375.00	☐ Chicago	21.00	24.00	75.00	375.00
☐ New York	21.00	24.00	75.00	375.00	☐ St. Louis	21.00	24.00	75.00	375.00
☐ Philadelphia	21.00	24.00	75.00	375.00	☐ Minneapolis	21.00	24.00	75.00	375.00
☐ Cleveland	21.00	24.00	75.00	375.00	☐ Kansas City	21.00	24.00	75.00	375.00
☐ Richmond	21.00	24.00	75.00	375.00	☐ Dallas	21.00	24.00	75.00	375.00
☐ Atlanta	21.00	24.00	75.00	375.00	☐ San Francisco	21.00	24.00	75.00	375.00

SERIES OF 1950E, SIGNATURES OF GRANAHAN-FOWLER, GREEN SEAL

BANK	A.B.P.	V.FINE	UNC.	★UNC.	BANK	A.B.P.	V.FINE	UNC.	★UNC.
☐ Boston	21.00	25.00	100.00	750.00	☐ Chicago	21.00	25.00	100.00	750.00
					☐ San Francisco	21.00	25.00	100.00	750.00

TWENTY DOLLAR NOTES (1963)
FEDERAL RESERVE NOTES

SERIES OF 1963, SIGNATURES OF GRANAHAN-FOWLER, GREEN SEAL

BANK	A.B.P.	V.FINE	UNC.	★UNC.	BANK	A.B.P.	V.FINE	UNC.	★UNC.
☐ Boston	21.00	25.00	80.00	150.00	☐ Chicago	21.00	25.00	80.00	150.00
☐ New York	21.00	25.00	80.00	150.00	☐ St. Louis	21.00	25.00	80.00	150.00
☐ Cleveland	21.00	25.00	80.00	150.00	☐ Kansas City	21.00	25.00	80.00	150.00
☐ Richmond	21.00	25.00	80.00	150.00	☐ Dallas	21.00	25.00	80.00	150.00
☐ Atlanta	21.00	25.00	80.00	150.00	☐ San Francisco	21.00	25.00	80.00	150.00

SERIES OF 1963A, SIGNATURES OF GRANAHAN-FOWLER, GREEN SEAL

BANK	A.B.P.	V.FINE	UNC.	★UNC.	BANK	A.B.P.	V.FINE	UNC.	★UNC.
☐ Boston	21.00	24.00	70.00	125.00	☐ Chicago	21.00	24.00	70.00	125.00
☐ New York	21.00	24.00	70.00	125.00	☐ St. Louis	21.00	24.00	70.00	125.00
☐ Philadelphia	21.00	24.00	70.00	125.00	☐ Minneapolis	21.00	24.00	70.00	125.00
☐ Cleveland	21.00	24.00	70.00	125.00	☐ Kansas City	21.00	24.00	70.00	125.00
☐ Richmond	21.00	24.00	70.00	125.00	☐ Dallas	21.00	24.00	70.00	125.00
☐ Atlanta	21.00	24.00	70.00	125.00	☐ San Francisco	21.00	24.00	70.00	125.00

TWENTY DOLLAR NOTES (1969)
FEDERAL RESERVE NOTES

SERIES OF 1969, SIGNATURES OF ELSTON-KENNEDY, GREEN SEAL

BANK	A.B.P.	V.FINE	UNC.	★UNC.	BANK	A.B.P.	V.FINE	UNC.	★UNC.
☐ Boston	—	23.00	55.00	100.00	☐ Chicago	—	23.00	55.00	100.00
☐ New York	—	23.00	55.00	100.00	☐ St. Louis	—	23.00	55.00	100.00
☐ Philadelphia	—	23.00	55.00	100.00	☐ Minneapolis	—	23.00	55.00	100.00
☐ Cleveland	—	23.00	55.00	100.00	☐ Kansas City	—	23.00	55.00	100.00
☐ Richmond	—	23.00	55.00	100.00	☐ Dallas	—	23.00	55.00	100.00
☐ Atlanta	—	23.00	55.00	100.00	☐ San Francisco	—	23.00	55.00	100.00

SERIES OF 1969A, SIGNATURES OF KABIS-CONNALLY, GREEN SEAL

BANK	A.B.P.	V.FINE	UNC.	★UNC.	BANK	A.B.P.	V.FINE	UNC.	★UNC.
☐ Boston	—	23.00	60.00	110.00	☐ Chicago	—	23.00	60.00	110.00
☐ New York	—	23.00	60.00	110.00	☐ St. Louis	—	23.00	60.00	110.00
☐ Philadelphia	—	23.00	60.00	110.00	☐ Minneapolis	—	23.00	60.00	110.00
☐ Cleveland	—	23.00	60.00	110.00	☐ Kansas City	—	23.00	60.00	110.00
☐ Richmond	—	23.00	60.00	110.00	☐ Dallas	—	23.00	60.00	110.00
☐ Atlanta	—	23.00	60.00	110.00	☐ San Francisco	—	23.00	60.00	110.00

SERIES OF 1969B, SIGNATURES OF BANUELOS-CONNALLY, GREEN SEAL

BANK	A.B.P.	V.FINE	UNC.	★UNC.	BANK	A.B.P.	V.FINE	UNC.	★UNC.
☐ New York	—	23.00	150.00	500.00	☐ Chicago	—	23.00	175.00	500.00
☐ Cleveland	—	23.00	175.00	—	☐ St. Louis	—	23.00	175.00	—
☐ Richmond	—	23.00	175.00	—	☐ Minneapolis	—	23.00	250.00	—
☐ Atlanta	—	23.00	175.00	500.00	☐ Kansas City	—	23.00	250.00	500.00
					☐ Dallas	—	23.00	200.00	—
					☐ San Francisco	—	23.00	175.00	500.00

SERIES of 1969C, SIGNATURES OF BANUELOS-SHULTZ, GREEN SEAL

BANK	A.B.P.	V.FINE	UNC.	★UNC.	BANK	A.B.P.	V.FINE	UNC.	★UNC.
☐ Boston	—	23.00	70.00	150.00	☐ Chicago	—	23.00	70.00	150.00
☐ New York	—	23.00	70.00	150.00	☐ St. Louis	—	23.00	70.00	150.00
☐ Philadelphia	—	23.00	70.00	150.00	☐ Minneapolis	—	23.00	70.00	150.00
☐ Cleveland	—	23.00	70.00	150.00	☐ Kansas City	—	23.00	70.00	150.00
☐ Richmond	—	23.00	70.00	150.00	☐ Dallas	—	23.00	70.00	150.00
☐ Atlanta	—	23.00	70.00	150.00	☐ San Francisco	—	23.00	70.00	150.00

TWENTY DOLLAR NOTES (1974)
FEDERAL RESERVE NOTES

SERIES OF 1974, SIGNATURES OF NEFF-SIMON, GREEN SEAL

BANK	A.B.P.	V.FINE	UNC.	★UNC.	BANK	A.B.P.	V.FINE	UNC.	★UNC.
☐ Boston	—	23.00	60.00	125.00	☐ Chicago	—	23.00	60.00	125.00
☐ New York	—	23.00	60.00	125.00	☐ St. Louis	—	23.00	60.00	125.00
☐ Philadelphia	—	26.00	60.00	125.00	☐ Minneapolis	—	26.00	60.00	125.00
☐ Cleveland	—	26.00	60.00	125.00	☐ Kansas City	—	26.00	60.00	125.00
☐ Richmond	—	26.00	60.00	125.00	☐ Dallas	—	26.00	60.00	125.00
☐ Atlanta	—	23.00	60.00	125.00	☐ San Francisco	—	23.00	60.00	125.00

TWENTY DOLLAR NOTES (1977)
FEDERAL RESERVE NOTES
SERIES OF 1977, SIGNATURES OF MORTON-BLUMENTHAL, GREEN SEAL

BANK	A.B.P.	V.FINE	UNC.	★UNC.	BANK	A.B.P.	V.FINE	UNC.	★UNC.
☐ Boston	—	22.00	55.00	100.00	☐ Chicago	—	22.00	55.00	100.00
☐ New York	—	22.00	55.00	100.00	☐ St. Louis	—	22.00	55.00	100.00
☐ Philadelphia	—	22.00	55.00	100.00	☐ Minneapolis	—	25.00	55.00	100.00
☐ Cleveland	—	22.00	55.00	100.00	☐ Kansas City	—	25.00	55.00	100.00
☐ Richmond	—	25.00	55.00	100.00	☐ Dallas	—	25.00	55.00	100.00
☐ Atlanta	—	25.00	55.00	100.00	☐ San Francisco	—	22.00	55.00	100.00

TWENTY DOLLAR NOTES (1981)
FEDERAL RESERVE NOTES
SERIES OF 1981, SIGNATURES OF BUCHANAN-REGAN, GREEN SEAL

BANK	A.B.P.	V.FINE	UNC.	★UNC.	BANK	A.B.P.	V.FINE	UNC.	★UNC.
☐ Boston	—	21.00	80.00	150.00	☐ Chicago	—	21.00	80.00	150.00
☐ New York	—	21.00	80.00	150.00	☐ St. Louis	—	21.00	80.00	150.00
☐ Philadelphia	—	21.00	80.00	150.00	☐ Minneapolis	—	22.00	80.00	150.00
☐ Cleveland	—	21.00	80.00	150.00	☐ Kansas City	—	22.00	80.00	150.00
☐ Richmond	—	21.00	80.00	150.00	☐ Dallas	—	22.00	80.00	150.00
☐ Atlanta	—	21.00	80.00	150.00	☐ San Francisco	—	21.00	80.00	150.00

SERIES OF 1981A, SIGNATURES OF ORTEGA-REGAN, GREEN SEAL

★Notes not issued for all banks

BANK	A.B.P.	V.FINE	UNC.	★UNC.	BANK	A.B.P.	V.FINE	UNC.	★UNC.
☐ Boston	—	21.00	70.00	—	☐ Chicago	—	21.00	70.00	—
☐ New York	—	21.00	70.00	—	☐ St. Louis	—	21.00	70.00	—
☐ Philadelphia	—	21.00	70.00	—	☐ Minneapolis	—	22.00	70.00	—
☐ Cleveland	—	21.00	70.00	200.00	☐ Kansas City	—	22.00	70.00	—
☐ Richmond	—	21.00	70.00	—	☐ Dallas	—	22.00	70.00	—
☐ Atlanta	—	21.00	70.00	200.00	☐ San Francisco	—	21.00	70.00	200.00

TWENTY DOLLAR NOTES (1985)
FEDERAL RESERVE NOTES
SERIES OF 1985, SIGNATURES OF ORTEGA-BAKER, GREEN SEAL

★Notes not issued for all banks

BANK	A.B.P.	V.FINE	UNC.	★UNC.	BANK	A.B.P.	V.FINE	UNC.	★UNC.
☐ Boston	—	21.00	55.00	75.00	☐ Chicago	—	21.00	55.00	75.00
☐ New York	—	21.00	55.00	75.00	☐ St. Louis	—	21.00	55.00	—
☐ Philadelphia	—	21.00	55.00	75.00	☐ Minneapolis	—	21.00	55.00	—
☐ Cleveland	—	21.00	55.00	75.00	☐ Kansas City	—	21.00	55.00	75.00
☐ Richmond	—	21.00	55.00	75.00	☐ Dallas	—	21.00	55.00	75.00
☐ Atlanta	—	21.00	55.00	—	☐ San Francisco	—	21.00	55.00	75.00

TWENTY DOLLAR NOTES (1988)
FEDERAL RESERVE NOTES
SERIES OF 1988A, SIGNATURES OF VILLALPANDO-BRADY, GREEN SEAL

★Notes not issued for all banks

BANK	A.B.P.	V.FINE	UNC.	★UNC.	BANK	A.B.P.	V.FINE	UNC.	★UNC.
☐ Boston	—	21.00	50.00	—	☐ Chicago	—	21.00	50.00	100.00
☐ New York	—	21.00	50.00	100.00	☐ St. Louis	—	21.00	50.00	—
☐ Philadelphia	—	21.00	50.00	100.00	☐ Minneapolis	—	21.00	50.00	—
☐ Cleveland	—	21.00	50.00		☐ Kansas City	—	21.00	50.00	—
☐ Richmond	—	21.00	50.00	—	☐ Dallas	—	21.00	50.00	100.00
☐ Atlanta	—	21.00	50.00	100.00	☐ San Francisco	—	21.00	50.00	—

TWENTY DOLLAR NOTES (1990)
FEDERAL RESERVE NOTES
SERIES OF 1990, SIGNATURES OF VILLALPANDO-BRADY, GREEN SEAL

★Notes not issued for all banks

BANK	A.B.P.	V.FINE	UNC.	★UNC.	BANK	A.B.P.	V.FINE	UNC.	★UNC.
☐ Boston	—	21.00	40.00	75.00	☐ Chicago	—	21.00	40.00	75.00
☐ New York	—	21.00	40.00	75.00	☐ St. Louis	—	21.00	40.00	75.00
☐ Philadelphia	—	21.00	40.00	—	☐ Minneapolis	—	21.00	40.00	75.00
☐ Cleveland	—	21.00	40.00	75.00	☐ Kansas City	—	21.00	40.00	—
☐ Richmond	—	21.00	40.00	75.00	☐ Dallas	—	21.00	40.00	—
☐ Atlanta	—	21.00	40.00	75.00	☐ San Francisco	—	21.00	40.00	—

TWENTY DOLLAR NOTES (1993)
FEDERAL RESERVE NOTES
SERIES OF 1993, SIGNATURES OF WITHROW-BENTSEN, GREEN SEAL

★Notes are not issued for all banks

BANK	A.B.P.	V.FINE	UNC.	★UNC.	BANK	A.B.P.	V.FINE	UNC.	★UNC.
☐ Boston	—	21.00	35.00	60.00	☐ Chicago	—	21.00	35.00	—
☐ New York	—	21.00	35.00	60.00	☐ St. Louis	—	21.00	35.00	—
☐ Philadelphia	—	21.00	35.00	—	☐ Kansas City	—	21.00	35.00	—
☐ Cleveland	—	21.00	35.00	60.00	☐ Dallas	—	21.00	35.00	—
☐ Richmond	—	21.00	35.00	60.00	☐ San Francisco	—	21.00	35.00	60.00
☐ Atlanta	—	21.00	35.00	60.00					

TWENTY DOLLAR NOTES (1995)
FEDERAL RESERVE NOTES
SERIES OF 1995, SIGNATURES OF WITHROW-RUBIN, GREEN SEAL

★Notes not issued for all banks

BANK	A.B.P.	V.FINE	UNC.	★UNC.	BANK	A.B.P.	V.FINE	UNC.	★UNC.
☐ Boston	—	22.00	34.00	42.00	☐ Chicago	—	22.00	34.00	42.00
☐ New York	—	22.00	34.00	42.00	☐ St. Louis	—	22.00	34.00	42.00
☐ Philadelphia	—	22.00	34.00	42.00	☐ Minneapolis	—	22.00	36.00	42.00
☐ Cleveland	—	22.00	36.00	42.00	☐ Kansas City	—	22.00	36.00	42.00
☐ Richmond	—	22.00	34.00	42.00	☐ Dallas	—	22.00	34.00	42.00
☐ Atlanta	—	22.00	34.00	42.00	☐ San Francisco	—	22.00	34.00	42.00

TWENTY DOLLAR NOTES (1915–1918)
FEDERAL RESERVE BANK NOTES
(ALL HAVE BLUE SEALS)

(Large Size)

Face Design: Portrait of President Cleveland left, name of bank and city center, blue seal right.

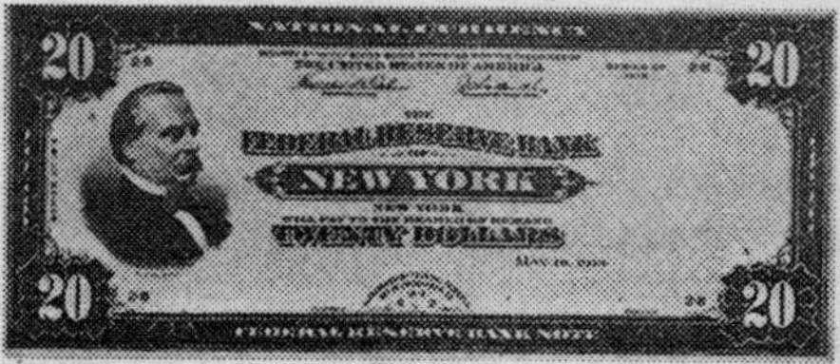

Back Design: Locomotive and steamship, similar to 1914 note.

BANK	SERIES	GOV'T SIGNATURES	BANK SIGNATURES	A.B.P.	GOOD	V.FINE	UNC.
☐Atlanta	1915	Teehee-Burke	Bell-Wellborn	510.00	825.00	1725.00	8300.00
	1915	Teehee-Burke	Pike-McCord	710.00	1025.00	1725.00	8800.00
☐Atlanta	1918	Elliott-Burke	Bell-Wellborn	350.00	525.00	1500.00	5000.00
☐Chicago	1915	Teehee-Burke	McLallen-McDougal	350.00	525.00	1500.00	5000.00
☐St. Louis	1918	Teehee-Burke	Attebery-Wells	350.00	525.00	1500.00	5000.00

BANK	SERIES	GOV'T SIGNATURES	BANK SIGNATURES	A.B.P.	GOOD	V.FINE	UNC.
☐Kansas City	1915	Teehee-Burke	Anderson-Miller	350.00	475.00	1550.00	5000.00
☐Kansas City	1915	Teehee-Burke	Cross-Miller	350.00	475.00	1525.00	5000.00
☐Dallas	1915	Teehee-Burke	Hoopes-Van Zandt	350.00	475.00	1525.00	5000.00
☐Dallas	1915	Teehee-Burke	Gilbert-Van Zandt	370.00	725.00	4075.00	8100.00
☐Dallas	1915	Teehee-Burke	Talley-Van Zandt	370.00	725.00	4175.00	8300.00

TWENTY DOLLAR NOTES (1929)
FEDERAL RESERVE BANK NOTES

(Small Size)

Face Design: Portrait of President Jackson center, name of bank and city left, blue seal right.

Back Design: The White House.

BANK	A.B.P.	V.FINE	UNC.	★UNC.	BANK	A.B.P.	V.FINE	UNC.	★UNC.
☐ Boston	25.00	90.00	335.00	4000.00	☐ Chicago	23.00	90.00	225.00	3500.00
☐ New York	25.00	90.00	250.00	3200.00	☐ St. Louis	23.00	90.00	300.00	3500.00
☐ Philadelphia	25.00	90.00	300.00	3500.00	☐ Minneapolis	23.00	90.00	275.00	3800.00
☐ Cleveland	25.00	90.00	300.00	4000.00	☐ Kansas City	23.00	90.00	1000.00	3800.00
☐ Richmond	25.00	90.00	450.00	3500.00	☐ Dallas	23.00	225.00	1500.00	5000.00
☐ Atlanta	25.00	90.00	630.00	4000.00	☐ San Francisco	29.00	90.00	1000.00	5000.00

FIFTY DOLLAR NOTES

ORDER OF ISSUE

FIFTY DOLLAR NOTES (1862–1863)
UNITED STATES NOTES
(ALSO KNOWN AS LEGAL TENDER NOTES)

(Large Size)

Face Design: Portrait of Hamilton to left.

Back Design

SERIES	SIGNATURES	SEAL	A.B.P.	GOOD	V.FINE	UNC.
□1862	Chittenden-Spinner*	Red	2300.00	3600.00	12,000.00	135,000.00
□1862	Chittenden-Spinner**	Red	2300.00	3600.00	12,000.00	135,000.00
□1863	Chittenden-Spinner**	Red	2300.00	3600.00	12,000.00	135,000.00

*First Obligation: Similar to 1862 $5 note.
**Second Obligation: Shown above.

FIFTY DOLLAR NOTES (1869) UNITED STATES NOTES
(ALSO KNOWN AS LEGAL TENDER NOTES)
(Large Size)

Face Design: Portrait of Henry Clay to right.

Back Design

SERIES	SIGNATURES	SEAL	A.B.P.	GOOD	V.FINE	UNC.
□1869	Allison-Spinner	Red	3300.00	4700.00	25,000.00	56,000.00

Only twenty-four pieces of this note remain unredeemed.

FIFTY DOLLAR NOTES (1874–1880)
UNITED STATES NOTES

(Large Size)

Face Design: Franklin to left.

Back Design

SERIES	SIGNATURES	SEAL	A.B.P.	GOOD	V.FINE	UNC.
□1874	Allison-Spinner	Sm. Red	1000.00	1600.00	5900.00	27,000.00
□1875	Allison-Wyman	Sm. Red	4000.00	16,500.00	75,000.00	RARE
□1878	Allison-Gilfillan	Sm. Red	1200.00	1650.00	6000.00	37,500.00
□1880	Bruce-Gilfillan	Lg. Brown	900.00	1350.00	4900.00	25,000.00
□1880	Bruce-Wyman	Lg. Brown	1100.00	2350.00	4700.00	12,500.00
□1880	Rosecrans-Jordan	Lg. Red	1100.00	2350.00	10500.00	26,500.00
□1880	Rosecrans-Hyatt	Red Plain	VERY RARE 63575.00			
□1880	Rosecrans-Hyatt	Red Spike	1200.00	1800.00	6700.00	45,000.00
□1880	Rosecrans-Huston	Lg. Red	18100.00	2500.00	12,000.00	35,000.00
□1880	Rosecrans-Huston	Lg. Brown	750.00	1150.00	5100.00	12,000.00
□1880	Tillman-Morgan	Sm. Red	1150.00	1600.00	3600.00	15,000.00
□1880	Bruce-Roberts	Sm. Red	4150.00	76000.00	25600.00	70,000.00
□1880	Lyons-Roberts	Sm. Red	750.00	1000.00	3600.00	12,500.00

FIFTY DOLLAR NOTES (1875) NATIONAL BANK NOTES
FIRST CHARTER PERIOD (Large Size)

Face Design: Washington crossing Delaware left, Washington at Valley Forge, right.

Back Design: Embarkation of the Pilgrims.

SERIES	SIGNATURES	SEAL	A.B.P.	GOOD	V.FINE	UNC.
☐ Original	Chittenden-Spinner	Red w/r	1300.00	1850.00	4900.00	20,500.00
☐ Original	Colby-Spinner	Red w/r	1300.00	1850.00	4900.00	20,500.00
☐ Original	Allison-Spinner	Red w/r	1300.00	1850.00	4900.00	20,500.00
☐ 1875	Allison-New	Red w/s	1300.00	1850.00	4900.00	20,500.00
☐ 1875	Allison-Wyman	Red w/s	1300.00	1850.00	4900.00	20,500.00
☐ 1875	Allison-Gilfillan	Red w/s	1300.00	1850.00	4900.00	20,500.00
☐ 1875	Scofield-Gilfillan	Red w/s	1300.00	1850.00	4900.00	20,500.00
☐ 1875	Bruce-Gilfillan	Red w/s	1300.00	1850.00	4900.00	20,500.00
☐ 1875	Bruce-Wyman	Red w/s	1300.00	1850.00	4900.00	20,500.00
☐ 1875	Rosecrans-Huston	Red w/s	1300.00	1850.00	4900.00	20,500.00
☐ 1875	Rosecrans-Nebeker	Red w/s	1300.00	1850.00	4900.00	20,500.00
☐ 1875	Tillman-Morgan	Red w/s	1300.00	1850.00	4900.00	20,500.00

FIFTY DOLLAR NOTES (1882) NATIONAL BANK NOTES
SECOND CHARTER PERIOD (Large Size)

First Issue (Brown seal and brown back)
Back Design
Face Design: Similar to First Charter Period note.

SERIES	SIGNATURES	SEAL	A.B.P.	GOOD	V.FINE	UNC.
□1882	Bruce-Gilfillan	Brown	400.00	600.00	2000.00	9000.00
□1882	Bruce-Wyman	Brown	400.00	600.00	2000.00	9000.00
□1882	Bruce-Jordan	Brown	400.00	600.00	2000.00	9000.00
□1882	Rosecrans-Jordan	Brown	400.00	600.00	2000.00	9000.00
□1882	Rosecrans-Hyatt	Brown	400.00	600.00	2000.00	9000.00
□1882	Rosecrans-Huston	Brown	400.00	600.00	2000.00	9000.00
□1882	Rosecrans-Nebeker	Brown	400.00	600.00	2000.00	9000.00
□1882	Rosecrans-Morgan	Brown	475.00	850.00	2550.00	9800.00
□1882	Tillman-Morgan	Brown	400.00	600.00	2000.00	9000.00
□1882	Tillman-Roberts	Brown	400.00	600.00	2000.00	9000.00
□1882	Bruce-Roberts	Brown	400.00	600.00	2000.00	9000.00
□1882	Lyons-Roberts	Brown	400.00	600.00	2000.00	9000.00
□1882	Vernon-Treat	Brown	525.00	925.00	2750.00	9800.00

FIFTY DOLLAR NOTES (1882) NATIONAL BANK NOTES
SECOND CHARTER PERIOD (Large Size)

Second Issue (Blue seal, green back with date "1882–1908".)
Face Design: Washington crossing Delaware left, Washington at Valley Forge right.

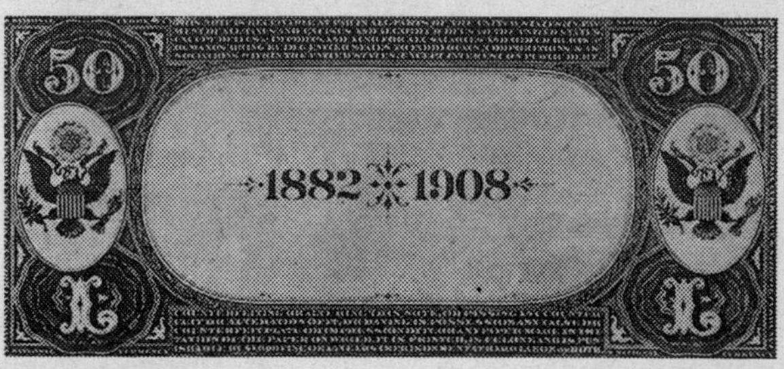

Back Design

SERIES	SIGNATURES	SEAL	A.B.P.	GOOD	V.FINE	UNC.
□1882	Rosecrans-Huston	Blue	360.00	525.00	1200.00	4900.00
□1882	Rosecrans-Nebeker	Blue	360.00	525.00	1200.00	4900.00
□1882	Tillman-Morgan	Blue	360.00	525.00	1200.00	4900.00
□1882	Tillman-Roberts	Blue	360.00	525.00	1200.00	4900.00
□1882	Bruce-Roberts	Blue	360.00	525.00	1200.00	4900.00
□1882	Lyons-Roberts	Blue	360.00	525.00	1200.00	4900.00
□1882	Vernon-Treat	Blue	360.00	525.00	1200.00	4900.00
□1882	Napier-McClung	Blue	360.00	525.00	1200.00	4900.00

Third Issue (As above, "FIFTY DOLLARS" replaces 1882–1908—excessively rare!)

□1882	Lyons-Roberts		20,000.00	25,000.00	45,000.00	95,000.00

FIFTY DOLLAR NOTES (1902) NATIONAL BANK NOTES
THIRD CHARTER PERIOD (Large Size)

First Issues (Red seal and numbers)
Face Design: Portrait of Sherman left. Name of bank center. Treasury Seal and numbers.

SERIES	SIGNATURES	SEAL	A.B.P.	GOOD	V.FINE	UNC.
□1902	Lyons-Roberts	Red	350.00	525.00	1550.00	8000.00
□1902	Lyons-Treat	Red	350.00	525.00	1550.00	8000.00
□1902	Vernon-Treat	Red	350.00	525.00	1550.00	8000.00

Second Issue (Treasury Seal)
Numbers remain blue, date "1902–1908" added on back.

□1902	Lyons-Roberts	Blue	125.00	185.00	650.00	2300.00
□1902	Lyons-Treat	Blue	125.00	185.00	650.00	2300.00
□1902	Vernon-Treat	Blue	125.00	185.00	650.00	2300.00
□1902	Vernon-McClung	Blue	125.00	185.00	650.00	2300.00
□1902	Napier-McClung	Blue	125.00	185.00	650.00	2300.00
□1902	Napier-Thompson	Blue	125.00	185.00	650.00	2300.00
□1902	Napier-Burke	Blue	125.00	185.00	650.00	2300.00
□1902	Parker-Burke	Blue	125.00	185.00	650.00	2300.00
□1902	Teehee-Burke	Blue	125.00	185.00	650.00	2300.00

Third Issue (Treasury Seal)
Numbers remain blue, date "1902–1908" removed from back.

□1902	Lyons-Roberts	Blue	130.00	180.00	575.00	2100.00
□1902	Lyons-Treat	Blue	130.00	180.00	575.00	2100.00
□1902	Vernon-Treat	Blue	130.00	180.00	575.00	2100.00
□1902	Vernon-McClung	Blue	130.00	180.00	575.00	2100.00
□1902	Napier-McClung	Blue	130.00	180.00	575.00	2100.00
□1902	Napier-Thompson	Blue	130.00	180.00	575.00	2100.00
□1902	Napier-Burke	Blue	130.00	180.00	575.00	2100.00
□1902	Parker-Burke	Blue	130.00	180.00	575.00	2100.00
□1902	Teehee-Burke	Blue	130.00	180.00	575.00	2100.00
□1902	Elliott-Burke	Blue	130.00	180.00	575.00	2100.00
□1902	Elliott-White	Blue	130.00	180.00	575.00	2100.00

SERIES	SIGNATURES	SEAL	A.B.P.	GOOD	V.FINE	UNC.
□1902	Speelman-White	Blue	130.00	180.00	550.00	3000.00
□1902	Woods-White	Blue	130.00	180.00	550.00	3000.00

FIFTY DOLLAR NOTES (1929) NATIONAL BANK NOTES (Small Size)

Face Design: Portrait of President Grant center. Bank left, brown seal right. Brown serial numbers, black Charter Numbers.

Back Design: The Capitol.

SERIES	SIGNATURES	SEAL	A.B.P.	V.FINE	UNC.
□1929, Type I*	Jones-Wood	Brown	65.00	110.00	500.00
□1929, Type II*	Jones-Wood	Brown	80.00	300.00	800.00

*See Page 92. Type I—Charter Number in black. Type II—Similar. Charter Number added in brown.

FIFTY DOLLAR NOTES (1878–1880)
SILVER CERTIFICATES

(Large Size)

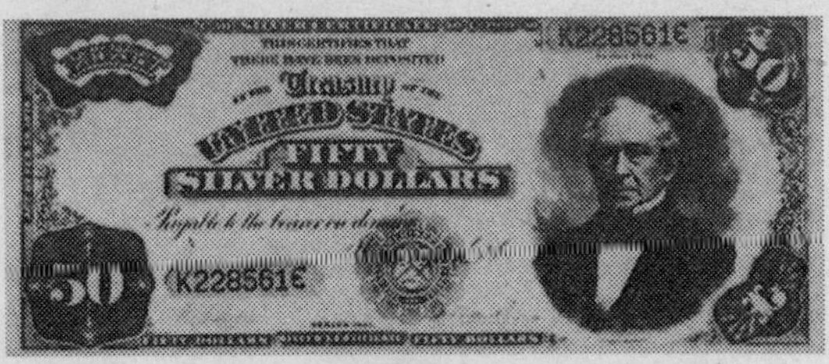

Face Design: Portrait of Edward Everett.

Back Design

SERIES	SIGNATURES	SEAL	A.B.P.	GOOD	V.FINE	UNC.
☐1878	Varied	Red	15000.00	—	—	VERY RARE
☐1880	Scofield-Gilfillan	Brown	15000.00	22,000.00	50,000.00	150,000.00
☐1880	Bruce-Gilfillan	Brown	7500.00	12,500.00	32,000.00	125,000.00
☐1880	Bruce-Wyman	Brown	4500.00	7600.00	38,000.00	95,000.00
☐1880	Rosecrans-Huston	Brown	2500.00	3600.00	15,000.00	150,000.00
☐1880	Rosecrans-Nebeker	Red	1500.00	2700.00	13,500.00	85,000.00

FIFTY DOLLAR NOTES (1891) SILVER CERTIFICATES
(Large Size)

Face Design: Portrait of Edward Everett.

Back Design

SERIES	SIGNATURES	SEAL	A.B.P.	GOOD	V.FINE	UNC.
□1891	Rosecrans-Nebeker	Red	650.00	3500.00	9500.00	18000.00
□1891	Tillman-Morgan	Red	650.00	1000.00	3600.00	14000.00
□1891	Bruce-Roberts	Red	650.00	1000.00	3500.00	14500.00
□1891	Lyons-Roberts	Red	650.00	1000.00	3900.00	20000.00
□1891	Vernon-Treat	Red	650.00	1000.00	3600.00	26400.00
□1891	Parker-Burke	Bluc	650.00	1000.00	3600.00	17000.00

FIFTY DOLLAR NOTES (1882) GOLD CERTIFICATES
(Large Size)

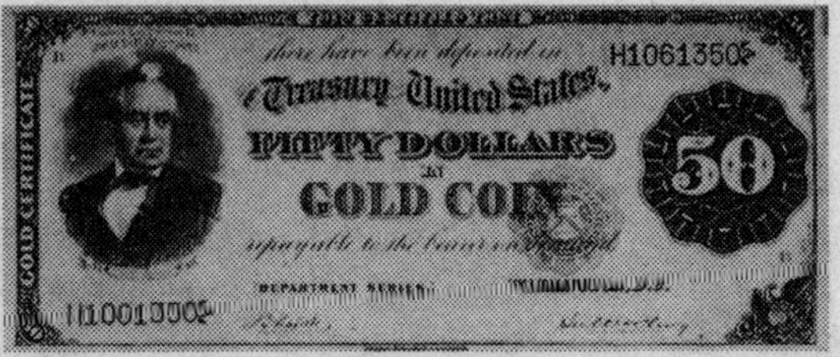

Face Design: Portrait of Silas Wright to left.

Back Design: Bright yellow color.

SERIES	SIGNATURES	SEAL	A.B.P.	GOOD	V.FINE	UNC.
□1882	Bruce-Gilfillan	Brown	2550.00	3875.00	30000.00	75,000.00
□1882	Bruce-Wyman	Brown	2550.00	3875.00	30000.00	82,500.00
□1882	Rosecrans-Hyatt	Red	1250.00	1875.00	14000.00	65,000.00
□1882	Rosecrans-Huston	Brown	600.00	8000.00	21000.00	250,000.00
□1882	Lyons-Roberts	Red	2450.00	4400.00	30000.00	85,000.00
□1882	Lyons-Treat	Red	465.00	900.00	2600.00	20,000.00
□1882	Vernon-Treat	Red	420.00	700.00	2600.00	20,000.00
□1882	Vernon-McClung	Red	450.00	900.00	2600.00	20,000.00
□1882	Napier-McClung	Red	350.00	600.00	1800.00	15,000.00

FIFTY DOLLAR NOTES (1913) GOLD CERTIFICATES (Large Size)

Face Design: Portrait of President Grant.

Back Design: Bright yellow color.

SERIES	SIGNATURES	SEAL	A.B.P.	GOOD	V.FINE	UNC.
□1913	Parker-Burke	Gold	180.00	275.00	1600.00	4200.00
□1913	Teehee-Burke	Gold	180.00	250.00	950.00	3200.00
□1922	Speelman-White	Gold	205.00	275.00	700.00	4100.00

FIFTY DOLLAR NOTES (1928) GOLD CERTIFICATES
(Small Size)

Back Design: Same as 1929 note.

SERIES	SIGNATURES	SEAL	A.B.P.	GOOD	V.FINE	UNC.
□1928	Woods-Mellon	Gold	65.00	90.00	350.00	2200.00

FIFTY DOLLAR NOTES (1891) TREASURY OR COIN NOTES
(Large Size)

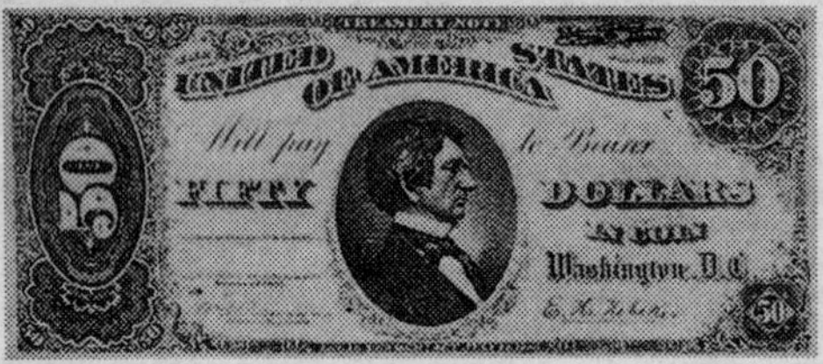

Face Design: Portrait of William H. Seward. Only twenty-five pieces remain unredeemed.
Back Design: Green.

SERIES	SIGNATURES	SEAL	A.B.P.	GOOD	V.FINE	UNC.
□1891	Rosecrans-Nebeker	Red	6000.00	8200.00	37,500.00	175,000.00

FIFTY DOLLAR NOTES (1914)
FEDERAL RESERVE NOTES

(Large Size)

SERIES OF 1914, SIGNATURES OF BURKE-McADOO, RED SEAL AND RED SERIAL NUMBERS

BANK	A.B.P.	V.FINE	UNC.	CITY	A.B.P.	V.FINE	UNC.
☐Boston	475.00	1800.00	5950.00	☐ Chicago	475.00	1650.00	6100.00
☐New York	475.00	1650.00	5950.00	☐ St. Louis	475.00	1575.00	6000.00
☐Philadelphia	475.00	1650.00	5950.00	☐ Minneapolis	475.00	1600.00	6050.00
☐Cleveland	475.00	1650.00	6100.00	☐ Kansas City	475.00	1630.00	6300.00
☐Richmond	475.00	1650.00	6050.00	☐ Dallas	475.00	1600.00	6050.00
☐Atlanta	475.00	1650.00	6100.00	☐ San Francisco	475.00	1600.00	6050.00

FIFTY DOLLAR NOTES (1914)
FEDERAL RESERVE NOTES
1914, BLUE TREASURY SEAL AND BLUE NUMBERS

DATE	BANK	SIGNATURES	SEAL	A.B.P.	GOOD	V.FINE	UNC.
1914	Boston	Burke-McAdoo	Blue	65.00	90.00	465.00	1825.00
1914	Boston	Burke-Glass	Blue	65.00	90.00	465.00	1825.00
1914	Boston	Burke-Huston	Blue	160.00	315.00	2090.00	3925.00
1914	Boston	White-Mellon	Blue	65.00	75.00	290.00	1475.00
1914	New York	Burke-McAdoo	Blue	65.00	90.00	580.00	2125.00
1914	New York	Burke-Glass	Blue	65.00	80.00	390.00	1675.00
1914	New York	Burke-Huston	Blue	65.00	75.00	290.00	1475.00
1914	New York	White-Mellon	Blue	65.00	75.00	335.00	1475.00

DATE	BANK	SIGNATURES	SEAL	A.B.P.	GOOD	V.FINE	UNC.
1914	Philadelphia	Burke-McAdoo	Blue	65.00	95.00	540.00	2075.00
1914	Philadelphia	Burke-Glass	Blue	65.00	115.00	890.00	2475.00
1914	Philadelphia	Burke-Huston	Blue	65.00	75.00	340.00	1575.00
1914	Philadelphia	White-Mellon	Blue	65.00	75.00	290.00	1475.00
1914	Cleveland	Burke-McAdoo	Blue	65.00	75.00	340.00	1575.00
1914	Cleveland	Burke-Glass	Blue	65.00	115.00	570.00	2175.00
1914	Cleveland	Burke-Huston	Blue	65.00	90.00	440.00	1775.00
1914	Cleveland	White-Mellon	Blue	65.00	75.00	370.00	1475.00
1914	Richmond	Burke-McAdoo	Blue	65.00	115.00	590.00	2175.00
1914	Richmond	Burke-Glass	Blue	65.00	140.00	890.00	2475.00
1914	Richmond	Burke-Huston	Blue	65.00	90.00	390.00	1675.00
1914	Richmond	White-Mellon	Blue	65.00	115.00	540.00	2075.00
1914	Atlanta	Burke-McAdoo	Blue	65.00	115.00	590.00	2175.00
1914	Atlanta	Burke-Glass	Blue	110.00	215.00	1590.00	2975.00
1914	Atlanta	Burke-Huston	Blue	65.00	75.00	290.00	1475.00
1914	Atlanta	White-Mellon	Blue	65.00	115.00	590.00	2175.00
1914	Chicago	Burke-McAdoo	Blue	65.00	75.00	315.00	1525.00
1914	Chicago	Burke-Glass	Blue	65.00	75.00	315.00	1525.00
1914	Chicago	Burke-Huston	Blue	65.00	90.00	440.00	1775.00
1914	Chicago	White-Mellon	Blue	65.00	90.00	440.00	1775.00
1914	St. Louis	Burke-McAdoo	Blue	65.00	115.00	540.00	2075.00
1914	St. Louis	Burke-Glass	Blue	65.00	90.00	440.00	1775.00
1914	St. Louis	Burke-Huston	Blue	65.00	75.00	330.00	1575.00
1914	St. Louis	White-Mellon	Blue	135.00	315.00	2090.00	3975.00
1914	Minneapolis	Burke-McAdoo	Blue	65.00	115.00	565.00	2125.00
1914	Minneapolis	Burke-Glass	Blue	135.00	315.00	2090.00	3975.00
1914	Minneapolis	Burke-Huston	Blue	110.00	265.00	1940.00	3475.00
1914	Minneapolis	White-Mellon	Blue	135.00	315.00	2090.00	3975.00
1914	Kansas City	Burke-McAdoo	Blue	65.00	95.00	490.00	1975.00
1914	Kansas City	White-Mellon	Blue		ONLY 1 KNOWN—RARE		
1914	Dallas	Burke-McAdoo	Blue	65.00	115.00	565.00	2125.00
1914	Dallas	Burke-Glass	Blue	135.00	315.00	2090.00	3975.00
1914	Dallas	Burke-Huston	Blue	135.00	315.00	2090.00	3975.00
1914	Dallas	White Mellon	Blue	135.00	315.00	2090.00	3975.00
1914	San Francisco	Burke-McAdoo	Blue	65.00	80.00	390.00	1675.00
1914	San Francisco	Burke-Glass	Blue	135.00	315.00	2090.00	3975.00
1914	San Francisco	Burke-Huston	Blue	65.00	80.00	390.00	1675.00
1914	San Francisco	White-Mellon	Blue	65.00	110.00	540.00	2075.00

FIFTY DOLLAR NOTES (1928)
FEDERAL RESERVE NOTES

(Small Size)
Face Design: Portrait of President Grant center. Black Federal Reserve Seal with number to left. Green Treasury Seal to right.
Back Design: Same as 1929 note.

FIFTY DOLLAR NOTES (1928)
FEDERAL RESERVE NOTES

SERIES OF 1928, SIGNATURES OF WOODS-MELLON, GREEN SEAL

BANK	A.B.P.	V.FINE	UNC.	★UNC.	BANK	A.B.P.	V.FINE	UNC.	★UNC.
☐ Boston	75.00	130.00	1000.00	—	☐ Chicago	70.00	125.00	800.00	—
☐ New York	75.00	130.00	700.00	—	☐ St. Louis	70.00	125.00	900.00	—
☐ Philadelphia	75.00	130.00	900.00	—	☐ Minneapolis	70.00	125.00	1250.00	—
☐ Cleveland	70.00	130.00	700.00	—	☐ Kansas City	75.00	130.00	1000.00	—
☐ Richmond	70.00	130.00	900.00	—	☐ Dallas	75.00	130.00	1000.00	—
☐ Atlanta	70.00	130.00	900.00	—	☐ San Francisco	75.00	130.00	800.00	—

SERIES OF 1928A, SIGNATURES OF WOODS-MELLON, GREEN SEAL

BANK	A.B.P.	V.FINE	UNC.	★UNC.	BANK	A.B.P.	V.FINE	UNC.	★UNC.
☐ Boston	65.00	985.00	550.00	—	☐ Chicago	65.00	110.00	500.00	—
☐ New York	65.00	985.00	550.00	—	☐ St. Louis	65.00	110.00	550.00	—
☐ Philadelphia	65.00	985.00	550.00	—	☐ Minneapolis	65.00	120.00	750.00	—
☐ Cleveland	65.00	985.00	550.00	—	☐ Kansas City	65.00	120.00	1200.00	—
☐ Richmond	65.00	985.00	550.00	—	☐ Dallas	65.00	120.00	1000.00	—
☐ Atlanta	65.00	985.00	550.00	—	☐ San Francisco	65.00	110.00	800.00	—

FIFTY DOLLAR NOTES (1934)
FEDERAL RESERVE NOTES

SERIES OF 1934, SIGNATURES OF JULIAN-MORGENTHAU, GREEN SEAL

BANK	A.B.P.	V.FINE	UNC.	★UNC.	BANK	A.B.P.	V.FINE	UNC.	★UNC.
☐ Boston	60.00	80.00	300.00	750.00	☐ Chicago	60.00	80.00	300.00	750.00
☐ New York	60.00	80.00	300.00	750.00	☐ St. Louis	60.00	80.00	300.00	750.00
☐ Philadelphia	60.00	80.00	300.00	750.00	☐ Minneapolis	60.00	80.00	300.00	750.00
☐ Cleveland	60.00	80.00	300.00	750.00	☐ Kansas City	60.00	80.00	300.00	750.00
☐ Richmond	60.00	80.00	300.00	750.00	☐ Dallas	60.00	80.00	300.00	750.00
☐ Atlanta	60.00	80.00	300.00	750.00	☐ San Francisco	60.00	80.00	300.00	750.00

SERIES OF 1934A, SIGNATURES OF JULIAN-MORGENTHAU, GREEN SEAL

BANK	A.B.P.	V.FINE	UNC.	★UNC.	BANK	A.B.P.	V.FINE	UNC.	★UNC.
☐ Boston	58.00	90.00	400.00	1500.00	☐ Chicago	58.00	90.00	400.00	1500.00
☐ New York	58.00	90.00	400.00	1500.00	☐ St. Louis	58.00	90.00	400.00	1500.00
☐ Philadelphia	58.00	90.00	400.00	1500.00	☐ Minneapolis	58.00	100.00	400.00	1500.00
☐ Cleveland	58.00	90.00	400.00	1500.00	☐ Kansas City	58.00	100.00	400.00	1500.00
☐ Richmond	58.00	90.00	400.00	1500.00	☐ Dallas	58.00	100.00	400.00	1500.00
☐ Atlanta	58.00	90.00	400.00	1500.00	☐ San Francisco	58.00	90.00	400.00	1500.00

SERIES OF 1934B, SIGNATURES OF JULIAN-VINSON, GREEN SEAL

BANK	A.B.P.	V.FINE	UNC.	★UNC.	BANK	A.P.B.	V.FINE	UNC.	★UNC.
					☐ Chicago	55.00	85.00	400.00	—
					☐ St. Louis	55.00	85.00	400.00	—
☐ Philadelphia	58.00	85.00	400.00	3500.00	☐ Minneapolis	65.00	105.00	400.00	—
☐ Cleveland	58.00	85.00	400.00	3500.00	☐ Kansas City	65.00	105.00	400.00	3500.00
☐ Richmond	58.00	85.00	400.00	3500.00	☐ Dallas	65.00	105.00	400.00	—
☐ Atlanta	58.00	85.00	400.00	—	☐ San Francisco	55.00	85.00	400.00	—

SERIES OF 1934C, SIGNATURES OF JULIAN-SNYDER, GREEN SEAL

BANK	A.B.P.	V.FINE	UNC.	★UNC.	BANK	A.B.P.	V.FINE	UNC.	★UNC.
☐ Boston	58.00	90.00	300.00	—	☐ Chicago	58.00	90.00	300.00	2000.00
☐ New York	58.00	90.00	300.00	2000.00	☐ St. Louis	58.00	90.00	300.00	—
☐ Philadelphia	58.00	90.00	300.00	2000.00	☐ Minneapolis	58.00	90.00	300.00	2000.00
☐ Cleveland	58.00	85.00	300.00	2000.00	☐ Kansas City	58.00	85.00	300.00	—
☐ Richmond	58.00	85.00	300.00	2000.00	☐ Dallas	58.00	85.00	300.00	2000.00
☐ Atlanta	58.00	85.00	300.00	—	☐				

SERIES OF 1934D, SIGNATURES OF CLARK-SNYDER, GREEN SEAL

BANK	A.B.P.	V.FINE	UNC.	★UNC.	BANK	A.B.P.	V.FINE	UNC.	★UNC.
☐ Boston	68.00	105.00	500.00	5000.00	☐ Chicago	55.00	75.00	500.00	4000
☐ New York	53.00	75.00	500.00	5000.00					
☐ Philadelphia	53.00	75.00	500.00	4000.00	☐ Minneapolis	55.00	75.00	500.00	—
☐ Richmond	68.00	105.00	500.00	—	☐ Dallas	65 .00	105.00	500.00	—
☐ Atlanta	68.00	105.00	500.00	5000.00					

FIFTY DOLLAR NOTES (1950)
FEDERAL RESERVE NOTES

SERIES OF 1950, SIGNATURES OF CLARK-SNYDER, GREEN SEAL

BANK	A.B.P.	V.FINE	UNC.	★UNC.	BANK	A.P.B.	V.FINE	UNC.	★UNC.
☐ Boston	58.00	90.00	350.00	1000.00	☐ Chicago	55.00	90.00	350.00	1000.00
☐ New York	58.00	90.00	350.00	1000.00	☐ St. Louis	55.00	90.00	350.00	1000.00
☐ Philadelphia	58.00	90.00	350.00	1000.00	☐ Minneapolis	55.00	90.00	350.00	1000.00
☐ Cleveland	53.00	85.00	350.00	1000.00	☐ Kansas City	55.00	90.00	350.00	1000.00
☐ Richmond	53.00	85.00	350.00	1000.00	☐ Dallas	55.00	90.00	350.00	1000.00
☐ Atlanta	53.00	85.00	350.00	1000.00	☐ San Francisco	55.00	90.00	350.00	1000.00

SERIES OF 1950A, SIGNATURES OF PRIEST-HUMPHERY, GREEN SEAL

BANK	A.B.P.	V.FINE	UNC.	★UNC.	BANK	A.B.P.	V.FINE	UNC.	★UNC.
☐ Boston	55.00	75.00	300.00	850.00	☐ Chicago	55.00	75.00	300.00	850.00
☐ New York	55.00	75.00	300.00	850.00	☐ St. Louis	55.00	75.00	300.00	850.00
☐ Philadelphia	55.00	75.00	300.00	850.00	☐ Minneapolis	55.00	75.00	300.00	850.00
☐ Cleveland	55.00	75.00	300.00	850.00	☐ Kansas City	55.00	75.00	300.00	850.00
☐ Richmond	55.00	75.00	300.00	850.00	☐ Dallas	55.00	75.00	300.00	850.00
☐ Atlanta	55.00	75.00	300.00	850.00	☐ San Francisco	55.00	75.00	300.00	850.00

SERIES OF 1950B, SIGNATURES OF PRIEST-ANDERSON, GREEN SEAL

BANK	A.B.P.	V.FINE	UNC.	★UNC.	BANK	A.B.P.	V.FINE	UNC.	★UNC.
☐ Boston	52.00	70.00	250.00	700.00	☐ Chicago	52.00	70.00	250.00	700.00
☐ New York	52.00	70.00	250.00	700.00	☐ St. Louis	52.00	70.00	250.00	700.00
☐ Philadelphia	52.00	70.00	250.00	700.00	☐ Minneapolis	52.00	70.00	250.00	700.00
☐ Cleveland	52.00	70.00	250.00	700.00	☐ Kansas City	52.00	70.00	250.00	700.00
☐ Richmond	52.00	70.00	250.00	700.00	☐ Dallas	52.00	70.00	250.00	700.00
☐ Atlanta	52.00	70.00	250.00	700.00	☐ San Francisco	52.00	70.00	250.00	700.00

SERIES OF 1950C, SIGNATURES OF SMITH-DILLON, GREEN SEAL

BANK	A.B.P.	V.FINE	UNC.	★UNC.	BANK	A.B.P.	V.FINE	UNC.	★UNC.
☐ Boston	52.00	70.00	225.00	650.00	☐ Chicago	52.00	70.00	225.00	650.00
☐ New York	52.00	70.00	225.00	650.00	☐ St. Louis	52.00	70.00	225.00	650.00
☐ Philadelphia	52.00	70.00	225.00	650.00	☐ Minneapolis	52.00	70.00	225.00	650.00
☐ Cleveland	52.00	70.00	225.00	650.00	☐ Kansas City	52.00	70.00	225.00	650.00
☐ Richmond	52.00	70.00	225.00	650.00	☐ Dallas	52.00	70.00	225.00	650.00
☐ Atlanta	52.00	70.00	225.00	650.00	☐ San Francisco	52.00	70.00	225.00	650.00

SERIES OF 1950D, SIGNATURES OF GRANAHAN-DILLON, GREEN SEAL

BANK	A.B.P.	V.FINE	UNC.	★UNC.	BANK	A.B.P.	V.FINE	UNC.	★UNC.
☐ Boston	65.00	105.00	225.00	600.00	☐ Chicago	58.00	95.00	225.00	600.00
☐ New York	65.00	105.00	225.00	600.00	☐ St. Louis	58.00	95.00	225.00	600.00
☐ Philadelphia	65.00	105.00	225.00	600.00	☐ Minneapolis	58.00	95.00	225.00	600.00
☐ Cleveland	58.00	95.00	225.00	600.00	☐ Kansas City	58.00	95.00	225.00	600.00
☐ Richmond	58.00	95.00	225.00	600.00	☐ Dallas	65.00	105.00	225.00	600.00
☐ Atlanta	58.00	95.00	225.00	600.00	☐ San Francisco	65.00	105.00	225.00	600.00

SERIES OF 1950E, SIGNATURES OF GRANAHAN-FOWLER, GREEN SEAL

BANK	A.B.P.	V.FINE	UNC.	★UNC.	BANK	A.B.P.	V.FINE	UNC.	★UNC.
					☐ Chicago	75.00	125.00	1200.00	5000.00
☐ New York	75.00	125.00	900.00	2000.00					
					☐ San Francisco	80.00	125.00	900.00	3000.00

FIFTY DOLLAR NOTES (1963)
FEDERAL RESERVE NOTES
SERIES OF 1963,
(THERE WERE NOT ANY NOTES PRINTED FOR THIS SERIES.)

SERIES OF 1963A, SIGNATURES OF GRANAHAN-FOWLER, GREEN SEAL

BANK	A.B.P.	V.FINE	UNC.	BANK	A.B.P.	V.FINE	UNC.
☐ Boston	51.00	65.00	300.00	☐ Chicago	51.00	65.00	300.00
☐ New York	51.00	65.00	300.00	☐ St. Louis	51.00	90.00	300.00
☐ Philadelphia	51.00	65.00	300.00	☐ Minneapolis	51.00	90.00	300.00
☐ Cleveland	51.00	65.00	300.00	☐ Kansas City	51.00	90.00	300.00
☐ Richmond	51.00	65.00	300.00	☐ Dallas	51.00	65.00	300.00
☐ Atlanta	51.00	65.00	300.00	☐ San Francisco	51.00	65.00	300.00

FIFTY DOLLAR NOTES (1969)
FEDERAL RESERVE NOTES
(WORDING IN GREEN TREASURY SEAL IS CHANGED FROM LATIN TO ENGLISH)

SERIES OF 1969, SIGNATURES OF ELSTON-KENNEDY, GREEN SEAL

BANK	A.B.P.	V.FINE	UNC.	BANK	A.B.P.	V.FINE	UNC.
☐ Boston	51.00	75.00	225.00	☐ Chicago	51.00	75.00	225.00
☐ New York	51.00	75.00	225.00	☐ St. Louis	51.00	90.00	250.00
☐ Philadelphia	51.00	75.00	225.00	☐ Minneapolis	51.00	90.00	250.00
☐ Cleveland	51.00	75.00	225.00	☐ Kansas City	51.00	90.00	250.00
☐ Richmond	51.00	75.00	225.00	☐ Dallas	51.00	75.00	225.00
☐ Atlanta	51.00	90.00	225.00	☐ San Francisco	51.00	75.00	225.00

SERIES OF 1969A, SIGNATURES OF KABIS-CONNALLY, GREEN SEAL

BANK	A.B.P.	V.FINE	UNC.	BANK	A.B.P.	V.FINE	UNC.
☐ Boston	51.00	60.00	210.00	☐ Chicago	51.00	60.00	210.00
☐ New York	51.00	60.00	210.00	☐ St. Louis	51.00	65.00	220.00
☐ Philadelphia	51.00	60.00	210.00	☐ Minneapolis	51.00	65.00	220.00
☐ Cleveland	51.00	60.00	210.00	☐ Kansas City	51.00	65.00	220.00
☐ Richmond	51.00	60.00	210.00	☐ Dallas	51.00	60.00	210.00
☐ Atlanta	51.00	60.00	210.00	☐ San Francisco	51.00	60.00	210.00

SERIES OF 1969B, SIGNATURES OF BANUELOS-CONNALLY, GREEN SEAL

BANK	A.B.P.	V.FINE	UNC.	BANK	A.B.P.	V.FINE	UNC.
☐ Boston	51.00	65.00	750.00	☐ Chicago	51.00	65.00	750.00
☐ New York	51.00	65.00	300.00				
☐ Richmond	51.00	65.00	750.00	☐ Dallas	51.00	65.00	750.00
☐ Atlanta	51.00	75.00	750.00				

SERIES OF 1969C, SIGNATURES OF BANUELOS-SHULTZ, GREEN SEAL

BANK	A.B.P.	V.FINE	UNC.	BANK	A.B.P.	V.FINE	UNC.
☐ Boston	51.00	75.00	190.00	☐ Chicago	51.00	65.00	175.00
☐ New York	51.00	75.00	190.00	☐ St. Louis	51.00	65.00	175.00
☐ Philadelphia	51.00	75.00	190.00	☐ Minneapolis	51.00	65.00	190.00
☐ Cleveland	51.00	65.00	175.00	☐ Kansas City	51.00	65.00	175.00
☐ Richmond	51.00	65.00	175.00	☐ Dallas	51.00	65.00	175.00
☐ Atlanta	51.00	65.00	175.00	☐ San Francisco	51.00	65.00	175.00

FIFTY DOLLAR NOTES (1974)
FEDERAL RESERVE NOTES

SERIES OF 1974, SIGNATURES OF NEFF-SIMON, GREEN SEAL

BANK	A.B.P.	V.FINE	UNC.	BANK	A.B.P.	V.FINE	UNC.
☐ Boston	51.00	70.00	200.00	☐ Chicago	51.00	70.00	200.00
☐ New York	51.00	70.00	200.00	☐ St. Louis	51.00	70.00	200.00
☐ Philadelphia	51.00	70.00	200.00	☐ Minneapolis	51.00	75.00	200.00
☐ Cleveland	51.00	70.00	200.00	☐ Kansas City	51.00	75.00	200.00
☐ Richmond	51.00	70.00	200.00	☐ Dallas	51.00	70.00	200.00
☐ Atlanta	51.00	70.00	200.00	☐ San Francisco	51.00	70.00	200.00

FIFTY DOLLAR NOTES (1977)
FEDERAL RESERVE NOTES

SERIES OF 1977, SIGNATURES OF MORTON-BLUMENTHAL, GREEN SEAL

BANK	A.B.P.	V.FINE	UNC.	BANK	A.B.P.	V.FINE	UNC.
☐ Boston	—	60.00	175.00	☐ Chicago	—	60.00	175.00
☐ New York	—	60.00	175.00	☐ St. Louis	—	60.00	175.00
☐ Philadelphia	—	60.00	175.00	☐ Minneapolis	—	60.00	175.00
☐ Cleveland	—	60.00	175.00	☐ Kansas City	—	60.00	175.00
☐ Richmond	—	60.00	175.00	☐ Dallas	—	60.00	175.00
☐ Atlanta	—	60.00	175.00	☐ San Francisco	—	60.00	175.00

FIFTY DOLLAR NOTES (1981)
FEDERAL RESERVE NOTES

SERIES OF 1981, SIGNATURES OF BUCHANAN-REGAN, GREEN SEAL

BANK	A.B.P.	V.FINE	UNC.	BANK	A.B.P.	V.FINE	UNC.
☐ Boston	—	54.00	200.00	☐ Chicago	—	54.00	200.00
☐ New York	—	54.00	200.00	☐ St. Louis	—	54.00	200.00
☐ Philadelphia	—	54.00	200.00	☐ Minneapolis	—	56.00	200.00
☐ Cleveland	—	54.00	200.00	☐ Kansas City	—	56.00	200.00
☐ Richmond	—	54.00	200.00	☐ Dallas	—	56.00	200.00
☐ Atlanta	—	54.00	200.00	☐ San Francisco	—	54.00	200.00

SERIES OF 1981A, SIGNATURES OF ORTEGA-REGAN, GREEN SEAL

BANK	A.B.P.	V.FINE	UNC.	BANK	A.B.P.	V.FINE	UNC.
☐ Boston	—	54.00	225.00	☐ Chicago	—	54.00	225.00
☐ New York	—	54.00	225.00	☐ St. Louis	—	54.00	225.00
☐ Philadelphia	—	54.00	225.00	☐ Minneapolis	—	56.00	225.00
☐ Cleveland	—	54.00	225.00	☐ Kansas City	—	56.00	225.00
☐ Richmond	—	54.00	225.00	☐ Dallas	—	56.00	225.00
☐ Atlanta	—	54.00	225.00	☐ San Francisco	—	54.00	225.00

FIFTY DOLLAR NOTES (1985)
FEDERAL RESERVE NOTES

SERIES OF 1985, SIGNATURES OF ORTEGA-BAKER, GREEN SEAL

BANK	A.B.P.	V.FINE	UNC.	BANK	A.B.P.	V.FINE	UNC.
☐ Boston	—	55.00	125.00	☐ Chicago	—	55.00	125.00
☐ New York	—	55.00	125.00	☐ St. Louis	—	55.00	125.00
☐ Philadelphia	—	55.00	125.00	☐ Minneapolis	—	55.00	125.00
☐ Cleveland	—	55.00	125.00	☐ Kansas City	—	55.00	125.00
☐ Richmond	—	55.00	125.00	☐ Dallas	—	55.00	125.00
☐ Atlanta	—	55.00	125.00	☐ San Francisco	—	55.00	125.00

FIFTY DOLLAR NOTES (1988)
FEDERAL RESERVE NOTES

SERIES OF 1988, SIGNATURES OF ORTEGA-BRADY, GREEN SEAL

BANK	A.B.P.	V.FINE	UNC.	BANK	A.B.P.	V.FINE	UNC.
☐ Boston	—	55.00	150.00	☐ Chicago	—	55.00	150.00
☐ New York	—	55.00	150.00	☐ St. Louis	—	55.00	150.00
☐ Philadelphia	—	55.00	150.00	☐ Minneapolis	—	55.00	150.00
☐ Cleveland	—	55.00	150.00	☐ Kansas City	—	55.00	150.00
☐ Richmond	—	55.00	150.00	☐ Dallas	—	55.00	150.00
☐ Atlanta	—	55.00	150.00	☐ San Francisco	—	55.00	150.00

FIFTY DOLLAR NOTES (1990)
FEDERAL RESERVE NOTES

SERIES OF 1990, SIGNATURES OF VILLALPANDO-BRADY, GREEN SEAL

BANK	A.B.P.	V.FINE	UNC.	BANK	A.B.P.	V.FINE	UNC.
☐ Boston	—	55.00	100.00	☐ Chicago	—	55.00	100.00
☐ New York	—	55.00	100.00	☐ St. Louis	—	55.00	100.00
☐ Philadelphia	—	55.00	100.00	☐ Minneapolis	—	55.00	100.00
☐ Cleveland	—	55.00	100.00	☐ Kansas City	—	55.00	100.00
☐ Richmond	—	55.00	100.00	☐ Dallas	—	55.00	100.00
☐ Atlanta	—	55.00	100.00	☐ San Francisco	—	55.00	100.00

FIFTY DOLLAR NOTES (1993)

FEDERAL RESERVE NOTES

SERIES OF 1993, SIGNATURES OF WITHROW-BENTSEN, GREEN SEAL

BANK	A.B.P.	V.FINE	UNC.	BANK	A.B.P.	V.FINE	UNC.
☐ Boston	—	55.00	90.00	☐ Chicago	—	55.00	90.00
☐ New York	—	55.00	90.00	☐ St. Louis	—	55.00	90.00
☐ Philadelphia	—	55.00	90.00	☐ Minneapolis	—	55.00	90.00
☐ Cleveland	—	55.00	90.00	☐ Kansas City	—	55.00	90.00
☐ Richmond	—	55.00	90.00	☐ Dallas	—	55.00	90.00
☐ Atlanta	—	55.00	90.00	☐ San Francisco	—	55.00	90.00

FIFTY DOLLAR NOTES (1996)

FEDERAL RESERVE NOTES

SERIES OF 1995, SIGNATURES OF WITHROW-BENTSEN, GREEN SEAL

BANK	A.B.P.	V.FINE	UNC.	BANK	A.B.P.	V.FINE	UNC.
☐ Boston	—	55.00	70.00	☐ Chicago	—	55.00	70.00
☐ New York	—	55.00	70.00	☐ St. Louis	—	55.00	70.00
☐ Philadelphia	—	55.00	70.00	☐ Minneapolis	—	55.00	70.00
☐ Cleveland	—	55.00	70.00	☐ Kansas City	—	55.00	70.00
☐ Richmond	—	55.00	70.00	☐ Dallas	—	55.00	70.00
☐ Atlanta	—	55.00	70.00	☐ San Francisco	—	55.00	70.00

FIFTY DOLLAR NOTES (1918)

FEDERAL RESERVE BANK NOTES

(Large Size)

Face Design: Portrait of President Grant to left, Federal Reserve Bank in center, blue seal right.

Back Design: Female figure of Panama between merchant ship and battleship. Plates were made for all twelve Federal Reserve Districts. Only St. Louis bank issued. Less than thirty notes are known today.

BANK	SERIES	GOV'T SIGNATURES	BANK SIGNATURES	A.B.P.	VF	UNC.
□St. Louis	1918	Teehee-Burke	Attebery-Wells	900.00	5200.00	20,000.00

FIFTY DOLLAR NOTES (1929)

FEDERAL RESERVE BANK NOTES

(Small Size)

Face Design: Portrait of Grant center, name of bank left, brown serial numbers, black letter for Federal Reserve District.

Back Design: Same as 1929 $50 note.

BANK	SERIES	SIGNATURES	SEAL	A.B.P.	V.FINE	UNC.	★UNC.
☐ New York	1929	Jones-Woods	Brown	80.00	160.00	450.00	4000.00
☐ Cleveland	1929	Jones-Woods	Brown	84.00	170.00	450.00	4500.00
☐ Chicago	1929	Jones-Woods	Brown	80.00	160.00	550.00	6000.00
☐ Minneapolis	1929	Jones-Woods	Brown	80.00	160.00	750.00	5000.00
☐ Kansas City	1929	Jones-Woods	Brown	80.00	140.00	450.00	2000.00
☐ Dallas	1929	Jones-Woods	Brown	84.00	190.00	2500.00	6000.00
☐ San Francisco	1929	Jones-Woods	Brown	139.00	265.00	1000.00	6000.00

ONE HUNDRED DOLLAR NOTES

ORDER OF ISSUE

ONE HUNDRED DOLLAR NOTES (1862–1863)
UNITED STATES NOTES
(ALSO KNOWN AS LEGAL TENDER NOTES)

(Large Size)

Face Design: Eagle with spread wings left, three discs with "100," red seal numbers.

Back Design: Green, two variations of the wording in obligation.

SERIES	SIGNATURES	SEAL	A.B.P.	GOOD	V.FINE	UNC.
□1862	Chittenden-Spinner*	Red	3750.00	5250.00	19,500.00	78,000.00
□1862	Chittenden-Spinner**	Red	3750.00	5250.00	19,500.00	78,000.00
□1863	Chittenden-Spinner**	Red	3750.00	5250.00	19,500.00	78,000.00

*First Obligation: Similar to 1875–1907 $5 note.
**Second Obligation: Shown above.

ONE HUNDRED DOLLAR NOTES (1869–1880)
UNITED STATES NOTES

(Large Size)

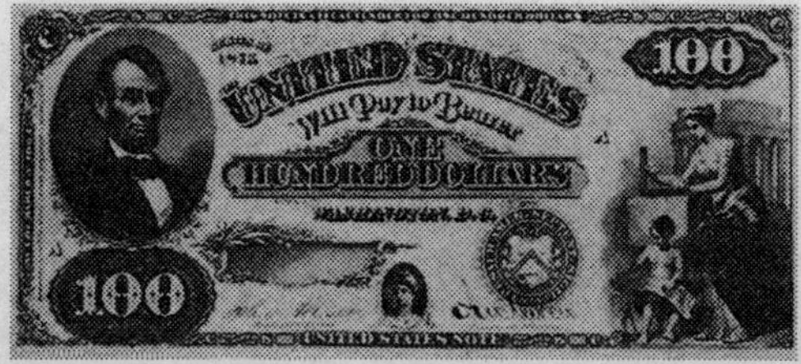

Face Design: Portrait of President Lincoln.

Back Design: First Issue

Back Design: Second Issue.

SERIES	SIGNATURES	SEAL	A.B.P.	GOOD	V.FINE	UNC.
□1869	Allison-Spinner	Red	3800.00	5500.00	24,500.00	62,000.00

The following notes have a modified back design.

(Small Size)

Second Issue

SERIES	SIGNATURES	SEAL	A.B.P.	GOOD	V.FINE	UNC.
□1875	Allison-New	Sm. Red	2100.00	3800.00	15,000.00	50,000.00
□1875	Allison-Wyman	Sm. Red	3500.00	5900.00	20,000.00	77,500.00
□1878	Allison-Gilfillan	Sm. Red	1800.00	3100.00	17,500.00	47,000.00
□1880	Bruce-Gilfillan	Lg. Brown	1300.00	2400.00	14,000.00	89,500.00
□1880	Bruce-Wyman	Lg. Brown	1300.00	2500.00	14,000.00	89,500.00
□1880	Rosecrans-Jordan	Lg. Red	1300.00	2300.00	24,000.00	42,500.00
□1880	Rosecrans-Hyatt	Red Plain	1800.00	3300.00	23,500.00	100,000.00
□1880	Rosecrans-Hyatt	Red Spike	1300.00	2300.00	14,000.00	42,500.00
□1880	Rosecrans-Huston	Lg. Red	1300.00	2300.00	11,500.00	65,000.00
□1880	Rosecrans-Huston	Lg. Brown	1300.00	2800.00	14,500.00	38,500.00
□1880	Tillman-Morgan	Sm. Red	1200.00	1800.00	9000.00	25,500.00
□1880	Bruce-Roberts	Sm. Red	1200.00	1800.00	8000.00	24,500.00
□1880	Lyons-Roberts	Sm. Red	1200.00	1800.00	8000.00	24,500.00

ONE HUNDRED DOLLAR NOTES (1966) U.S. NOTES (ALSO KNOWN AS LEGAL TENDER NOTES)

(Small Size)

Face Design: Portrait of Franklin, red seal, red serial numbers.

Back Design: Independence Hall.

SERIES	SIGNATURES	SEAL	A.B.P.	V.FINE	UNC.	*UNC
☐1966*	Granahan-Fowler	Red	125.00	165.00	500.00	2000.00
☐1966A	Elston-Kennedy	Red	125.00	230.00	1250.00	—

*This is the first note to be issued with the new Treasury Seal with wording in English instead of Latin.

ONE HUNDRED DOLLAR NOTES (1875)
NATIONAL BANK NOTES

FIRST CHARTER PERIOD (Large Size)

Face Design: Perry leaving the Saint Lawrence, left.

Back Design: Border green, center black, signing of the Declaration of Independence.

SERIES	SIGNATURES	SEAL	A.B.P.	GOOD	V.FINE	UNC.
☐Original	Chittenden-Spinner	Red	1600.00	2500.00	6500.00	39,500.00
☐Original	Colby-Spinner	Red	1600.00	2500.00	6500.00	39,500.00
☐Original	Allison-Spinner	Red	1600.00	2500.00	6500.00	39,500.00
☐1875	Allison-New	Red	1400.00	2500.00	6500.00	41,000.00
☐1875	Allison-Wyman	Red	1400.00	2500.00	6500.00	41,000.00
☐1875	Allison-Gilfillan	Red	1400.00	2500.00	6500.00	41,000.00
☐1875	Scofield-Gilfillan	Red	1400.00	2500.00	6500.00	41,000.00
☐1875	Bruce-Gilfillan	Red	1400.00	2500.00	6500.00	41,000.00
☐1875	Bruce-Wyman	Red	1400.00	2500.00	6500.00	41,000.00
☐1875	Rosecrans-Huston	Red	1400.00	2500.00	6500.00	41,000.00
☐1875	Tillman-Morgan	Red	1400.00	2500.00	6500.00	41,000.00

ONE HUNDRED DOLLAR NOTES (1882)
NATIONAL BANK NOTES

SECOND CHARTER PERIOD (Large Size)

First Issue (Brown seal and brown backs.)

SERIES	SIGNATURES	SEAL	A.B.P.	GOOD	V.FINE	UNC.
□1882	Bruce-Gilfillan	Brown	450.00	675.00	2100.00	10000.00
□1882	Bruce-Wyman	Brown	450.00	675.00	2100.00	10000.00
□1882	Bruce-Jordan	Brown	450.00	675.00	2100.00	10000.00
□1882	Rosecrans-Jordan	Brown	450.00	675.00	2100.00	10000.00
□1882	Rosecrans-Hyatt	Brown	450.00	675.00	2100.00	10000.00
□1882	Rosecrans-Huston	Brown	450.00	675.00	2100.00	10000.00
□1882	Rosecrans-Nebeker	Brown	450.00	675.00	2100.00	10000.00
□1882	Rosecrans-Morgan	Brown	450.00	1100.00	2600.00	10600.00
□1882	Tillman-Morgan	Brown	450.00	675.00	2100.00	10000.00
□1882	Tillman-Roberts	Brown	450.00	675.00	2100.00	10000.00
□1882	Bruce-Roberts	Brown	450.00	675.00	2100.00	10000.00
□1882	Lyons-Roberts	Brown	450.00	675.00	2100.00	10000.00

SECOND CHARTER PERIOD (Large Size)

Second Issue (Blue seal, green back with date "1882–1908")

Back Design: Green with date "1882–1908" center.

SERIES	SIGNATURES	SEAL	A.B.P.	GOOD	V.FINE	UNC.
□1882	Rosecrans-Huston	Blue	300.00	550.00	1650.00	5100.00
□1882	Rosecrans-Nebeker	Blue	300.00	550.00	1650.00	5100.00
□1882	Tillman-Morgan	Blue	300.00	550.00	1650.00	5100.00
□1882	Tillman-Roberts	Blue	300.00	550.00	1650.00	5100.00
□1882	Bruce-Roberts	Blue	300.00	550.00	1650.00	5100.00
□1882	Lyons-Roberts	Blue	300.00	550.00	1650.00	5100.00
□1882	Vernon-Treat	Blue	300.00	550.00	1650.00	5100.00
□1882	Napier-McClung	Blue	300.00	550.00	1650.00	5100.00
This note was also issued with (value) ONE HUNDRED DOLLARS on the back. Very rare.		—	45,000.00	60,000.00	95,000.00	—

ONE HUNDRED DOLLAR NOTES (1902)
NATIONAL BANK NOTES
THIRD CHARTER PERIOD (Large Size)

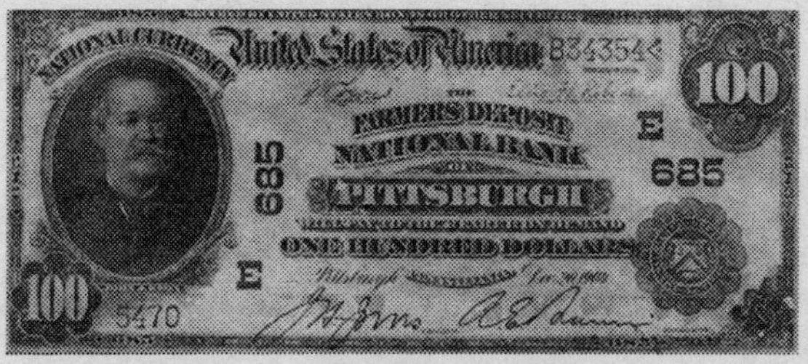

Face Design: Portrait of John J. Knox left.

Back Design: Male figures with shield and flags.

First Issue (Red seal)

SERIES	SIGNATURES	SEAL	A.B.P.	GOOD	V.FINE	UNC.
□1902	Lyons-Roberts	Red	465.00	700.00	2050.00	10,500.00
□1902	Lyons-Treat	Red	375.00	550.00	1850.00	9000.00
□1902	Vernon-Treat	Red	375.00	550.00	1850.00	9000.00

Second Issue*

Design is similar to previous note. Seal and serial numbers are now blue; back of note has date "1902–1908" added.

SERIES	SIGNATURES	SEAL	A.B.P.	GOOD	V.FINE	UNC.
		Blue	165.00	225.00	675.00	2500.00

Third Issue*

Design continues as previous notes. Seal and serial numbers remain blue, date "1902–1908" removed from back.

SERIES	SIGNATURES	SEAL	A.B.P.	GOOD	V.FINE	UNC.
		Blue	150.00	210.00	595.00	2400.00

* The notes of the **Second and Third Issue** appeared with various signatures: Lyons-Roberts, Lyons-Treat, Vernon-Treat, Vernon-McClung, Napier-McClung, Parker-Burke, Teehee-Burke, Elliott-Burke, Elliott-White, Speelman-White, Woods-White.

ONE HUNDRED DOLLAR NOTES (1929)
NATIONAL BANK NOTES

(Small Size)

Face Design: Portrait of Franklin center. Name of bank and city left. Brown seal right.

SERIES	SIGNATURES	SEAL	A.B.P.	V.FINE	UNC.
□1929	Type I Jones-Woods	Brown	125.00	175.00	600.00
□1929	Type II Jones-Woods	Brown	150.00	275.00	1500.00

ONE HUNDRED DOLLAR NOTES (1878)
SILVER CERTIFICATES

SERIES	SIGNATURES	SEAL	A.B.P.	GOOD	V.FINE	UNC.
□1878	Scofield-Gilfillan-White	Red				UNIQUE
□1878	Scofield-Gilfillan-Hopper	Red		NO SPECIMENS KNOWN		
□1878	Scofield-Gilfillan-Hillhouse	Red		NO SPECIMENS KNOWN		
□1878	Scofield-Gilfillan-Anthony	Red				UNIQUE
□1878	Scofield-Gilfillan-Wyman (printed signature of Wyman)	Red		NO SPECIMENS KNOWN		
□1878	Scofield-Gilfillan	Red			VERY RARE	
□1880	Scofield-Gilfillan	Brown		EXTREMELY RARE		
□1880	Bruce-Gilfillan	Brown	2750.00	4150.00	17,500.00	60,000.00
□1880	Bruce-Wyman	Brown	1750.00	3150.00	15,000.00	50,000.00
□1880	Rosecrans-Huston	Brown	1750.00	3150.00	15,000.00	200,000.00
□1880	Rosecrans-Nebeker	Brown	1750.00	3150.00	15,000.00	175,000.00

ONE HUNDRED DOLLAR NOTES (1891)
SILVER CERTIFICATES

(Large Size)

Face Design: Portrait of President Monroe.

SERIES	SIGNATURES	SEAL	A.B.P.	GOOD	V.FINE	UNC.
□1891	Rosecrans-Nebeker	Red	1730.00	3200.00	11,000.00	35,000.00
□1891	Tillman-Morgan	Red	1730.00	3200.00	11,000.00	35,000.00

This note was also issued in the Series of 1878 and 1880. They are very rare.

ONE HUNDRED DOLLAR NOTES (1882–1922)
GOLD CERTIFICATES

(Large Size)

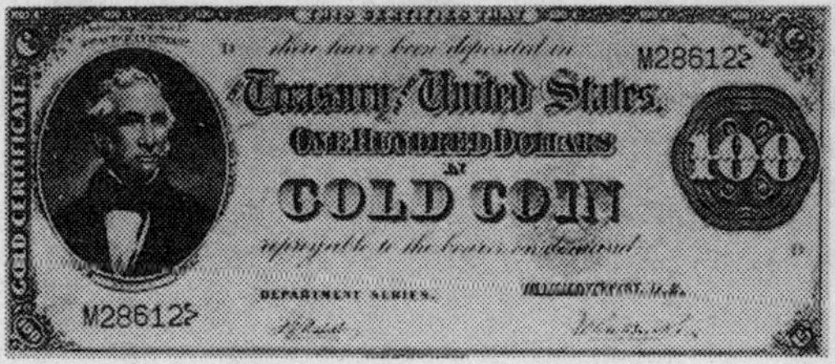

Face Design: Portrait of Thomas H. Benton.

SERIES	SIGNATURES	SEAL	A.B.P.	GOOD	V.FINE	UNC.
□1882	Bruce-Gilfillan	Brown	1540.00	2885.00	18000.00	250,000.00
□1882	Bruce-Wyman	Brown	3500.00	7000.00	48100.00	275,000.00
□1882	Rosecrans-Hyatt	Lg. Red	3500.00	6000.00	45000.00	250,000.00
□1882	Rosecrans-Huston	Lg. Brown	3500.00	5000.00	30000.00	250,000.00
□1882	Lyons-Roberts	Sm. Red	200.00	260.00	1825.00	6000.00
□1882	Lyons-Treat	Sm. Red	200.00	460.00	2625.00	28,000.00
□1882	Vernon-Treat	Sm. Red	200.00	360.00	2025.00	8000.00
□1882	Vernon-McClung	Sm. Red	200.00	360.00	2100.00	0000.00
□1882	Napier-McClung	Sm. Red	200.00	285.00	2025.00	8000.00
□1882	Napier-Thompson	Sm. Red	210.00	385.00	1725.00	10,250.00
□1882	Napier-Burke	Sm. Red	200.00	250.00	975.00	8000.00
□1882	Parker-Burke	Sm. Red	200.00	250.00	975.00	8000.00
□1882	Teehee-Burke	Sm. Red	200.00	250.00	975.00	8000.00
□1922	Speelman-White	Sm. Red	200.00	260.00	875.00	8000.00

ONE HUNDRED DOLLAR NOTES (1928)
GOLD CERTIFICATES

(Small Size)

Face Design: Portrait of Franklin center. Yellow seal to left. Yellow numbers.

SERIES	SIGNATURES	SEAL	A.B.P.	GOOD	V.FINE	UNC.
□1928	Woods-Mellon	Gold	145.00	220.00	535.00	3200.00

ONE HUNDRED DOLLAR NOTES (1890–1891)
TREASURY OR COIN NOTES

(Large Size)

Face Design: Portrait of Commodore Farragut to right.

Back Design: Large "100," called "Watermelon Note."

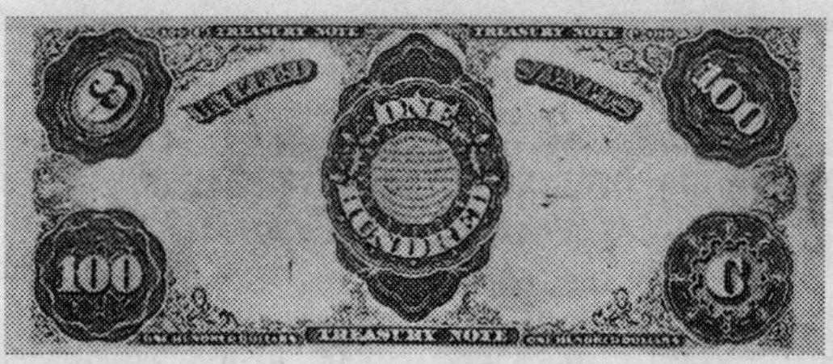

Back Design: ONE HUNDRED in scalloped medallion.

SERIES	SIGNATURES	SEAL	A.B.P.	GOOD	V.FINE	UNC.
□1890	Rosecrans-Huston	Brown	6200.00	10,100.00	65,000.00	175,000.00+
□1890	Rosecrans-Nebeker	Red	6200.00	10,100.00	65,000.00	175,000.00+

ONE HUNDRED DOLLAR NOTES (1914)
FEDERAL RESERVE NOTES

(Large Size)

Face Design: Portrait of Franklin in center.
Back Design: Group of five allegorical figures.

SERIES OF 1914, SIGNATURES OF BURKE-McADOO, RED SEAL AND RED SERIAL NUMBERS

BANK	A.B.P.	GOOD	V.FINE	UNC.	BANK	A.B.P.	GOOD	V.FINE	UNC.
☐ Boston	300.00	500.00	1600.00	6000.00	☐Chicago	300.00	500.00	1600.00	6000.00
☐ New York	300.00	500.00	1600.00	6000.00	☐St. Louis	300.00	500.00	1600.00	6000.00
☐ Philadelphia	300.00	500.00	1600.00	6000.00	☐Minneapolis	300.00	500.00	1600.00	6000.00
☐ Cleveland	300.00	500.00	1600.00	6000.00	☐Kansas City	300.00	500.00	1600.00	6000.00
☐ Richmond	300.00	500.00	1600.00	6000.00	☐Dallas	300.00	500.00	1600.00	6000.00
☐ Atlanta	300.00	500.00	1600.00	6000.00	☐San Francisco	300.00	500.00	1600.00	6000.00

SERIES OF 1914, DESIGN CONTINUES AS PREVIOUS NOTE, BLUE SEAL AND BLUE SERIAL NUMBERS

This note was issued with various signatures for each bank (Burke-McAdoo, Burke-Glass, Burke-Huston, White-Mellon).

BANK	A.B.P.	V.FINE	UNC.	BANK	A.B.P.	V.FINE	UNC.
☐Boston	175.00	525.00	1550.00	☐ Chicago	205.00	525.00	1550.00
☐New York	175.00	525.00	1550.00	☐ St. Louis	205.00	525.00	1550.00
☐Philadelphia	175.00	525.00	1550.00	☐ Minneapolis	205.00	525.00	1550.00
☐Cleveland	175.00	525.00	1550.00	☐ Kansas City	205.00	525.00	1550.00
☐Richmond	175.00	525.00	1550.00	☐ Dallas	205.00	525.00	1550.00
☐Atlanta	175.00	525.00	1550.00	☐ San Francisco	205.00	525.00	1550.00

ONE HUNDRED DOLLAR NOTES (1928)
FEDERAL RESERVE NOTES

(Small Size)

Face Design: Portrait of Franklin, black Federal Reserve Seal left with number, green Treasury Seal right.

SERIES OF 1928, SIGNATURES OF WOODS-MELLON, GREEN SEAL

BANK	A.B.P.	V.FINE	UNC.	BANK	A.B.P.	V.FINE	UNC.
☐Boston	120.00	215.00	750.00	☐ Chicago	120.00	205.00	1255.00
☐New York	120.00	175.00	750.00	☐ St. Louis	120.00	180.00	1255.00
☐Philadelphia	120.00	175.00	750.00	☐ Minneapolis	120.00	180.00	1800.00
☐Cleveland	120.00	215.00	750.00	☐ Kansas City	120.00	185.00	1255.00
☐Richmond	120.00	215.00	750.00	☐ Dallas	170.00	205.00	2500.00
☐Atlanta	120.00	215.00	750.00	☐ San Francisco	120.00	185.00	1230.00

SERIES OF 1928A, SIGNATURES OF WOODS-MELLON, GREEN SEAL

The number is in black and the Federal Reserve Seal is changed to a letter.

(Small Size)

BANK	A.B.P.	V.FINE	UNC.	BANK	A.B.P.	V.FINE	UNC.
☐Boston	120.00	220.00	600.00	☐ Chicago	120.00	170.00	600.00
☐New York	120.00	190.00	600.00	☐ St. Louis	120.00	170.00	600.00
☐Philadelphia	120.00	220.00	600.00	☐ Minneapolis	120.00	190.00	600.00
☐Cleveland	120.00	185.00	600.00	☐ Kansas City	120.00	210.00	000.00
☐Richmond	120.00	230.00	600.00	☐ Dallas	120.00	170.00	600.00
☐Atlanta	170.00	210.00	600.00	☐ San Francisco	120.00	170.00	600.00

ONE HUNDRED DOLLAR NOTES (1934)
FEDERAL RESERVE NOTES

SERIES OF 1934, SIGNATURES OF JULIAN-MORGENTHAU, GREEN SEAL

BANK	A.B.P.	V.FINE	UNC.	BANK	A.B.P.	V.FINE	UNC.
☐ Boston	115.00	140.00	300.00	☐ Chicago	115.00	140.00	300.00
☐ New York	115.00	140.00	300.00	☐ St. Louis	115.00	140.00	300.00

☐ Philadelphia	115.00	140.00	300.00	☐ Minneapolis	115.00	140.00	300.00
☐ Cleveland	115.00	140.00	300.00	☐ Kansas City	115.00	140.00	300.00
☐ Richmond	115.00	140.00	300.00	☐ Dallas	115.00	140.00	300.00
☐ Atlanta	115.00	140.00	300.00	☐ San Francisco	115.00	140.00	300.00

SERIES OF 1934A, SIGNATURES OF JULIAN-MORGENTHAU, GREEN SEAL

BANK	A.B.P.	V.FINE	UNC.	BANK	A.B.P.	V.FINE	UNC.
☐ Boston	110.00	130.00	400.00	☐ Chicago	120.00	130.00	400.00
☐ New York	110.00	130.00	400.00	☐ St. Louis	120.00	130.00	400.00
☐ Philadelphia	110.00	130.00	400.00	☐ Minneapolis	120.00	130.00	400.00
☐ Cleveland	110.00	130.00	400.00	☐ Kansas City	120.00	130.00	400.00
☐ Richmond	110.00	130.00	400.00	☐ Dallas	120.00	130.00	400.00
☐ Atlanta	110.00	130.00	400.00	☐ San Francisco	120.00	130.00	400.00

SERIES OF 1934B, SIGNATURES OF JULIAN-VINSON, GREEN SEAL

BANK	A.B.P.	V.FINE	UNC.	BANK	A.B.P.	V.FINE	UNC.
☐ Boston	120.00	185.00	500.00	☐ Chicago	125.00	200.00	500.00
☐ New York	120.00	185.00	500.00	☐ St. Louis	125.00	200.00	500.00
☐ Philadelphia	125.00	200.00	500.00	☐ Minneapolis	125.00	200.00	500.00
☐ Cleveland	125.00	200.00	500.00	☐ Kansas City	120.00	185.00	500.00
☐ Richmond	125.00	200.00	500.00	☐ Dallas	120.00	185.00	500.00
☐ Atlanta	125.00	200.00	500.00	☐ San Francisco	120.00	185.00	500.00

SERIES OF 1934C, SIGNATURES OF JULIAN-SNYDER, GREEN SEAL

BANK	A.B.P.	V.FINE	UNC.	BANK	A.B.P.	V.FINE	UNC.
☐ Boston	120.00	185.00	500.00	☐ Chicago	120.00	220.00	500.00
☐ New York	120.00	185.00	500.00	☐ St. Louis	120.00	200.00	500.00
☐ Philadelphia	120.00	185.00	500.00	☐ Minneapolis	120.00	200.00	500.00
☐ Cleveland	120.00	200.00	500.00	☐ Kansas City	120.00	200.00	500.00
☐ Richmond	120.00	200.00	500.00	☐ Dallas	120.00	200.00	500.00
☐ Atlanta	120.00	200.00	500.00	☐ San Francisco	120.00	200.00	500.00

SERIES OF 1934D, SIGNATURES OF JULIAN-SNYDER, GREEN SEAL

BANK	A.B.P.	V.FINE	UNC.	BANK	A.B.P.	V.FINE	UNC.
☐ New York	110.00	5000.00	8000.00	☐ St. Louis	110.00	250.00	900.00
☐ Philadelphia	110.00	300.00	1000.00	☐ Dallas	110.00	300.00	1000.00
☐ Atlanta	110.00	300.00	1000.00				
☐ Chicago	110.00	300.00	1000.00				

ONE HUNDRED DOLLAR NOTES (1950)

FEDERAL RESERVE NOTES

SERIES OF 1950, SIGNATURES OF CLARK-SNYDER, GREEN SEAL

BANK	A.B.P.	V.FINE	UNC.	UNC.★	BANK	A.B.P.	V.FINE	UNC.	UNC.★
☐ Boston	110.00	130.00	500.00	1500.00	☐ Chicago	110.00	130.00	500.00	1500.00
☐ New York	110.00	130.00	500.00	1500.00	☐ St. Louis	110.00	130.00	500.00	1500.00
☐ Philadelphia	105.00	115.00	500.00	1500.00	☐ Minneapolis	105.00	115.00	500.00	1500.00
☐ Cleveland	110.00	130.00	500.00	1500.00	☐ Kansas City	110.00	130.00	500.00	1500.00
☐ Richmond	110.00	130.00	500.00	1500.00	☐ Dallas	110.00	130.00	500.00	1500.00
☐ Atlanta	110.00	130.00	500.00	1500.00	☐ San Francisco	105.00	115.00	500.00	1500.00

SERIES OF 1950A, SIGNATURES OF PRIEST-HUMPHERY, GREEN SEAL

BANK	A.B.P.	V.FINE	UNC.	UNC.★	BANK	A.B.P.	V.FINE	UNC.	UNC.★
☐ Boston	105.00	130.00	300.00	750.00	☐ Chicago	105.00	130.00	300.00	750.00
☐ New York	105.00	130.00	300.00	750.00	☐ St. Louis	105.00	120.00	300.00	750.00
☐ Philadelphia	105.00	120.00	300.00	750.00	☐ Minneapolis	105.00	130.00	300.00	750.00
☐ Cleveland	105.00	120.00	300.00	750.00	☐ Kansas City	105.00	130.00	300.00	750.00
☐ Richmond	105.00	120.00	300.00	750.00	☐ Dallas	105.00	120.00	300.00	750.00
☐ Atlanta	105.00	130.00	300.00	750.00	☐ San Francisco	105.00	120.00	300.00	750.00

SERIES OF 1950B, SIGNATURES OF PRIEST-ANDERSON, GREEN SEAL

BANK	A.B.P.	V.FINE	UNC.	UNC.★	BANK	A.B.P.	V.FINE	UNC.	UNC.★
☐ Boston	110.00	130.00	245.00	720.00	☐ Chicago	100.00	110.00	245.00	720.00
☐ New York	110.00	130.00	245.00	720.00	☐ St. Louis	100.00	130.00	245.00	720.00
☐ Philadelphia	100.00	110.00	245.00	720.00	☐ Minneapolis	100.00	130.00	245.00	720.00
☐ Cleveland	110.00	130.00	245.00	720.00	☐ Kansas City	100.00	130.00	245.00	720.00
☐ Richmond	110.00	130.00	245.00	720.00	☐ Dallas	100.00	130.00	245.00	720.00
☐ Atlanta	100.00	110.00	245.00	720.00	☐ San Francisco	100.00	130.00	245.00	720.00

SERIES OF 1950C, SIGNATURES OF SMITH-DILLON, GREEN SEAL

BANK	A.B.P.	V.FINE	UNC.	UNC.★	BANK	A.B.P.	V.FINE	UNC.	UNC.★
☐ Boston	105.00	125.00	300.00	650.00	☐ Chicago	105.00	115.00	300.00	650.00
☐ New York	105.00	125.00	300.00	650.00	☐ St. Louis	105.00	125.00	300.00	650.00
☐ Philadelphia	105.00	125.00	300.00	650.00	☐ Minneapolis	105.00	125.00	300.00	650.00
☐ Cleveland	105.00	115.00	300.00	650.00	☐ Kansas City	105.00	125.00	300.00	650.00
☐ Richmond	105.00	115.00	300.00	650.00	☐ Dallas	105.00	125.00	300.00	650.00
☐ Atlanta	105.00	115.00	300.00	650.00	☐ San Francisco	105.00	125.00	300.00	650.00

SERIES OF 1950D, SIGNATURES OF GRANAHAN-DILLON, GREEN SEAL

BANK	A.B.P.	V.FINE	UNC.	UNC.★
☐ Boston	105.00	145.00	285.00	960.00
☐ New York	105.00	145.00	285.00	960.00
☐ Philadelphia	105.00	125.00	260.00	960.00
☐ Cleveland	105.00	125.00	260.00	960.00
☐ Richmond	105.00	125.00	260.00	960.00
☐ Atlanta	105.00	125.00	260.00	960.00
☐ Chicago	105.00	145.00	285.00	915.00
☐ St. Louis	105.00	145.00	285.00	915.00
☐ Minneapolis	105.00	145.00	285.00	915.00
☐ Kansas City	105.00	125.00	260.00	915.00
☐ Dallas	105.00	125.00	260.00	915.00
☐ San Francisco	105.00	125.00	260.00	915.00

SERIES OF 1950E, SIGNATURES OF GRANAHAN-FOWLER, GREEN SEAL

BANK	A.B.P.	V.FINE	UNC.
☐ New York	130.00	225.00	950.00
☐ Chicago	130.00	225.00	1250.00
☐ San Francisco	130.00	225.00	950.00

ONE HUNDRED DOLLAR NOTES (1963)
FEDERAL RESERVE NOTES
SERIES OF 1963, (THERE WERE NOT ANY NOTES PRINTED FOR THIS SERIES.)

SERIES OF 1963A, SIGNATURES OF GRANAHAN-FOWLER, GREEN SEAL

BANK	A.B.P.	V.FINE	UNC.	UNC.★
☐ Boston	105.00	125.00	275.00	675.00
☐ New York	105.00	125.00	275.00	675.00
☐ Philadelphia	102.00	115.00	275.00	675.00
☐ Cleveland	102.00	115.00	275.00	675.00
☐ Richmond	102.00	115.00	275.00	675.00
☐ Atlanta	102.00	115.00	275.00	675.00
☐ Chicago	105.00	125.00	275.00	675.00
☐ St. Louis	105.00	125.00	275.00	675.00
☐ Minneapolis	105.00	125.00	275.00	675.00
☐ Kansas City	105.00	125.00	275.00	675.00
☐ Dallas	105.00	125.00	275.00	675.00
☐ San Francisco	105.00	125.00	275.00	675.00

ONE HUNDRED DOLLAR NOTES (1969)
FEDERAL RESERVE NOTES
SERIES OF 1969, SIGNATURES OF ELSTON-KENNEDY, GREEN SEAL

BANK	A.B.P.	V.FINE	UNC.	UNC.★
☐ Boston	102.00	110.00	225.00	400.00
☐ New York	102.00	110.00	225.00	400.00
☐ Philadelphia	102.00	110.00	225.00	400.00
☐ Cleveland	102.00	110.00	225.00	400.00
☐ Richmond	102.00	110.00	225.00	400.00
☐ Atlanta	102.00	110.00	225.00	400.00
☐ Chicago	102.00	110.00	225.00	400.00
☐ St. Louis	102.00	110.00	225.00	400.00
☐ Minneapolis	102.00	110.00	225.00	400.00
☐ Kansas City	102.00	110.00	225.00	400.00
☐ Dallas	102.00	110.00	225.00	400.00
☐ San Francisco	102.00	110.00	225.00	400.00

SERIES OF 1969A, SIGNATURES OF KABIS-CONNALLY, GREEN SEAL

BANK	A.B.P.	V.FINE	UNC.	UNC.★	BANK	A.B.P.	V.FINE	UNC.	UNC.★
☐ Boston	—	110.00	225.00	375.00	☐ Chicago	—	110.00	225.00	375.00
☐ New York	—	110.00	225.00	375.00	☐ St. Louis	—	110.00	225.00	375.00
☐ Philadelphia	—	110.00	225.00	375.00	☐ Minneapolis	—	110.00	225.00	375.00
☐ Cleveland	—	110.00	225.00	375.00	☐ Kansas City	—	110.00	225.00	375.00
☐ Richmond	—	110.00	225.00	375.00	☐ Dallas	—	110.00	225.00	375.00
☐ Atlanta	—	110.00	225.00	375.00	☐ San Francisco	—	110.00	225.00	375.00

SERIES OF 1969B, (THERE WERE NOT ANY NOTES PRINTED FOR THIS SERIES.)

SERIES OF 1969C, SIGNATURES OF BANUELOS-SHULTZ, GREEN SEAL

BANK	A.B.P.	V.FINE	UNC.	UNC.★	BANK	A.B.P.	V.FINE	UNC.	UNC.★
☐ Boston	—	110.00	225.00	400.00	☐ Chicago	—	110.00	225.00	400.00
☐ New York	—	110.00	225.00	400.00	☐ St. Louis	—	110.00	225.00	400.00
☐ Philadelphia	—	110.00	225.00	400.00	☐ Minneapolis	—	110.00	225.00	400.00
☐ Cleveland	—	110.00	225.00	400.00	☐ Kansas City	—	110.00	225.00	400.00
☐ Richmond	—	110.00	225.00	400.00	☐ Dallas	—	110.00	225.00	400.00
☐ Atlanta	—	110.00	225.00	400.00	☐ San Francisco	—	110.00	225.00	400.00

ONE HUNDRED DOLLAR NOTES (1974)
FEDERAL RESERVE NOTES

SERIES OF 1974, SIGNATURES OF NEFF-SIMON, GREEN SEAL

BANK	A.B.P.	V.FINE	UNC.	UNC.★	BANK	A.B.P.	V.FINE	UNC.	UNC.★
☐ Boston	—	110.00	245.00	350.00	☐ Chicago	—	110.00	200.00	350.00
☐ New York	—	110.00	245.00	350.00	☐ St. Louis	—	110.00	200.00	350.00
☐ Philadelphia	—	110.00	245.00	350.00	☐ Minneapolis	—	110.00	200.00	350.00
☐ Cleveland	—	110.00	245.00	350.00	☐ Kansas City	—	110.00	200.00	350.00
☐ Richmond	—	110.00	245.00	350.00	☐ Dallas	—	110.00	200.00	350.00
☐ Atlanta	—	110.00	245.00	350.00	☐ San Francisco	—	110.00	200.00	350.00

ONE HUNDRED DOLLAR NOTES (1977)
FEDERAL RESERVE NOTES

SERIES OF 1977, SIGNATURES OF MORTON-BLUMENTHAL, GREEN SEAL

BANK	A.B.P.	V.FINE	UNC.	UNC.★	BANK	A.B.P.	V.FINE	UNC.	UNC.★
☐ Boston	—	110.00	200.00	325.00	☐ Chicago	—	110.00	200.00	325.00
☐ New York	—	110.00	200.00	325.00	☐ St. Louis	—	110.00	200.00	325.00
☐ Philadelphia	—	110.00	200.00	325.00	☐ Minneapolis	—	110.00	200.00	325.00
☐ Cleveland	—	110.00	200.00	325.00	☐ Kansas City	—	110.00	200.00	325.00
☐ Richmond	—	110.00	200.00	325.00	☐ Dallas	—	110.00	200.00	325.00
☐ Atlanta	—	110.00	200.00	325.00	☐ San Francisco	—	110.00	200.00	325.00

ONE HUNDRED DOLLAR NOTES (1981)
FEDERAL RESERVE NOTES
SERIES OF 1981, SIGNATURES OF BUCHANAN-REGAN, GREEN SEAL

BANK	A.B.P.	V.FINE	UNC.	BANK	A.B.P.	V.FINE	UNC.
☐ Boston	—	110.00	275.00	☐ Chicago	—	110.00	275.00
☐ New York	—	110.00	275.00	☐ St. Louis	—	110.00	275.00
☐ Philadelphia	—	110.00	275.00	☐ Minneapolis	—	110.00	275.00
☐ Cleveland	—	110.00	275.00	☐ Kansas City	—	110.00	275.00
☐ Richmond	—	110.00	275.00	☐ Dallas	—	110.00	275.00
☐ Atlanta	—	110.00	275.00	☐ San Francisco	—	110.00	275.00

SERIES OF 1981A, SIGNATURES OF ORTEGA-REGAN, GREEN SEAL

BANK	A.B.P.	V.FINE	UNC.	BANK	A.B.P.	V.FINE	UNC.
☐ Boston	—	110.00	250.00	☐ Chicago	—	110.00	250.00
☐ New York	—	110.00	250.00	☐ St. Louis	—	110.00	250.00
☐ Philadelphia	—	110.00	250.00	☐ Minneapolis	—	110.00	250.00
☐ Cleveland	—	110.00	250.00	☐ Kansas City	—	110.00	250.00
☐ Richmond	—	110.00	250.00	☐ Dallas	—	110.00	250.00
☐ Atlanta	—	110.00	250.00	☐ San Francisco	—	110.00	250.00

ONE HUNDRED DOLLAR NOTES (1985)
FEDERAL RESERVE NOTES
SERIES OF 1985, SIGNATURES OF ORTEGA-REGAN, GREEN SEAL

BANK	A.B.P.	V.FINE	UNC.	BANK	A.B.P.	V.FINE	UNC.
☐ Boston	—	110.00	190.00	☐ Chicago	—	110.00	190.00
☐ New York	—	110.00	190.00	☐ St. Louis	—	110.00	190.00
☐ Philadelphia	—	110.00	190.00	☐ Minneapolis	—	110.00	190.00
☐ Cleveland	—	110.00	190.00	☐ Kansas City	—	110.00	190.00
☐ Richmond	—	110.00	190.00	☐ Dallas	—	110.00	190.00
☐ Atlanta	—	110.00	190.00	☐ San Francisco	—	110.00	190.00

ONE HUNDRED DOLLAR NOTES (1988)
FEDERAL RESERVE NOTES
SERIES OF 1988, SIGNATURES OF ORTEGA-BRADY, GREEN SEAL

BANK	A.B.P.	V.FINE	UNC.	BANK	A.B.P.	V.FINE	UNC.
☐ Boston	—	110.00	180.00	☐ Chicago	—	110.00	180.00
☐ New York	—	110.00	180.00	☐ St. Louis	—	110.00	180.00
☐ Philadelphia	—	110.00	180.00	☐ Minneapolis	—	110.00	180.00
☐ Cleveland	—	110.00	180.00	☐ Kansas City	—	110.00	180.00
☐ Richmond	—	110.00	180.00	☐ Dallas	—	110.00	180.00
☐ Atlanta	—	110.00	180.00	☐ San Francisco	—	110.00	180.00

ONE HUNDRED DOLLAR NOTES (1990)
FEDERAL RESERVE NOTES
SERIES OF 1990, SIGNATURES OF VILLALPANDO-BRADY, GREEN SEAL

BANK	A.B.P.	V.FINE	UNC.	BANK	A.B.P.	V.FINE	UNC.
☐ Boston	—	—	150.00	☐ Chicago	—	—	150.00
☐ New York	—	—	150.00	☐ St. Louis	—	—	150.00
☐ Philadelphia	—	—	150.00	☐ Minneapolis	—	—	150.00
☐ Cleveland	—	—	150.00	☐ Kansas City	—	—	150.00
☐ Richmond	—	—	150.00	☐ Dallas	—	—	150.00
☐ Atlanta	—	—	150.00	☐ San Francisco	—	—	150.00

ONE HUNDRED DOLLAR NOTES (1993)
FEDERAL RESERVE NOTES
SERIES OF 1993, SIGNATURES OF WITHROW-BENTSEN, GREEN SEAL

BANK	A.B.P.	V.FINE	UNC.	BANK	A.B.P.	V.FINE	UNC.
☐ Boston	—	—	145.00	☐ Chicago	—	—	145.00
☐ New York	—	—	145.00	☐ St. Louis	—	—	145.00
☐ Philadelphia	—	—	145.00	☐ Minneapolis	—	—	145.00
☐ Cleveland	—	—	145.00	☐ Kansas City	—	—	145.00
☐ Richmond	—	—	145.00	☐ Dallas	—	—	145.00
☐ Atlanta	—	—	145.00	☐ San Francisco	—	—	145.00

ONE HUNDRED DOLLAR NOTES (1996)
FEDERAL RESERVE NOTES
SERIES OF 1996, SIGNATURES OF WITHROW-RUBIN, GREEN SEAL

BANK	A.B.P.	V.FINE	UNC.	BANK	A.B.P.	V.FINE	UNC.
☐ Boston	—	—	130.00	☐ Chicago	—	—	130.00
☐ New York	—	—	130.00	☐ St. Louis	—	—	130.00
☐ Philadelphia	—	—	130.00	☐ Minneapolis	—	—	130.00
☐ Cleveland	—	—	130.00	☐ Kansas City	—	—	130.00
☐ Richmond	—	—	130.00	☐ Dallas	—	—	130.00
☐ Atlanta	—	—	130.00	☐ San Francisco	—	—	130.00

ONE HUNDRED DOLLAR NOTES (1929)
FEDERAL RESERVE BANK NOTES
(ISSUED ONLY IN SERIES OF 1929)

(Small Size)

Face Design: Portrait of Franklin, brown seal and numbers.

Back Design

BANK & CITY	SIGNATURES	SEAL	A.B.P.	V.FINE	UNC.
☐New York	Jones-Woods	Brown	110.00	160.00	450.00
☐Cleveland	Jones-Woods	Brown	110.00	160.00	450.00
☐Richmond	Jones-Woods	Brown	110.00	170.00	800.00
☐Chicago	Jones-Woods	Brown	110.00	160.00	450.00
☐Minneapolis	Jones-Woods	Brown	110.00	175.00	550.00
☐Kansas City	Jones-Woods	Brown	110.00	135.00	575.00
☐Dallas	Jones-Woods	Brown	110.00	200.00	2000.00

FIVE HUNDRED, ONE THOUSAND, FIVE THOUSAND, AND TEN THOUSAND DOLLAR NOTES

(Production of notes in denominations above one hundred dollars was discontinued in 1969.)

FEDERAL RESERVE
FIVE HUNDRED DOLLAR NOTES

	A.B.P.	V.FINE	UNC.	BANK
□ 1928	700.00	875.00	2000.00	ALL BANKS
□ 1934	675.00	825.00	1500.00	ALL BANKS
□ 1934A	675.00	825.00	1500.00	ALL BANKS EXCEPT BOSTON/ATLANTA
□ 1934B	—	RARE	RARE	ATLANTA ONLY
□ 1934C	—	RARE	RARE	BOSTON ONLY
Gold Certs.				
□ 1928	1000.00	4500.00	20,000.00	

ONE THOUSAND DOLLAR NOTES

	A.B.P.	V.FINE	UNC.
□ 1928	1200.00	1600.00	3800.00
□ 1934	1200.00	1500.00	2400.00
□ 1934A	1200.00	1500.00	2400.00
Gold:			
□ 1928	1300.00	6000.00	30,000.00
□ 1934	RARE	RARE	RARE

FIVE THOUSAND DOLLAR NOTES

	A.B.P.	V.FINE	UNC.	BANK
□ 1928	10,000.00	30,000.00	60,000.00	
□ 1934	8000.00	28,000.00	40,000.00	
□ 1934A	—	RARE	RARE	ST. LOUIS ONLY
□ 1934B	—	RARE	RARE	NEW YORK
□ Gold Certs.			VERY RARE	

TEN THOUSAND DOLLAR NOTES

	A.B.P.	V.FINE	UNC.	BANK
□ 1928	20,000.00	45,000.00	120,000.00	
□ 1934	15,000.00	37,500.00	60,000.00	
□ 1934A	—	RARE	RARE	CHICAGO ONLY
□ Gold Certs.			VERY RARE	

SPECIAL REPORT: UNCUT SHEETS

As very few notes exist in the form of full uncut sheets, this is a limited area for the collector. Also, the prices are high, well out of range for most hobbyists.

Uncut sheets available on the market are of Small Size Notes exclusively. In most instances it is not known precisely how they reached public hands. Some were undoubtedly presented as souvenir gifts to Treasury Department officials. In any event, uncut sheets have never been illegal to own, since the notes they comprise are precisely the same as those released into general circulation.

The sheets differ in the number of notes, from a low of six in National Currency sheets to a high of eighteen for some sheets of United States (Legal Tender) Notes and Silver Certificates. Others have twelve notes. These differences are due entirely to the printing method being used at their time of manufacture. Any given note was always printed in sheets of the same size, with the same number of specimens per sheet. If you have an uncut sheet with twelve notes, it means that all notes from the series were printed twelve to a sheet.

The condition standards for uncut sheets are the same as those for single notes. Obviously, an uncut sheet did not circulate as money, but some specimens became worn or damaged as a result of careless storage, accident, or other causes. These impaired sheets do turn up in the market, but there is not much demand for them. Almost every buyer of uncut sheets wants Uncirculated condition. Quite often an uncut sheet will be framed when you buy it. This should be considered a plus, as the frame has probably kept the sheet in immaculate condition. Just to be entirely safe, however, it is wise to examine the reverse side of the sheet for possible staining or other problems.

The following prices were current for uncut sheets in Uncirculated grade at publication time. Gem Uncirculated sheets in absolutely pristine condition command higher prices than those shown.

SILVER CERTIFICATES

DENOMINATION	SERIES	NO. OF NOTES PER SHEET	CURRENT PRICE RANGE IN UNC. CONDITION
$1	1928	12	1950.00–2800.00
$1	1934	12	2400.00–3000.00
$5	1934	12	1400.00–2000.00
$10	1934	12	3900.00–5000.00
$1	1935	12	700.00–1000.00
$5	1953	18	1200.00–1600.00
$10	1953	18	3900.00–4800.00

UNITED STATES NOTES (LEGAL TENDER NOTES)

DENOMINATION	SERIES	NO. OF NOTES PER SHEET	CURRENT PRICE RANGE IN UNC. CONDITION
$1	1928	12	9000.00–10,500.00
$2	1928	12	900.00–1150.00
$5	1928	12	1450.00–2250.00
$2	1953	18	800.00–1200.00
$5	1953	18	1500.00–2100.00

NATIONAL CURRENCY

DENOMINATION	SERIES	NO. OF NOTES PER SHEET	CURRENT PRICE RANGE IN UNC. CONDITION
$5	1929	6	750.00–2500.00
$10	1929	6	775.00–2600.00
$20	1929	6	825.00–3000.00
$50	1929	6	4000.00–8000.00
$100	1929	6	5000.00–10,000.00
EMERGENCY NOTES:			
Hawaii $1	1935A		4500.00–7000.00
No. Africa $1	1935A		5000.00–9000.00

MULES (MIXED PLATE NUMBERS)

All U.S. currency has plate numbers on the face and back. These plate numbers are in the lower right corner somewhat close to the fine scroll design. They refer to the number of the engraved plate used to print the sheet of notes. Each plate can be used for about 100,000 impressions. It is then destroyed and a new plate with the next number in sequence is put into use.

During the term of Treasury officials Julian and Morgenthau, the plate numbers were changed from almost a microscopic to a larger size, far easier to read. Due to this improvement the series designation then in use was an advance on United States Notes, Silver Certificates, and Federal Reserve Notes. The signatures remained Julian-Morgenthau. National Currency and Gold Certificates were not affected, as these were discontinued earlier.

During the changeover period in printing, plates were sometimes mixed up, producing a note with a large number on one side and a small number on the other side. Notes of this variety are called "mules," or "mule notes." This is from a term applied to coins struck with the obverse or reverse die of one year and the opposite side from a die of another year.

Many collectors are eager to add one or more of these mule notes to their collection. Some of the most common mule notes are:

$2 UNITED STATES NOTES
1928-C, 1928-D

$5 UNITED STATES NOTES
1928-B, 1928-C, 1928-D, 1928-E

$1 SILVER CERTIFICATES
1935, 1935-A

$5 SILVER CERTIFICATES
1934, 1934-A, 1934-B, 1934-C

$10 SILVER CERTIFICATES
1934, 1934A

Mules were also issued in the Federal Reserve Note Series. However, these are not as popular with collectors as the United States Notes and Silver Certificates because of the higher denominations and the twelve districts involved.

The schedule below shows some of the most common mule notes and their values in new condition. The combination of the prefix and suffix letters of the serial numbers on notes is known as "Blocks." For instance: A—A Block, B—A Block.

			UNC.
$2 UNITED STATES NOTE	1928-D	B—A	600.00
		C—A	100.00
		*—A	125.00
$5 UNITED STATES NOTE	1928-B	E—A	150.00
		*—A	575.00
	1928-C	E—A	130.00
		*—A	150.00
$1 SILVER CERTIFICATE	1935	N—A	
		Thru	200.00
		P—A	
	1935-A	M—A	
		Thru	100.00
		V—A	
		C—B	100.00
$5 SILVER CERTIFICATE	1934-A	D—A	
		Thru	100.00
		G—A	
		*—A	200.00
$10 SILVER CERTIFICATE	1934	A—A	110.00
		*—A	150.00
	1934-A	A—A	250.00

Front **SIZES DIFFERENT** **Back**

INTRODUCTION TO UNITED STATES FRACTIONAL CURRENCY

Events following the outbreak of the Civil War resulted in a shortage of circulating coinage. Trade was hampered as many merchants, especially in large cities, were unable to make change and only customers presenting the exact amount for a purchase could buy—but they were generally as short on coins as the shop proprietors. Various attempts were made to solve this problem by issuing credit slips (which most customers didn't care for), tokens (which they also didn't care for), and using postage stamps as money. Finally, in 1862, the government stepped in, recognizing that the economy was being seriously hurt, and issued a series of small paper notes as equivalents of coinage denominations. They carried designs adapted from the current postage stamps of the day and were known as Postage Currency or Postal Currency. The more popular title is now Fractional Currency. There were five separate issues of Fractional Currency, three of which occurred during the Civil War and two thereafter, the final one as late as 1874. That a need existed for coin substitutes as late as the 1870s demonstrates the drain placed upon coinage during the war and the long period of recovery. A total of six denominations were issued, from 3¢ to 50¢, comprising 23 designs and more than 100 varieties. Because of its small size and lack of visual impact, Fractional Currency was long shunned by collectors. In recent years it has enjoyed an unprecedented surge of popularity, which, if continued, promises to drive prices beyond present levels. All told, more than $360,000,000 worth of Fractional Currency was circulated. It would be extremely plentiful today but for the fact that most notes were redeemed, leaving only about

$2,000,000 outstanding. This is what collectors have to work with, and a good deal of these are badly preserved.

FIRST ISSUE—Postage Currency August 21st, 1862
5-10-25-50
SECOND ISSUE—Fractional Currency October 10th, 1863
5-10-25-50
THIRD ISSUE—Fractional Currency December 5th, 1864
3-5-10-15-25-50
FOURTH ISSUE—Fractional Currency July 14th, 1869
10-15-25-50
FIFTH ISSUE—Fractional Currency February 26th, 1874
10-25-50

THE FRACTIONAL CURRENCY SHIELD

Fractional currency shields were sold by the Treasury Department in 1866. Specimen notes printed only on one side were used. Very Good–condition shields are valued at $3000 to $3500. Choice condition shields in contemporary frames can sell for $4200. Shields with pink, green, or other backgrounds are more valuable.

FRACTIONAL CURRENCY NOTES

The following notes may be collected by issue or by denomination. We list them here by denomination for convenience. Also, since most of these notes were hastily cut from large sheets, the margin size can vary. Specimens are narrow margined while proofs have wide margins. Prices listed are for Nice "well centered" Uncirculated notes.

THREE-CENT NOTES

THIRD ISSUE

Face Design: Portrait of President Washington.

SPECIMEN	FACE	REVERSE
Light Port.	140.00	60.00
Dark Port.	90.00	60.00
PROOF		
Light Port	6000.00	225.00
Dark Port	260.00	225.00

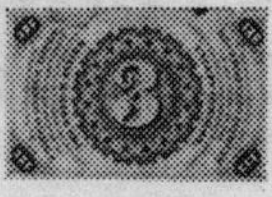

Back Design: Large "3" green.

REGULAR ISSUES	A.B.P.	GOOD	V.FINE	UNC.
☐ With Light Portrait	13.00	20.00	34.00	180.00
☐ With Dark Portrait	14.00	20.00	40.00	300.00

FIVE-CENT NOTES

FIRST ISSUE					
SPECIMEN	FACE	85.00	REVERSE	55.00
PROOF	FACE	290.00	REVERSE	245.00

Face Design: Portrait of President Jefferson, brown.

Back Design: "5" black.

REGULAR ISSUES	A.B.P.	GOOD	V.FINE	UNC.
☐Perforated edges, monogram ABNCO on back	8.00	12.00	28.00	300.00
☐Perforated edges, without monogram on back	8.00	11.00	46.00	410.00
☐Straight edges, monogram ABNCO on back	6.00	10.00	21.00	145.00
☐Straight edges, without monogram on back	8.00	11.00	25.00	250.00

FIVE-CENT NOTES

SECOND ISSUE	**SPECIMEN**	**FACE**	90.00	**REVERSE**	60.00
	PROOF	**FACE**	195.00	**REVERSE**	170.00

Face Design: Portrait of President Washington.

Back Design: Shield and brown, "5"s.

REGULAR ISSUES	**A.B.P.**	**GOOD**	**V.FINE**	**UNC.**
☐Value only in bronze on back	8.00	11.00	20.00	135.00
☐Surcharges 18-63 on back	8.00	10.00	20.00	135.00
☐Surcharges S-18-63 on back	11.00	15.00	20.00	140.00
☐Surcharges R-1-18-63 on back, fiber paper	10.00	16.00	55.00	500.00

FIVE-CENT NOTES

THIRD ISSUE	**SPECIMEN**	**FACE**	90.00	**REVERSE**	60.00
	PROOF	**FACE**	250.00	**REVERSE**	175.00

Face Design: Portrait of Spencer M. Clark.

Back Design: Green or red.

REGULAR ISSUES	**A.B.P.**	**GOOD**	**V.FINE**	**UNC.**
☐Without letter "A" on face, red back	8.00	11.00	22.00	250.00
☐With letter "A" on face, red back	8.00	12.00	26.00	265.00
☐Without letter "A" on face, green back	6.00	10.00	18.00	160.00
☐With letter "A" on face, green back	6.00	10.00	19.00	160.00

This note was authorized to have the portraits of the explorers Lewis and Clark on the face. Mr. Spencer M. Clark, who was then head of the Bureau of Currency, flagrantly placed his own portrait on this note. This caused Congress to pass legislation forbidding the likeness of any living person on U.S. currency.

TEN-CENT NOTES

FIRST ISSUE	**SPECIMEN**	**FACE**	80.00	**REVERSE**	60.00
	PROOF	**FACE**	250.00	**REVERSE**	225.00

Face Design: Portrait of President Washington.

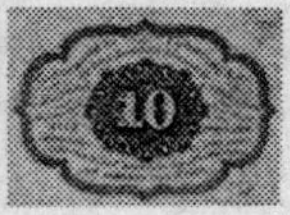

Back Design: "10," black.

REGULAR ISSUES	A.B.P.	GOOD	V.FINE	UNC.
□Perforated edges, monogram ABNCO on back	8.00	9.00	28.00	410.00
□Perforated edges, without monogram on back	8.00	9.00	30.00	425.00
□Plain edges, monogram ABNCO on back	6.00	11.00	17.00	200.00
□Plain edges, without monogram on back	7.00	12.00	38.00	275.00

TEN-CENT NOTES

SECOND ISSUE					
	SPECIMEN	FACE	90.00	REVERSE	60.00
	PROOF	FACE	225.00	REVERSE	185.00

Face Design: Portrait of President Washington.

Back Design: "10," green.

REGULAR ISSUE	A.B.P.	GOOD	V.FINE	UNC.
□Value only surcharge on back	4.00	7.00	19.00	130.00
□Surcharge 18-63 on back	4.00	7.00	19.00	130.00
□Surcharge S-18-63 on back	5.00	8.00	21.00	135.00
□Surcharge I-18-63 on back	9.00	21.00	42.00	275.00
□Surcharge 0-63 on back	140.00	410.00	1100.00	2200.00
□Surcharge T-1-18-63 on back, fiber paper	12.00	20.00	100.00	450.00

TEN-CENT NOTES

THIRD ISSUE					
	SPECIMEN	FACE	105.00	REVERSE	100.00
	PROOF	FACE	230.00	REVERSE	185.00

Face Design: Portrait of President Washington.

Back Design: "10," green or red.

REGULAR ISSUES	A.B.P.	GOOD	V.FINE	UNC.
□Printed signatures Colby-Spinner, green back	6.00	10.00	18.00	130.00
□As above, figure "1" near left margin on face	6.00	11.00	18.00	140.00
□Printed signatures Colby-Spinner, red back	7.00	11.00	22.00	280.00
□As above, figure "1" near left margin, red back	7.00	14.00	32.00	300.00
□Autographed signatures Colby-Spinner, red back	11.00	17.00	27.00	300.00
□Autographed signatures Jeffries-Spinner, red back	11.00	17.00	52.00	310.00

TEN-CENT NOTES

FOURTH ISSUE	**SPECIMEN**	**FACE**	325.00	**REVERSE**	RARE
	PROOF	**FACE**	325.00	**REVERSE**	RARE

Face Design:
Bust of Liberty.

Back Design:
Green with TEN and "10."

REGULAR ISSUES	**A.B.P.**	**GOOD**	**V.FINE**	**UNC.**
☐Large red seal, watermarked paper	7.00	10.00	17.00	115.00
☐Large red seal, pink fibers in paper	7.00	10.00	18.00	115.00
☐Large seal, pink fibers in paper, right end blue	7.00	10.00	21.00	115.00
☐Large brown seal	16.00	30.00	85.00	210.00
☐Small red seal, pink fibers, right end blue	7.00	10.00	27.00	160.00

TEN-CENT NOTES

FIFTH ISSUE	**PROOF**	**FACE**	**RARE**	**REVERSE**	$400.00

Face Design:
William Meredith.

Back Design:
Green.

REGULAR ISSUES

	A.B.P.	**GOOD**	**V.FINE**	**UNC.**
☐Green seal, long narrow key	6.00	8.00	15.00	100.00
☐Red seal, long narrow key	6.00	7.00	12.00	50.00
☐Red seal, short stubby key	6.00	7.00	12.00	50.00

FIFTEEN-CENT NOTES

FACES AND BACKS PRINTED SEPARATELY

THIRD ISSUE ALL ARE SPECIMENS AND UNISSUED.

Face Design:
Sherman and President Grant.

Back Design:
Green or red.

	SPECIMEN UNC.	**PROOF UNC.**
☐ With printed signatures Colby-Spinner	300.00	650.00
☐ With autographed signatures Colby-Spinner	2000.00	7500.00
☐ With autographed signatures Jeffries-Spinner	280.00	550.00
☐ With autographed signatures Allison-Spinner	320.00	550.00
☐ Green back	180.00	250.00
☐ Red back	165.00	250.00

FIFTEEN-CENT NOTES

FOURTH ISSUE **PROOF** **FACE** **RARE** **REVERSE** 475.00

Face Design: Bust of Columbia.

Back Design: Green with "15"s.

REGULAR ISSUES	**A.B.P.**	**GOOD**	**V.FINE**	**UNC.**
☐Large seal, watermarked paper	20.00	31.00	57.00	200.00
☐Large seal, pink fibers in paper	20.00	32.00	62.00	210.00
☐Large seal, pink fibers in paper, right end blue	20.00	32.00	57.00	205.00
☐Large brown seal	26.00	46.00	180.00	RARE
☐Smaller red seal, pink fibers, right end blue	20.00	31.00	60.00	210.00

TWENTY-FIVE-CENT NOTES

FIRST ISSUE	**SPECIMEN**	**FACE**	95.00	**REVERSE**	65.00
	PROOF	**FACE**	275.00	**REVERSE**	220.00

Face Design: Five 5¢ Jefferson Stamps.

Back Design: Black, large "25."

REGULAR ISSUES	**A.B.P.**	**GOOD**	**V.FINE**	**UNC.**
☐Perforated edges, monogram ABNCO on back	9.00	12.00	32.00	425.00
☐Perforated edges, without monogram on back	8.00	13.00	57.00	535.00
☐Straight edges, monogram ABNCO on back	8.00	10.00	20.00	200.00
☐Straight edges, without monogram on back	9.00	15.00	67.00	585.00

TWENTY-FIVE-CENT NOTES

SECOND ISSUE	**SPECIMEN**	**FACE**	95.00	**REVERSE**	75.00
	PROOF	**FACE**	250.00	**REVERSE**	210.00

Time and climatic condition have changed the purple color on the back of this note into many variations.

Face Design: Portrait of President Washington.

Back Design: Purple with "25."

REGULAR ISSUES	A.B.P.	GOOD	V.FINE	UNC.
☐Value only surcharge on back	8.00	12.00	21.00	225.00
☐Surcharge 18-63 on back	8.00	13.00	21.00	250.00
☐Surcharge A-18-63 on back	8.00	12.00	21.00	250.00
☐Surcharge 1-18-63 on back	19.00	37.00	200.00	600.00
☐Surcharge 2-18-63 on back	8.00	12.00	25.00	310.00
☐Surcharge S-18-63 on back	9.00	16.00	25.00	310.00
☐Surcharge T-1-18-63 on back, fiber paper	11.00	21.00	80.00	360.00
☐Surcharge T-2-18-63 on back, fiber paper	11.00	21.00	80.00	350.00

TWENTY-FIVE-CENT NOTES

THIRD ISSUE	**SPECIMEN**	**FACE**	140.00	**REVERSE**	82.00
	PROOF	**FACE**	250.00	**REVERSE**	170.00

All notes have printed signatures of Colby-Spinner.

Face Design: Portrait of Fessenden.

Back Design: Green or red with "25"

	A.B.P.	GOOD	V.FINE	UNC.
☐Face—bust of Fessenden between solid bronze surcharges, fiber paper, back—green, surcharge M-2-6-5 in corners	125.00	200.00	800.00	3200.00
☐As above, with letter "A" in lower left corner of face	150.00	320.00	1000.00	4200.00
☐Face—Fessenden, open scroll bronze surcharges, fiber paper, back—green, surcharges M-2-6-5 in corners	12.00	21.00	90.00	440.00
☐As above with letter "A" in lower left corner of face	10.00	20.00	80.00	450.00
☐Face—Fessenden, open scroll surcharges, plain paper, back—green, value surcharges only	8.00	15.00	32.00	165.00
☐As before, letter "A" in lower left corner of face, back—green, plain paper	10.00	18.00	42.00	170.00
☐Face—Fessenden, red back, value surcharge only	12.00	21.00	46.00	250.00
☐As above, letter "A" in lower left corner of face	12.00	20.00	50.00	295.00

TWENTY-FIVE-CENT NOTES

FOURTH ISSUE SPECIMENS AND PROOFS RARE

Face Design: Portrait of President Washington and Treasury Seal.

Back Design: Green.

REGULAR ISSUES	A.B.P.	GOOD	V.FINE	UNC.
☐Large seal, plain watermarked paper	6.00	9.00	22.00	125.00
☐Large seal, pink silk fiber in paper	6.00	9.00	22.00	125.00
☐Large seal, pink fibers in paper, right end blue	6.00	8.50	24.00	135.00
☐Large brown seal, right end blue	35.00	70.00	282.00	1100.00
☐Smaller red seal, right end blue	6.00	10.00	24.00	125.00

TWENTY-FIVE-CENT NOTES

FIFTH ISSUE SPECIMENS AND PROOFS RARE

Face Design: Portrait of Walker and red seal.

Back Design: Black.

REGULAR ISSUES	A.B.P.	GOOD	V.FINE	UNC.
☐With long narrow key in Treasury Seal.	6.00	9.00	16.00	60.00
☐With short stubby key in Treasury Seal	6.00	9.00	16.00	60.00

FIFTY-CENT NOTES

FIRST ISSUE					
	SPECIMEN	FACE	135.00	REVERSE	100.00
	PROOF	FACE	275.00	REVERSE	220.00

Face Design: Five 10¢ Washington stamps.

Back Design: Green.

REGULAR ISSUES	A.B.P.	GOOD	V.FINE	UNC.
☐Perforated edges, monogram ABNCO on back	15.00	14.00	81.00	650.00
☐Perforated edges, without monogram on back	13.00	20.00	75.00	700.00
☐Straight edges, monogram ABNCO on back	8.00	10.00	30.00	350.00
☐Straight edges, without monogram	11.00	20.00	85.00	400.00

FIFTY-CENT NOTES

FIRST ISSUE	SPECIMEN	FACE	135.00	REVERSE	105.00
	PROOF	FACE	330.00	REVERSE	260.00

Face Design: Portrait of President Washington.

Back Design: Red.

REGULAR ISSUES	A.B.P.	GOOD	V.FINE	UNC.
☐Surcharge 18-63 on back	7.00	11.00	35.00	520.00
☐Surcharge A-18-63 on back	7.00	11.00	20.00	335.00
☐Surcharge O-1-18-63, fiber paper	9.00	25.00	80.00	550.00
☐Surcharge R-2-18-63, fiber paper	11.00	17.00	47.00	455.00
☐Surcharge T-1-18-63, fiber paper	7.00	15.00	47.00	450.00

FIFTY-CENT NOTES

THIRD ISSUE	SPECIMENS	FACE	150.00	REVERSE	110.00
	PROOFS FACE		325.00	REVERSE	275.00

Face Design: Justice with sword, shield, scales.

Back Design: Green or red.

The following notes have printed signatures of Colby-Spinner and have *green backs.*

REGULAR ISSUES	A.B.P.	GOOD	V.FINE	UNC.
☐Value surcharge and S-2-6-4 on back, fiber paper			12,000.00	25,000.00
☐Value surcharge and A-2-6-5 on back, fiber paper	16.00	32.00	90.00	1300.00
☐As above with "1" and letter "A" on face, A-2-6-5 on back	55.00	85.00	750.00	3100.00
☐As above with "1" only on face, A-2-6-5 on back	14.00	32.00	85.00	700.00
☐As above with letter "A" only on face, A-2-6-5 on back	14.00	37.00	85.00	675.00
☐A-2-6-5 on back, *narrowly spaced,* plain paper	10.00	12.00	70.00	500.00

	A.B.P.	GOOD	V.FINE	UNC.
☐As above, numeral "1" and letter "A" on face	10.00	22.00	75.00	525.00
☐As above, numeral "1" only on face	10.00	12.00	65.00	500.00
☐As above, letter "A" only on face	10.00	18.00	75.00	525.00
☐A-2-6-5 on back, *widely spaced,* plain paper	10.00	18.00	72.00	535.00
☐As above, numeral "1" and letter "A" on face	20.00	45.00	300.00	1200.00
☐As above, numeral "1" only on face	9.00	13.00	70.00	650.00
☐As above, letter "A" only on face	9.00	12.00	70.00	650.00
☐Without position letters or back surcharges	9.00	12.00	62.00	500.00
☐As above with numeral "1" and letter "A" on face	15.00	26.00	160.00	1525.00
☐As above with numeral "1" only on face	7.00	12.00	60.00	500.00
☐As above with letter "A" only on face	7.00	12.50	68.00	490.00

The following notes have printed signatures of Colby-Spinner and *red backs.*

	A.B.P.	GOOD	V.FINE	UNC.
☐Value surcharge and S-2-6-4 on back, fiber	150.00	175.00	15,000.00	33,000.00
☐As above, numeral "1" and letter "A"	150.00	350.00	2700.00	50,000.00
☐As above, numeral "1" only on face	125.00	200.00	850.00	30,000.00
☐As above, letter "A" only on face	135.00	225.00	850.00	30,000.00
☐Value surcharge and A-2-6-5 on back, plain	10.00	19.00	78.00	700.00
☐As above, numeral "1" and letter "A"	47.00	77.00	483.00	2130.00
☐As above, numeral "1" only on face	10.00	19.00	82.00	600.00
☐As above, letter "A" only on face	10.00	20.00	82.00	600.00
☐No surcharge on back, plain paper	10.00	20.00	85.00	680.00
☐As above, numeral "1" and letter "A" on face	25.00	50.00	258.00	2130.00
☐As above, numeral "1" only on face	13.00	24.00	145.00	950.00
☐As above, letter "A" only on face	13.00	30.00	110.00	700.00

The following notes have autographed signatures of Colby-Spinner and *red backs.*

	A.B.P.	GOOD	V.FINE	UNC.
☐Value surcharge and S-2-6-4 on back, fiber	37.00	90.00	200.00	1400.00
☐Value surcharge and A-2-6-5 on back, fiber	35.00	75.00	180.00	1100.00
☐Value surcharge only on back, plain paper	16.00	30.00	80.00	800.00

FIFTY-CENT NOTES

THIRD ISSUE	SPECIMEN	FACE	130.00	REVERSE	120.00
	PROOF	FACE	400.00	REVERSE	280.00

Face Design: Bust of Spinner with surcharges.
Back Design: Green or red.

The following notes have printed signatures of Colby-Spinner, and *green backs.*

REGULAR ISSUES	A.B.P.	GOOD	V.FINE	UNC.
☐Value surcharge and A-2-6-5 on back	9.00	27.00	100.00	350.00
☐As above, numeral "1" and letter "A" on face	22.00	41.00	225.00	710.00
☐As above, numeral "1" only on face	9.00	19.00	60.00	360.00
☐As above, letter "A" only on face	9.00	18.00	100.00	500.00
☐Value surcharge only on back	9.00	12.00	50.00	400.00
☐As above, numeral "1" and letter "A" on face	12.00	28.00	60.00	400.00
☐As above, numeral "1" only on face	9.00	14.00	50.00	400.00
☐As above, letter "A" only on face	9.00	14.00	50.00	450.00
TYPE II BACK DESIGN				
☐No back surcharge	9.00	18.00	55.00	375.00
☐Numeral "1" and letter "A" on face	20.00	37.00	90.00	450.00
☐Numeral "1" only on face	9.00	17.00	57.00	375.00
☐Letter "A" only on face	9.00	22.00	75.00	450.00

The following notes have a portrait of Spinner, printed signatures of Colby-Spinner, *red backs*, and are Type I.

REGULAR ISSUES	A.B.P.	GOOD	V.FINE	UNC.
☐Value surcharge and A-2-6-5 on back	10.00	45.00	60.00	350.00
☐As above with numeral "1" and letter "A"	20.00	45.00	145.00	800.00
☐As above with numeral "1" only on face	10.00	17.00	60.00	425.00
☐As above with letter "A" only on face	10.00	25.00	75.00	510.00

The following notes have autographed signatures, *red backs,* and are Type I.

	A.B.P.	GOOD	V.FINE	UNC.
☐Autographed signatures COLBY-SPINNER, back surcharged value and A-2-6-5	12.00	28.00	80.00	525.00
☐Autographed signatures ALLISON-SPINNER, back surcharged value and A-2-6-5	12.00	28.00	100.00	560.00
☐Autographed signatures ALLISON-NEW, back surcharged value and A-2-6-5	400.00	650.00	1600.00	5500.00

FIFTY-CENT NOTES

FOURTH ISSUE SPECIMENS AND PROOFS RARE

Face Design: Bust of Lincoln.

Back Design: Green.

	A.B.P.	GOOD	V.FINE	UNC.
☐Plain paper	16.00	23.00	65.00	525.00
☐Paper with pink fibers	16.00	23.00	70.00	550.00

FIFTY-CENT NOTES

FOURTH ISSUE SPECIMENS AND PROOFS RARE

Face Design: Bust of Stanton.

Back Design: Green with "50."

	A.B.P.	GOOD	V.FINE	UNC.
☐Red seal and signatures ALLISON-SPINNER, paper with pink fibers, blue ends	9.00	15.00	42.00	275.00

FIFTY-CENT NOTES

FOURTH ISSUE SPECIMENS AND PROOFS RARE

Face Design: Bust of Samuel Dexter.

Back Design: Green with "50."

	A.B.P.	GOOD	V.FINE	UNC.
☐Green seal, pink fibers, blue ends	8.00	12.00	23.00	190.00

FIFTY-CENT NOTES

FIFTH ISSUE SPECIMENS AND PROOFS RARE

Face Design: Bust of Crawford.

Back Design: Green with "50."

	A.B.P.	GOOD	V.FINE	UNC.
☐Signatures ALLISON-NEW, paper with pink fibers, blue ends	6.00	10.00	19.00	90.00

FIFTY-CENT NOTES

FIFTH ISSUE SPECIMENS AND PROOFS RARE

Face Design: Bust of Seward.

Back Design: Red & Brown with "$50–4%"

A.B.P.	GOOD	V.FINE	UNC.
75.00	100.00	700.00	1500.00

ERROR OR FREAK NOTES

Notes have been misprinted from time to time since the earliest days of currency. The frequency of misprintings and other abnormalities has increased in recent years due to heavier production and high-speed machinery. This has provided a major sub-hobby for note collectors. Freaks and errors have become very popular, their appeal and prices showing upward movement each year.

On the following pages we have pictured and described most of the more familiar and collectible Error Notes. Pricing is approximate only because many notes bearing the same general type of error differ in severity of error from one specimen to another. As a general rule, the less glaring or obvious errors carry a smaller premium value. Very valuable Error Notes include double denominations, or bills having the face of one denomination and reverse side of another.

Error and Freak Notes do turn up in everyday change. Specimens are located either in that fashion or from bank packs. As far as circulated specimens are concerned, some Error Notes have passed through so many hands before being noticed that the condition is not up to collector standards. This, of course, results in a very low premium valuation.

Values given below are for the specimens pictured and described. Different premiums may be attached to other specimens with similar errors, or notes showing the same errors but of different denominations.

MISMATCHED SERIAL NUMBERS

On ordinary notes, the serial number in the lower left of the obverse matches that in the upper right. When it fails to, even by the difference of a single digit, this is known as a "mismatched serial number." It occurs as the result of a cylinder or cylinders in the high-speed numbering machine becoming jammed. If more than one digit is mismatched, the value will be greater.

	V. FINE	UNC.
□$1 Federal Reserve Note, Series 1969, signatures Elston-Kennedy	120.00	275.00

	V. FINE	UNC.
□$1 Silver Certificate, Series 1957B, signatures Granahan-Dillon	120.00	230.00

	V. FINE	UNC.
□$1 Federal Reserve Note, Series 1977A, signatures Morton-Miller	120.00	225.00

INVERTED THIRD PRINT

The inverted third print is also known as "inverted overprint." The Treasury Seal, District Seal, Serial Numbers, and District Number are inverted on the obverse side of the note, or printed upside-down, caused by the sheet of notes (having already received the primary design on front and back) being fed upside-down into the press for this so-called "third print." (The back design is the "first print," the front is the "second print," and these various additions comprise the "third print." It is not possible to print these third print items at the same time as the obverse design, since they are not standard on every bill. At one time the signatures were included in the third print, but these are now engraved directly into the plate and are part of the second print.)

Though very spectacular, inverted third print errors are not particularly scarce and are especially plentiful in 1974 and 1976 series notes.

	V. FINE	UNC.
☐$5 Federal Reserve Note, Series 1974, signatures Neff-Simon	140.00	250.00

	V. FINE	UNC.
☐$2 Federal Reserve Note, Series 1976, signatures Neff-Simon	425.00	675.00

	V. FINE	UNC.
□$1 Federal Reserve Note, Series 1974, signatures Neff-Simon	165.00	350.00

	V. FINE	UNC.
□$50 Federal Reserve Note, Series 1977, signatures Morton-Blumenthal	425.00	600.00

	V. FINE	UNC.
□$20 Federal Reserve Note, Series 1974, signatures Neff-Simon	220.00	450.00

	V. FINE	UNC.
□$10 Federal Reserve Note, Series 1974, signatures Neff-Simon	200.00	380.00

COMPLETE OFFSET TRANSFER

Offset transfers are not, as is often believed, caused by still-wet printed sheets coming into contact under pressure. Though very slight offsetting can occur in that manner, it would not create notes as spectacular as those pictured here, in which the offset impression is almost as strong as the primary printing. These happen as a result of the printing press being started an instant or so before the paper is fed in. Instead of contacting the paper, the inked plate makes its impression upon the machine bed. When the paper is then fed through, it picks up this "ghost" impression from the bed, in addition to the primary impression it is supposed to receive. Each successive sheet going through the press will acquire the impression until all ink is totally removed from the machine bed. But, naturally, the first sheet will show the transfer strongest, and the others will be weaker and weaker. Obviously, the market value of such notes depends largely on the strength of the offset impression. The heavier and more noticeable it is, the more valuable the note will be—all other things being equal.

	V. FINE	UNC.
□$5 Federal Reserve Note, Series 1977, signatures Morton-Blumenthal, offset of reverse side of face		
Dark	125.00	310.00
Light	115.00	175.00

	V. FINE	UNC.
☐$1 Federal Reserve note, Series 1974, signatures Neff-Simon, offset of reverse side of face.		
Dark	100.00	350.00
Light	100.00	175.00

PARTIAL OFFSET TRANSFER

The most logical explanation for this error is that a sheet of paper fed into the press incorrectly became mangled or torn, and part of the inked plate contacted the printing press bed. Therefore, wet ink was left on those portions of the press bed not covered by paper. When the next sheet was fed through, it received the correct impression, plus it acquired a partial offset transfer by contacting this wet area of the press bed. Just as with offset transfers, the first sheet going through the press following an accident of this kind will receive the strongest transfer, and it will become gradually less noticeable on succeeding sheets.

	V. FINE	UNC.
☐$1 Federal Reserve Note, Series 1969D, signatures Banuelos-Schultz, offset of a portion of reverse side on face		
Dark	45.00	125.00
Light	40.00	120.00

PRINTED FOLD

Notes showing printed folds occur as the result of folds in the paper before printing, which probably happen most often when the sheet is being fed into the press. If the sheet is folded in such a manner that a portion of the reverse side is facing upward, as shown here, it will receive a part of the impression intended for its obverse. Naturally the positioning of these misplaced portions of printing is very random, depending on the nature and size of the fold.

	V. FINE	UNC.
☐$20 Federal Reserve Note, Series 1977, signatures Morton-Blumenthal, Federal Reserve District seal and District number printed on reverse	140.00	300.00

THIRD PRINT ON REVERSE

The cause of this error is obvious, the sheet having been fed through the press on the wrong side (back instead of front) for the third impression or "third print." In the so-called third print, the note receives the Treasury and Federal Reserve District seals, district numbers, and serial numbers.

	V. FINE	UNC.
☐$1 Federal Reserve Note, third print on reverse	150.00	315.00

BOARD BREAKS

The terminology of this error is misleading. It suggests that the fernlike unprinted areas were caused by a broken printing plate. Actually they must have resulted from something—probably linty matter—sticking to the printing ink. The assumption reached by the public, when it encounters such a note, is that the blank streaks were caused by the paper being folded in printing. This, however, is not possible, as that would yield an error of a much different kind (*see* Printed Fold).

It should be pointed out that board breaks are easily created by counterfeiters by erasing portions of the printed surface, and that the collector ought to examine such specimens closely.

	V. FINE	UNC.
☐$20 Federal Reserve Note, board breaks on reverse	85.00	200.00

MISSING SECOND PRINT

The "second print" is the front face, or obverse of the note—the "first print" being the reverse or back. A note with a missing second print has not received the primary impression on its obverse, though the back is normal and the front carries the standard third print matter (Treasury Seal, serial numbers, etc.). These errors, while they probably occur frequently, are so easily spotted by B.E.P. checkers that such notes are very scarce on the market.

	V. FINE	UNC.
□$10 Federal Reserve Note, missing second print	250.00	600.00

PRINTED FOLD

This note was folded nearly in half before receiving the third print, which fell across the waste margin on the reverse side. Had the note not been folded, this waste margin would have been removed in the cutting process. This note, when unfolded, is grotesque in shape.

	V. FINE	UNC.
□$1 Federal Reserve Note, printed fold with Federal Reserve District seal, district numbers, and serial numbers on reverse. (Naturally, this note lacks the "third print" matter, such as the Treasury Seal, that was supposed to appear on the righthand side of the obverse.)	300.00	600.00

	V. FINE	UNC.
☐$5 Federal Reserve Note. Printed fold with entire Federal Reserve District seal, portion of another Federal Reserve District seal, and portion of two different serial numbers on the reverse. It may be hard to imagine how a freak of this nature occurs. This note was folded diagonally along a line bisecting the Lincoln Memorial building slightly to the right of center. The lefthand portion of the reverse side was thereby drawn down across the lefthand side of the obverse, extending well below the bottom of the note. It reached far enough down to catch the district seal intended for the note beneath it, as well as a bit of the serial number. This is why the two serial numbers are different; they were supposed to go on two different notes. Obviously, when something this dramatic happens in printing, not only one error note is created but several—at least—at the same time. Not all necessarily reach circulation, however.	400.00	1000.00

THIRD PRINT BLACK INK MISSING OR LIGHT

Though the machinery used is ultramodern, U.S. currency notes are printed by the same basic technique used when printing was first invented more than 500 years ago. Ink is spread on the metal plates and these are pressed on the sheets as they go through the press. Because the inking is manually fed (as is the paper), an even flow is usually achieved. When an under-inked note is found, it is generally merely "light," giving a faded appearance. But sometimes the plate will be very improperly inked, due to mechanical misfunction or some other cause, resulting in whole areas being unprinted or so lightly printed that they cannot be seen without close inspection. These are not especially valuable notes but counterfeit specimens are frequently made.

	V. FINE	UNC.
□$1 Federal Reserve Note, Series 1977, signatures of Morton-Blumenthal. Federal Reserve District seal and District numbers missing from lefthand side, remainder of "third print" material light but distinct. If the lefthand serial number was strong, there might be suspicion of this being a counterfeit.	90.00	250.00

THIRD PRINT GREEN INK MISSING OR LIGHT

In this case, the green, rather than the black, ink was applied too lightly to the printing plate.

	V. FINE	UNC.
□$5 Federal Reserve Note, Series 1977, signatures of Morton-Blumenthal	40.00	160.00

NOTE FOLDED DURING OVERPRINT

This note was folded as it was being overprinted and failed to receive the District seal and District numbers at the left side of its obverse. This kind of error, like all involving missing portions of printing, has been extensively counterfeited.

	V. FINE	UNC.
□$2 Federal Reserve Note, Series 1976, signatures of Neff-Simon	90.00	200.00

FAULTY ALIGNMENT

Notes of this kind were formerly called "miscut," and sometimes still are. "Faulty alignment" is a more inclusive term which encompasses not only bad cutting but accidents in printing. If the sheet shifts around in the press, it will not receive the printed impressions exactly where they should be. Even if the cutting is normal, the resulting note will be misaligned; the cutting machine cannot correct botched printing. It is very easy to determine where the fault lies. If one side of the note has its design higher than the opposite side, this is a printing error. If the misalignment occurs equally on both sides, the problem was in cutting. Since the two sides are not printed in the same operation, it would be a one-in-a-million chance for them to become equally misaligned.

The value of such notes depends upon the degree of misalignment. Collectors are especially fond of specimens showing a portion—even if very slight, as with the one pictured of an adjoining note.

	V. FINE	UNC.
□$5 Federal Reserve Note, bottom left of reverse shaved (or "bled"), corresponding portion of adjoining note just visible at top. This ranks as a "dramatic" specimen.		
Slight	60.00	150.00
Dramatic	50.00	250.00

INSUFFICIENT PRESSURE

Under-inking of the printing plate is not the only cause of weak or partially missing impressions. If the press is not operating correctly and the inked plate meets the sheet with insufficient pressure, the result is similar to under-inking. This probably happens as a result of a sheet going through just as the press is being turned off for the day, or at other intervals. Supposedly all action ceases at the instant of turnoff, but considering the rapidity of this operation, it is likely that a random sheet could pass through and be insufficiently impressed. The note pictured here received normal "third print," as is generally the case with notes whose first or second print is made with insufficient pressure.

	V. FINE	UNC.
□$20 Federal Reserve Note, Series 1977, signatures of Morton-Blumenthal	140.00	325.00

PRINTED FOLD

This note, along with a large portion of the adjoining note, became folded after the second print. When it passed through the press to receive the third print or overprints (seals, serial numbers, etc.), these naturally failed to appear on the folded area.

	V. FINE	UNC.
□$1 Federal Reserve Note, printed fold with overprints partially missing		
Small	75.00	200.00
Large	175.00	400.00

DOUBLE IMPRESSION

Double impressions have traditionally been traced to the sheet of notes passing through the press twice, which would be the logical explanation. However, in considering the method by which currency is printed, it would seem more likely that double impression notes have not made two trips through the press. They probably result from the automatic paper feed jamming. The sheet just printed fails to be ejected, and the printing plate falls upon it a second time instead of on a fresh sheet. This does not merely create a strong impression, but a twin, or a ghost, impression, since the sheet is not positioned exactly the same way for the second strike. Though the paper feed may not be operating properly, there will still be some slight movement—enough to prevent the second impression from falling directly atop the first.

	V. FINE	UNC.
□$1 Federal Reserve Note, Series 1977A, signatures of Morton-Miller, double "second print" impression		
Partial	175.00	425.00
Complete	410.00	900.00

DOUBLE IMPRESSION OF OVERPRINTS ("DOUBLE THIRD PRINT")

This note is normal as far as the primary obverse and reverse printings are concerned. It received twin impressions of the overprints or "third print." This was not caused by jamming of the paper feed as discussed above. Naturally, the serial numbers are different, as the automatic numbering machine turns with every rise and fall of the press.

	V. FINE	UNC.
□$20 Federal Reserve Note, Series 1950, signatures of Priest-Humphrey, double impression of overprints.		
Partial	250.00	500.00
Complete	450.00	750.00

THIRD PRINT (OR OVERPRINTS) SHIFTED

Whenever the overprints (serial number, seals, etc.) are out of position, vertically or horizontally, this is known as "third print shifted" or "overprints shifted." In the example pictured, shifting is extreme. This is a premium value specimen which would command the higher of the two sums quoted. Normally, the overprinting on a "shifted" note fails to touch the portrait, or touches it only slightly. The cause of this kind of error is a sheet feeding incorrectly into the press for the overprinting operation. As striking and desirable as these notes are to collectors, they often go unnoticed by the public.

	V. FINE	UNC.
□$100 Federal Reserve Note, Series 1969C, signatures of Banuelos-Schultz, third print shifted.		
Slight	200.00	450.00
Dramatic	210.00	400.00

INK SMEARS

Ink smearing is one of the more common abnormalities of currency notes. Generally it can be attributed to malfunction of the automatic inking device which inks the printing plate. When performing properly, ink is applied at a steady, controlled pace to the printing plate. A very minor disorder in the machine can dispense enough extra ink to yield very spectacular "smeared notes," such as the one illustrated. The value of ink smear notes depends upon the area and intensity of the smear. They are quite easily faked, so the buyer should be cautious.

	V. FINE	UNC.
□$1 Federal Reserve Note, ink smear		
Small	35.00	95.00
Large	60.00	140.00

PRINTING FOLD

This note was crumpled along the right side prior to the third printing or application of overprints. Hence the "third print" matter on the lefthand side is normal, but portions of the overprint on the right appear on the note's reverse side.

	V. FINE	UNC.
□$20 Federal Reserve Note, Series 1977, signatures Morton-Blumenthal.	130.00	275.00

BLANK CREASE

It occasionally happens that a note becomes creased prior to the reverse or obverse printing in such a way that a small fold is created. During the printing procedure this fold hides a portion of the note's surface, which fails to receive the impression. These notes are actually double errors—the cutting machine cuts them without knowledge of the fold, and when the fold is opened out the bill is then of larger than normal size. Since "crease errors" are difficult to spot in the Bureau of Engraving and Printing's checking, they find their way into circulation in rather sizable numbers. It is difficult to place standard values on them because the price depends on the exact nature of the specimen. The wider the crease, the more valuable the note will be. Premium values are attached to notes with multiple creases that cause the blank unprinted area to fall across the portrait.

	V. FINE	UNC.
□Blank crease note, any denomination. Value stated is collector premium over and above face value. (If note has additional value because of series, signatures, etc., this too must be added.)		
Single crease	35.00	82.00
Multiple crease	40.00	85.00

MIXED DENOMINATION

The two notes pictured are normal in themselves, and if they were not owned together as a set, no premium value would be attached to them. The error (which may be dubious to term as such) lies with their serial numbers. The $5 Note has a serial number one digit higher than the $1, suggesting that it was fed into the printing machine intended to print overprints (or "third prints") on $1 bills. Even when this does happen (probably infrequently), it is very difficult to obtain "matching" notes of the kind illustrated, in which the serial numbers are only a single digit apart. Even if you had a $5 Note and $1 Note (or other combination of denominations) from sheets that were fed one after the other, the odds on getting one-digit-apart serial numbers are extremely small.

The value is given for an Uncirculated set only, as there would be no possibility of finding such matched notes except in a bank pack. Once released into circulation, they may never again be mated.

	UNC.
☐Mixed denomination pair from bank pack, $5 Federal Reserve Note within pack of $1 Federal Reserve Notes	4000.00

BLANK REVERSE

U.S. currency has its reverse printed before the obverse—in other words, back before front. The only logical explanation for blank reverse notes is that blank paper found its way into the batch of sheets on which reverses had already been printed. They were then fed—without detection—into the press for application of the obverse. They continued to escape notice during printing of the overprints, and miraculously got into circulation.

	V. FINE	UNC.
☐$100 Federal Reserve Note, blank reverse	385.00	750.00

	V. FINE	UNC.
□$20 Federal Reserve Note, Series 1977, signatures of Morton-Blumenthal Blank reverse	150.00	350.00

	V. FINE	UNC.
□$10 Federal Reserve Note, Series 1974, signatures of Neff-Simon Blank reverse	160.00	345.00

	V. FINE	UNC.
□$1 Federal Reserve Note, Series 1977, signatures of Morton-Blumenthal Blank reverse	150.00	300.00

DOUBLE DENOMINATION COUNTERFEIT

This is a counterfeit or faked error. We include it to show the kind of work done by counterfeiters, and how such items can be made to resemble genuine errors. This happens to be a counterfeit of an error note that cannot exist in its genuine state. Thus, there can be no hesitancy in proclaiming it a fake. Anyone who is even slightly familiar with the way currency is printed should instantly recognize this item as a fraud.

Nevertheless, fakers succeed in selling (often at high prices) specimens of this kind, probably because some collectors want the impossible for their albums. Genuine double or twin denomination notes have the obverse of one denomination and the reverse of a different denomination. They do not consist of two obverses or two reverses, such as the one pictured. The note illustrated carries four serial numbers. For it to be genuine, it would have had to pass through the "third print" (overprinting) process twice. Obviously it was made by gluing a $1 and $5 Note together. Much more deceptive paste-ups are created with the notes correctly paired so that the obverse of one and reverse of the other shows. Beware!

INVERTED OBVERSE

U.S. currency is printed reverse first. Therefore, when the back and front do not face in the same vertical direction (as they should), the note is known as an "inverted obverse." The term "inverted reverse" is never used. This, of course, results from the sheet being fed through upside-down for the obverse or second print. Though these specimens are scarce in Uncirculated condition, they often pass through many hands in circulation before being spotted. The uninformed public is not even aware that a note with faces in opposite directions is an error and has premium value.

	V. FINE	UNC.
□$2 Federal Reserve Note, Series 1976, signatures of Neff-Simon, inverted obverse	325.00	675.00

MISSING THIRD PRINT

This error is also known as "missing overprint." It consists of a note released into circulation without having gone through the "third print" operation.

	V. FINE	UNC.
□$1 Federal Reserve Note, Series 1977, signatures Morton-Blumenthal, missing third print	170.00	375.00

FOREIGN MATTER ON OBVERSE

Sometimes foreign matter, usually paper scraps of one kind or another, gets between the printing plate and the sheet. This naturally results in the area covered being blank on the note. Because of the extreme pressure exerted in printing, the foreign matter is occasionally "glued" to the note and travels with it into circulation. If the appendage is paper, it will normally be found to be of the same stock from which the note is made—apparently a shred from one of the sheet margins that worked its way into a batch of sheets awaiting printing. The value of such notes varies greatly, depending on the size of the foreign matter and its placement. It's rare to find notes in which foreign matter became attached before the first or second print. Nearly always, they found their way to the note after the second print and before the third.

	V. FINE	UNC.
□$1 Federal Reserve Note, Series 1974, signatures Neff-Simon, foreign matter on obverse	110.00	210.00

	V. FINE	UNC.
□$1 Silver Certificate, Series 1935E, signatures of Priest-Humphrey. Foreign matter on obverse. More valuable than the preceding because of the note's age and the foreign matter being larger.	320.00	600.00

MISSING PORTION OF REVERSE DESIGN (DUE TO ADHERENCE OF SCRAP PAPER)

In this instance, the foreign matter got in the way of the first print, or reverse printing. It prevented the covered area from being printed, but it later became dislodged and is no longer present. What appears on the illustration to be a strip of paper on the note is really the blank unprinted area once covered by the strip. Obviously a note that merely had a random strip of paper attached, over a normally printed design, would have no collector interest.

	V. FINE	UNC.
□$1 Federal Reserve Note, missing portion of reverse design due to adherence of scrap paper	110.00	250.00

OVERPRINT PARTIALLY MISSING

The overprint or third print on this note is normal on the righthand side and missing entirely on the left. This was caused by the note being folded (more or less in half, vertically) immediately before overprinting. Had the lefthand side been folded over the face, this would have interfered with the overprints on the righthand side. Instead, this specimen was folded over the reverse side, or downward, with the result that the missing portion of overprint did not strike the note at all—it simply hit the printing press bed. The reverse side of this note is normal.

	V. FINE	UNC.
□$1 Federal Reserve Note, Series 1963A, overprint partially missing	95.00	250.00

THIRD PRINT OFFSET ON REVERSE

This note is normal on the obverse but carries an "offset" of the third print or overprints on its reverse. It would appear that the overprints are showing through to the reverse, as if the note were printed on very thin paper. Actually, this "mirror image" is caused by a malfunction in the printing or paper-feeding machinery. The inked plate for printing the overprints contacted the machine bed without a sheet of paper being in place. Therefore, as the next sheet came through it received the normal overprint on its face and picked up the offset impression on its reverse from the machine bed. Each successive sheet going through the press also received an offset, but it naturally became fainter and fainter as the ink was absorbed. The value of a note of this kind depends on the intensity of the impression.

	V. FINE	UNC.
☐$5 Federal Reserve Note, offset impression of overprints on reverse	125.00	265.00

CONFEDERATE MONEY

The Civil War Centennial of 1961–65 has generally been credited with sparking an interest in the collecting and study of Confederate or C.S.A. Notes. This, however, is not totally borne out by facts, as C.S.A. currency had advanced steadily in value since the 1940s. It rides a crest of popularity today surpassing the early 1960s. This is due in part to the exhaustive research carried out since that time and numerous books and articles published. Even today, some C.S.A. Notes would still appear to be undervalued based on their availability vs. regular U.S. issues.

History. It became apparent upon the outbreak of the Civil War that both sides would experience extreme coinage shortages, and each took to the printing of notes that could be exchanged in lieu of bullion or "real money" (which always meant coined money until the 1860s). The South suffered more serious difficulties than the North, as it did not have as many skilled printers or engravers at its command. Also, with the war being fought on its territory rather than the North's, there was an ever-present danger of sabotage to plants printing money or engaging in related activities. The Confederacy tried by all available means to satisfy the currency demand and succeeded in distributing quite a large quantity of notes. Its shortage was taken up by notes issued by private banks, individual states, counties, railroads, and private merchants. Merchant tokens, to take the place of rapidly disappearing small change, poured forth in abundance during this period. All told, the Confederate Congress authorized the printing of about one and a half billion dollars' worth of paper currency. It is impossible to determine the total actually produced, but it would appear that this figure was far surpassed. At the war's conclusion, these notes were worthless, as the C.S.A. no longer existed and the federal government refused to redeem them. Many were discarded as scrap, but a surprising number were held faithfully by their owners who believed "the South will rise again." The South did indeed rise, industrially and economically, and those old C.S.A. Notes rose, too. They still aren't spendable, but many are worth sums in excess of face value as collectors' pieces. Until about 1900, however, practically no value was placed on Confederate currency—even by collectors.

Designs. Some surprising designs will be observed, including mythological gods and goddesses that seem to relate very little to the Southern artistic or cultural climate of the 1860s. Many scholarly efforts have been made to explain away the use of such motifs, but the simple fact is that they appeared not so much by choice as by necessity. Southern printers, not having the facilities of their Northern counterparts, were compelled to make do with whatever engravings or "stock cuts" were already on hand, as inappropriate as they might have proved. However, a number of original designs were created reflecting unmistakably regional themes and at times picturing heroes or leaders of the Confederacy. Slaves at labor, used as a symbol of the South's economic strength and its supposed advantage over the North, where labor was hired, was a frequent motif. Sailors were also depicted, as well as railroad trains and anything else that appeared symbolic of Southern industry. Probably the most notable single design, not intended to carry the satirical overtones it now possesses, is "General Francis Marion's Sweet Potato Breakfast" on the $10 1861 issue note.

In general, the C.S.A. Notes are not so badly designed a group as might be anticipated in light of conditions. The designing was, in fact, several leagues improved over the printing, which often left much to be desired. George Washington is depicted—not for being the first U.S. President but as a native son of Virginia. Jefferson Davis, President of the C.S.A., is among the more common portraits. He became even more disliked in the North than he otherwise might have been because of his picture turning up on currency. But after the war he took a moderate stand

and erased the old ill feelings; he even had words of praise for Lincoln. Other individuals whose portraits (not necessarily very faithful) will be encountered are:

- John C. Calhoun, U.S. Senator who led the battle for slavery and Southern Rights (later called "states rights")
- Alexander H. Stephen, Davis' Vice-President of the C.S.A.
- Judah P. Benjamin, holder of various official titles in the Southern government
- C.G. Memminger, Secretary of the Treasury and Secretary of War
- Lucy Pickens, wife of South Carolina's governor and the only woman (aside from mythological types) shown on C.S.A. currency
- John E. Ward
- R.M.T. Hunter

Printers. The study of printers of C.S.A. Notes is complex, made no less so by the fact that some contractors produced only plates, others did only printing (from plates procured elsewhere), and some did both. The principal Southern printer was the lithography firm of Hoyer & Ludwig of Richmond, Virginia. Also located in Richmond were Keatinge & Ball, which did commendable, if not exactly inspired, work, and B. Duncan, who also worked in Columbia, South Carolina. Another firm involved in quite a bit of note printing was J.T. Paterson of Columbia. The so-called "Southern Bank Note Company" was a fictitious name used to disguise the origin of notes prepared in the North. Some early notes were marked "National Bank Note Co., New York," but it was subsequently decided to remove correct Identification from the notes of this printer, undoubtedly on the latter's request (fearing prosecution for aiding the enemy).

Cancellations. Two varieties of cancels are commonly found on C.S.A. Notes. First is the Cut Cancel (CC), in which a knife or similar instrument has been used to make piercings in a design or pattern. Unless roughly executed, such cuts do not materially reduce a specimen's value. In the case of some notes, examples without cancellation are almost impossible to find. The COC, or Cut-Out Cancel, is more objectionable because, instead of merely leaving slits, a portion of the paper was removed. The reduction of value for a Cut-Out Cancel averages around 25 percent. These are considered "space fillers" if the issue is fairly common, but a rare note with a COC may be very desirable. Pen Cancellations (PC) are far less frequently encountered. These show the word "Canceled" written out by hand across the note's face, in ink. Unless the ink is heavy or blotchy, a Pen Cancel will not have too much bearing on value. As the note is not physically injured, it would seem to be the least offensive of the three varieties. Whenever a note is being sold, presence of a cancel, of whatever type, should be plainly spelled out. Some collectors are not interested in canceled specimens. In time, as the scarce issues become even scarcer, they will probably have to be accepted as a fact of life.

Signatures. The first six notes issued, the four from Montgomery and T5 & 6 from Richmond, were hand-signed by the Register and Treasurer themselves. Thereafter, because the Treasury Secretary felt hand signatures helped prevent counterfeiting, and because of the quantities of notes spewing forth, clerks were hired to sign "for Register" and "for Treasurer." There were about 200 different people who signed for each Treasury official, making for thousands of signature combinations. Mostly the clerks were women, many the wives or daughters of soldiers who had been killed in action. Since the notes were signed in Richmond through April of 1864 (when all operations were removed to Columbia, South Carolina), most of the signers were from there. Some moved to Columbia, and others were hired there.

It is most interesting to many people to find that they had relatives who signed Confederate money, and many people search for such notes. A complete listing of all the names from the Confederate Records appears in Colonel Criswell's extensive book, *Confederate and Southern States Currency.*

Condition Grades. While condition standards are basically the same for Confederate currency as other notes of their age, some allowance must be made for paper quality and deficiencies in printing and cutting. These matters have nothing to do with the preservation or wear and can be observed just as frequently in Uncirculated specimens as in those in average condition. Without a source of good paper, printers were obliged to use whatever was most easily and quickly obtainable. Often the paper was thin, or stiff, or contained networks of minute wrinkles which interfered with printing. Cutting was generally not done by machine, as in the North, but by hand with a pair of scissors—workers actually took the sheets and cut apart notes individually. When paper-cutting devices were employed, they were apparently not of the best quality. In any case, regular edges on C.S.A. Notes are uncommon, and their absence does not constitute grounds for classifying an otherwise perfect specimen in a condition grade below Uncirculated. When the occasional gem is located—a well-printed, well-preserved note on good paper, decently cut—its value is sure to be higher than those listed. The collector is not advised to confine himself to such specimens, as his activities would become seriously limited.

Uncirculated—UNC. An Uncirculated note shows no evidence of handling and is as close to "new condition" as possible. An Uncirculated specimen may, however, have pinholes or a finger smudge, which should be mentioned in a sales offering. If these are readily noticeable, the note deserves to be classified as "Almost Uncirculated." Crispness is hardly a criterion of uncirculation as this quality is expected in notes graded as low as Very Fine.

Almost Uncirculated—A.U. Similar to the above grade, but not quite as good as an Uncirculated specimen. The note bears no indication of having actually circulated but has minor flaws resulting from accident or mishandling, such as individuals' counting crinkles.

Extremely Fine—X.F. An X.F. note is on the borderline between Uncirculated and Circulated. It has not been heavily handled but may reveal several imperfections: a pinhole, finger smudge, counting crinkles, or a light wallet fold. The fold is not so heavy as to be termed a crease.

Very Fine—V.F. Has been in circulation but is not worn or seriously creased. It must still be clean and crisp, without stains or tears. Fine to Very Fine condition is considered the equivalent of "Average Circulated" but not "Average" condition (which is another term for poor).

Fine—F. A note that has been in circulation and shows it, but has no physical injuries or just slight ones.

Very Good—V.G. A well-circulated note bearing evidence of numerous foldings. It may possibly have creased corners and wrinkles as well as light staining, smudging, or pinholes, but major defects (such as a missing corner) would place it into an even lower category.

Good—G. Good notes have been heavily circulated, worn, possibly stained or scribbled on edges, could be frayed or "dog-eared." There may be holes larger than pin punctures, but not on the central portion of design. This is the lowest grade of condition acceptable to a collector, and only when nothing better is available. Unless very rare, such specimens are considered space-fillers only.

Average Buying Prices—A.B.P. The Average Buying Prices given here are the approximate sums paid by retail dealers for specimens in Good condition. As selling prices vary, so do buying prices, and in fact they usually vary more. A dealer who is overstocked on a certain note is sure to offer less than one who has no specimens on hand. The dealer's location, size of operation, and other circumstances will also influence the buying price. We present these figures merely as approximate guides to what sellers should expect.

Type Numbers. Each Confederate Note pictured has a "Type" number as well as a "regular" Criswell catalog number. The Criswell numbers are listed in the beginning of each of the price listings, and the Type numbers appear immediately following in parentheses. These numbers are used for identification and are cross-referenced in Grover Criswell's publications.

FOR MORE INFORMATION

Considered to have been the foremost authority on Confederate currency, the late Col. Grover Criswell has a variety of books available. His last release, *Confederate and Southern States Currency* ($75), covers all the currency issued by the Confederate States Central Government, the Southern States, the Indian Territories, the Florida Republic and Territory, and the Republic and Independent Government of Texas. This edition also gives interesting discovery information that you are sure to enjoy. There are also current market values listed, as well as rarities. This is the best reference available for the serious collector, libraries, and the casual reader.

CONFEDERATE STATES OF AMERICA—

1861 ISSUE, MONTGOMERY, ALABAMA
$1,000,000 authorized by "Act of March 9th."
Written dates "1861."
"NATIONAL BANK NOTE CO., NY"

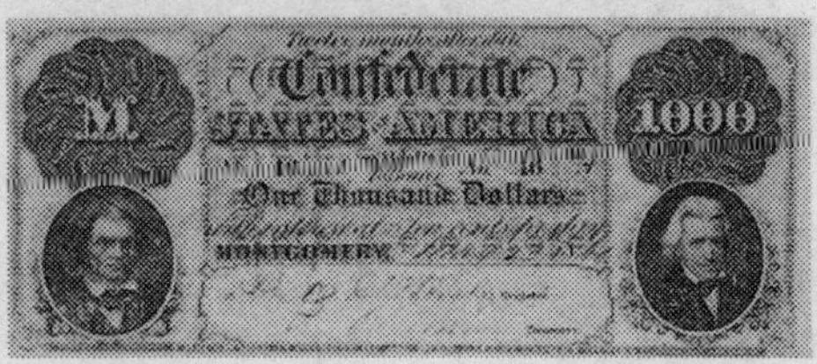

TYPE 1

Face Design: Green and black, bears "Interest Ten Cents Per Day," 607 issued. John C. Calhoun left, Andrew Jackson right.

CRISWELL	NOTE	A.B.P.	GOOD	UNC.
□1	$1000	5500.00	8000.00	50,000.00

"NATIONAL BANK NOTE CO., NY"

TYPE 2

Face Design: Green and black, bears "Interest Five Cents Per Day," 607 issued. Cattle crossing a brook.

CRISWELL	NOTE	A.B.P.	GOOD	UNC.
□2	$500	5500.00	8500.00	51,000.00

CONFEDERATE STATES OF AMERICA—
1861 ISSUE
"NATIONAL BANK NOTE CO., NY"

TYPE 3

Face Design: Green and black, bears "Interest One Cent Per Day." Railway train, Minerva left.

CRISWELL	NOTE	A.B.P.	GOOD	UNC.
□3	$100	2650.00	6000.00	29,000.00

"NATIONAL BANK NOTE CO., NY"

TYPE 4

Face Design: Green and black, bears "Interest Half A Cent Per Day." Negroes hoeing cotton.

CRISWELL	NOTE	A.B.P.	GOOD	UNC.
□4	$50	2650.00	4000.00	26,000.00

CONFEDERATE STATES OF AMERICA—1861 ISSUE
"AMERICAN BANK NOTE CO., NY"
(Though ostensibly by the "SOUTHERN BANK NOTE CO.")

TYPE 5

Face Design: Green and black, red fibre paper, bears "Interest One Cent Per Day." Railway train, Justice left and Minerva right.

CRISWELL	NOTE	A.B.P.	GOOD	UNC.
□5	$100	450.00	700.00	2700.00

TYPE 6

Face Design: Green and black, red fibre paper, bears "Interest Half A Cent Per Day." Pallas and Ceres seated on bale of cotton, Washington at right.

CRISWELL	NOTE	A.B.P.	GOOD	UNC.
□6	$50	320.00	500.00	2400.00

CONFEDERATE STATES OF AMERICA—1861 ISSUE
$20,000,000 authorized by "Act of May 16th, 1861"
(All lithographic date "July 25th, 1861")
"HOYER & LUDWIG, RICHMOND, VA"

TYPE 7

Face Design: Ceres and Proserpina flying, Washington left.

CRISWELL	NOTE	A.B.P.	GOOD	UNC.
□7-13	$100	375.00	500.00	2000.00

TYPE 8

Face Design: Washington, Tellus left.

CRISWELL	NOTE	A.B.P.	GOOD	UNC.
□14-22	$50	75.00	90.00	3600.00

CONFEDERATE STATES OF AMERICA—1861 ISSUE

TYPE XXI

Face Design: Exists in a variety of colors.

CRISWELL	NOTE	A.B.P.	GOOD	UNC.
□XXI	$20	60.00	125.00	300.00

The above type notes were bogus. For years it was thought they were a regular Confederate issue, and evidence exists that they were circulated as such. No collection of Confederate Notes is complete without one. There is no evidence as to who the printer was, but the authors have reason to believe he was located somewhere in Ohio. It is not a product of S.C. Upham, of Philadelphia, the well-known counterfeiter of Confederate Notes.

TYPE 9

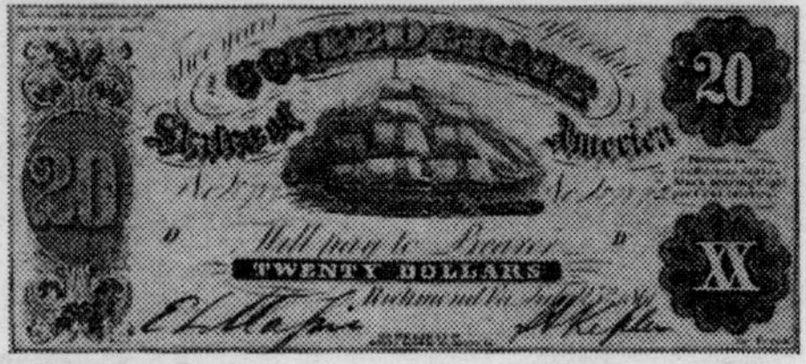

Face Design: Large sailing vessel, "20" at left.

CRISWELL	NOTE	A.B.P.	GOOD	UNC.
□23-33	$20	40.00	90.00	400.00

CONFEDERATE STATES OF AMERICA—1861 ISSUE

TYPE 10

Face Design: Liberty seated by eagle, with shield and flag.

There are at least forty-two minor varieties of this note, including a supposed ten or eleven stars on shield. Usually the stars are so indistinct that a note may show from six to fifteen stars. The other differences are minute changes in the size of the "10" in the upper corners. We list only the major type.

CRISWELL	NOTE	A.B.P.	GOOD	UNC.
□34-41	$10	70.00	125.00	3000.00

TYPE 11

Face Design: Liberty seated by eagle, sailor left.

CRISWELL	NOTE	A.B.P.	GOOD	UNC.
□42-45	$5	200.00	500.00	22,000.00

CONFEDERATE STATES OF AMERICA—1861 ISSUE
(Written date "July 25th, 1861")
"J. MANOUVRIER, NEW ORLEANS"

TYPE 12

Face Design: CONFEDERATE STATES OF AMERICA in blue on blue reverse.

CRISWELL	NOTE	A.B.P.	GOOD	UNC.
☐46-49	$5	440.00	1000.00	8000.00

$100,000,000 authorized by "Act of Aug. 19th, 1861."
$50,000,000 authorized by "Act of Dec. 24th, 1861."
"HOYER & LUDWIG, RICHMOND, VA"

TYPE 13

(Lithographic date "September 2nd, 2d, & s, 1861")

Face Design: Negroes loading cotton, sailor left.

CRISWELL	NOTE	A.B.P.	GOOD	UNC.
☐50-58	$100	50.00	80.00	3200.00

CONFEDERATE STATES OF AMERICA—1861 ISSUE

TYPE 14

Face Design: Moneta seated by treasure chests, sailor left.

CRISWELL	NOTE	A.B.P.	GOOD	UNC.
□59-78	$50	35.00	60.00	275.00

"SOUTHERN BANK NOTE CO., NEW ORLEANS"

TYPE 15

Face Design: Black and red on red fibre paper. Railway train, Justice right, Hope with anchor left.

CRISWELL	NOTE	A.B.P.	GOOD	UNC.
□79	$50	900.00	1500.00	12,500.00

CONFEDERATE STATES OF AMERICA—1861 ISSUE
"KEATINGE & BALL, RICHMOND, VA"

TYPE 16

Face Design: Black and green, red fibre paper. Portrait of Jefferson Davis.

CRISWELL	NOTE	A.B.P.	GOOD	UNC.
□80-98	$50	100.00	150.00	1300.00

"HOYER & LUDWIG, RICHMOND, VA"

TYPE 17

Face Design: Black with green ornamentation, plain paper. Ceres seated between Commerce and Navigation, Liberty left.

CRISWELL	NOTE	A.B.P.	GOOD	UNC.
□99-100	$20	210.00	285.00	2500.00

CONFEDERATE STATES OF AMERICA—1861 ISSUE
"HOYER & LUDWIG, RICHMOND, VA"

TYPE 18

Face Design: Large sailing vessel, sailor at capstan left.

CRISWELL	NOTE	A.B.P.	GOOD	UNC.
□101-136	$20	30.00	60.00	175.00

"SOUTHERN BANK NOTE CO., NEW ORLEANS"

TYPE 19

Face Design: Black and red on red fibre paper. Navigator seated by charts, Minerva left, blacksmith right.

CRISWELL	NOTE	A.B.P.	GOOD	UNC.
□137	$20	700.00	1200.00	6100.00

CONFEDERATE STATES OF AMERICA—1861 ISSUE
"B. DUNCAN, COLUMBIA, SC"

TYPE 20

Face Design: Industry seated between cupid and beehive, bust of A. H. Stephens left.

CRISWELL	NOTE	A.B.P.	GOOD	UNC.
□139-140	$20	40.00	60.00	250.00

"B. DUNCAN, RICHMOND, VA"

CRISWELL	NOTE	A.B.P.	GOOD	UNC.
□141-143	$20	35.00	50.00	250.00

"KEATINGE & BALL, COLUMBIA, SC"

TYPE 21

Face Design: Portrait of Alexander H. Stephens.

YELLOW-GREEN ORNAMENTATION

CRISWELL	NOTE	A.B.P.	GOOD	UNC.
□144	$20	150.00	240.00	2100.00

DARK-GREEN ORNAMENTATION

CRISWELL	NOTE	A.B.P.	GOOD	UNC.
□145-149	$20	110.00	225.00	1800.00

CONFEDERATE STATES OF AMERICA—1861 ISSUE
"SOUTHERN BANK NOTE CO., NEW ORLEANS"

TYPE 22

Face Design: Black and red, red fibre paper. Group of Indians, Thetis left, maiden with "X" at right.

CRISWELL	NOTE	A.B.P.	GOOD	UNC.
□150-152	$10	220.00	400.00	2400.00

"LEGGETT, KEATINGE & BALL, RICHMOND, VA"

TYPE 23

Face Design: Black and orange/red. Wagon load of cotton, harvesting sugar cane right. John E. Ward left.

CRISWELL	NOTE	A.B.P.	GOOD	UNC.
□153-155	$10	335.00	550.00	3700.00

CONFEDERATE STATES OF AMERICA—1861 ISSUE
"LEGGETT, KEATINGE & BALL, RICHMOND, VA"

TYPE 24

Face Design: Black and orange/red. R.M.T. Hunter left, vignette of child right.

CRISWELL	NOTE	A.B.P.	GOOD	UNC.
□156-160	$10	85.00	170.00	1000.00

"KEATINGE & BALL, RICHMOND, VA"

CRISWELL	NOTE	A.B.P.	GOOD	UNC.
□161-167	$10	60.00	130.00	925.00

"KEATINGE & BALL, RICHMOND, VA"

TYPE 25

Face Design: Hope with anchor, R.M.T. Hunter left, C. G. Memminger right.

CRISWELL	NOTE	A.B.P.	GOOD	UNC.
□168-171	$10	55.00	110.00	600.00

CONFEDERATE STATES OF AMERICA—1861 ISSUE
"KEATINGE & BALL, RICHMOND, VA"

TYPE 26

Face Design: Hope with anchor, R.M.T. Hunter left, C.G. Memminger right.

Face Design: *Solid red "X" and "X" overprint.

CRISWELL	NOTE	A.B.P.	GOOD	UNC.
□173-184	$10	60.00	110.00	750.00

*There are three types of red "X" and "X" overprints. That section of the note on which the overprints appear is illustrated in double size.

Face Design: *Coarse lace "X" and "X" red overprint.

CRISWELL	NOTE	A.B.P.	GOOD	UNC.
□189-210	$10	60.00	100.00	700.00

CONFEDERATE STATES OF AMERICA—1861 ISSUE

Face Design: Fine lace "X" and "X" red overprint.*

CRISWELL	NOTE	A.B.P.	GOOD	UNC.
□211–214	$10	55.00	100.00	680.00

TYPE 27

Face Design: Liberty seated by shield and eagle.

CRISWELL	NOTE	A.B.P.	GOOD	UNC.
□221-229,	$10	1650.00	6300.00	46,000.00

CONFEDERATE STATES OF AMERICA—1861 ISSUE
"HOYER & LUDWIG, RICHMOND, VA"

TYPE 28

Face Design: Ceres and Commerce with an urn.

CRISWELL	NOTE	A.B.P.	GOOD	UNC.
□230-234	$10	35.00	65.00	600.00

"J. T. PATERSON, COLUMBIA, SC"

CRISWELL	NOTE	A.B.P.	GOOD	UNC.
□235-236	$10	41.00	80.00	600.00

"B. DUNCAN, RICHMOND, VA"

TYPE 29

Face Design: Negro picking cotton.

CRISWELL	NOTE	A.B.P.	GOOD	UNC.
□237	$10	85.00	200.00	1650.00

CONFEDERATE STATES OF AMERICA—1861 ISSUE
"B. DUNCAN, COLUMBIA, SC"

TYPE 30

Face Design: Gen. Francis Marion's "Sweet Potato Dinner." R. M. T. Hunter left, Minerva right.

CRISWELL	NOTE	A.B.P.	GOOD	UNC.
□238	$10	40.00	80.00	325.00

NO ENGRAVER'S NAME

CRISWELL	NOTE	A.B.P.	GOOD	UNC.
□239-241	$10	40.00	50.00	310.00

"SOUTHERN BANK NOTE CO., NEW ORLEANS"

TYPE 31

Face Design: Black and red on red fibre paper. Minerva left; Agriculture, Commerce, Industry, Justice, and Liberty seated at center; statue of Washington right.

CRISWELL	NOTE	A.B.P.	GOOD	UNC.
□243-245	$5	110.00	240.00	1600.00

CONFEDERATE STATES OF AMERICA—1861 ISSUE
"LEGGETT, KEATINGE & BALL, RICHMOND, VA"

TYPE 32

Face Design: Black and orange/red. Machinist with hammer, boy in oval left.

CRISWELL	NOTE	A.B.P.	GOOD	UNC.
□246-249	$5	175.00	385.00	3600.00

"LEGGETT, KEATINGE & BALL, RICHMOND, VA"

TYPE 33

Face Design: Black and white note with blue-green ornamentation. C.G. Memminger, Minerva right.

CRISWELL	NOTE	A.B.P.	GOOD	UNC.
□250-256	$5	60.00	130.00	1300.00

CONFEDERATE STATES OF AMERICA—1861 ISSUE

"KEATINGE & BALL, RICHMOND, VA"

TYPE 34

Face Design: C.G. Memminger, Minerva right.

CRISWELL	NOTE	A.B.P.	GOOD	UNC.
□262-270	$5	45.00	100.00	800.00

"HOYER & LUDWIG, RICHMOND, VA"

TYPE 35

Face Design: Loading cotton left, Indian princess right.

CRISWELL	NOTE	A.B.P.	GOOD	UNC.
□271	$5	2200.00	6000.00	78,000.00

CONFEDERATE STATES OF AMERICA—1861 ISSUE
"HOYER & LUDWIG, RICHMOND, VA"

TYPE 36

Face Design: Ceres seated on bale of cotton, sailor left.

CRISWELL	NOTE	A.B.P.	GOOD	UNC.
□272	$5	30.00	60.00	350.00

"J. T. PATERSON & CO., COLUMBIA, SC"

CRISWELL	NOTE	A.B.P.	GOOD	UNC.
□274	$5	25.00	45.00	250.00
□276-282	$5	25.00	45.00	250.00

CONFEDERATE STATES OF AMERICA—1861 ISSUE
"B. DUNCAN, RICHMOND, VA"

TYPE 37

Face Design: Sailor seated beside bales of cotton, C.G. Memminger left, Justice and Ceres right.

CRISWELL	NOTE	A.B.P.	GOOD	UNC.
□284	$5	50.00	100.00	600.00

"B. DUNCAN, COLUMBIA, SC"

CRISWELL	NOTE	A.B.P.	GOOD	UNC.
□285	$5	50.00	125.00	600.00

"B. DUNCAN, COLUMBIA, SC"

TYPE 38

Face Design: Personification of South striking down Union, J.P. Benjamin left. Dated "September 2, 1861" through an error. No Confederate Note less than $5 was authorized in 1861.

CRISWELL	NOTE	A.B.P.	GOOD	UNC.
□286	$2	225.00	340.00	7000.00

CONFEDERATE STATES OF AMERICA—1862 ISSUE
$165,000,000 Authorized by "Act of April 17th."
"HOYER & LUDWIG, RICHMOND, VA."

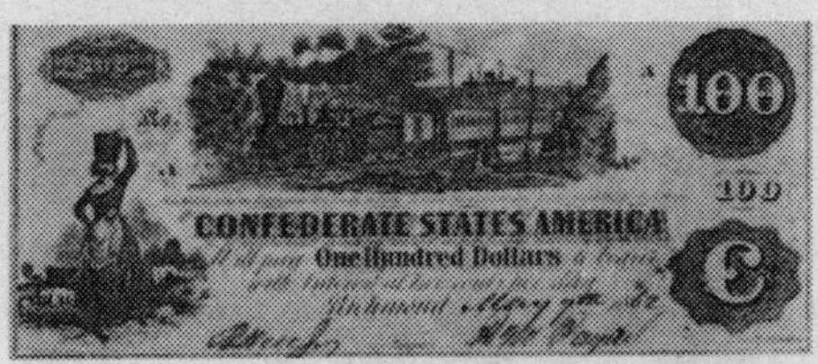

TYPE 39

Face Design: Railway train, straight steam from locomotive, milkmaid left. Bears "Interest at Two Cents Per Day."

CRISWELL	NOTE	A.B.P.	GOOD	UNC.
□287-289	$100	45.00	75.00	185.00

Dated May 5 to May 9, 1862

J.T. PATERSON, COLUMBIA, S.C. (At Lower Left)

□290-293	$100	38.00	60.00	140.00

VARIOUS WRITTEN DATES, MAY THROUGH OCTOBER, 1862

J.T. PATERSON, COLUMBIA, S.C. (At Lower Right)

□294-296	$100	38.00	70.00	145.00

VARIOUS WRITTEN DATES, MAY THROUGH OCTOBER, 1862

TYPE 40

"J.T. PATERSON, COLUMBIA, S.C."

Face Design: Railway train, diffused steam from locomotive, milkmaid left Bears "Interest at Two Cents Per Day."

CRISWELL	NOTE	A.B.P.	GOOD	UNC.
□298-309	$100	40.00	60.00	150.00

VARIOUS WRITTEN DATES, MAY THROUGH OCTOBER, 1862

CONFEDERATE STATES OF AMERICA—1862 ISSUE
"KEATINGE & BALL, COLUMBIA, S.C."
On the following notes there are two types of ornamental scrolls in the upper right corners.

TYPE 41

Face Design: "Hundred" overprint in orange/red. Bears "Interest at Two Cents Per Day." Negroes hoeing cotton, J.C. Calhoun left, Columbia right.

CRISWELL	NOTE	A.B.P.	GOOD	UNC.
□310-314	$100	55.00	85.00	230.00
Dated "August 26th, 1862" (Date all written, scroll No. 1.)				
□315-324	$100	45.00	85.00	180.00
Written dates, AUG. to DEC. "1862." ("186" of date is engraved.)				
□325-331	$100	45.00	80.00	175.00
Dated January 1 to January 8, 1863.				

CONFEDERATE STATES OF AMERICA—1862 ISSUE
$5,000,000 authorized by "Act of April 18th, 1862"
$5,000,000 authorized by "Act of September 23rd, 1862"
"B. DUNCAN, COLUMBIA, S.C."

TYPE 42

Face Design: Personification of South striking down Union, J.P. Benjamin left.

CRISWELL	NOTE	A.B.P.	GOOD	UNC.
☐334-337	$2	30.00	40.00	350.00

TYPE 43

Face Design: "2" and "Two" in green overprint. Personification of South striking down Union, J.P. Benjamin left.

CRISWELL	NOTE	A.B.P.	GOOD	UNC.
☐338	$2	40.00	80.00	1750.00

CONFEDERATE STATES OF AMERICA—1862 ISSUE

TYPE 44

Face Design: Steamship at sea. Lucy Holcombe Pickens right. Liberty left.

CRISWELL	NOTE	A.B.P.	GOOD	UNC.
□339-341	$1	40.00	65.00	265.00

TYPE 45

Face Design: "1" and "One" green overprint. Steamship at sea. Lucy Holcombe Pickens right. Liberty left.

CRISWELL	NOTE	A.B.P.	GOOD	UNC.
□342-342A	$1	55.00	95.00	1700.00

CONFEDERATE STATES OF AMERICA—1862 ISSUE
"HOYER & LUDWIG, RICHMOND, VA."

This is a Sept. 2, 1861 note, dated through error "September 2, 1862." No engravers' name, appears, but it is a product of Hoyer & Ludwig, Richmond, VA.

TYPE 46

Face Design: Ceres reclining on cotton bales. R.M.T. Hunter at right.

CRISWELL	NOTE	A.B.P.	GOOD	UNC.
□343-344	$10	35.00	70.00	500.00

(Essay Note, Printed Signatures.)

"KEATINGE & BALL, COLUMBUS, S.C."

TYPE 47

Face Design: Liberty seated on bale of cotton. R.M.T. Hunter right.

CRISWELL	NOTE	A.B.P.	GOOD	UNC.
□345	$20	EXTREMELY RARE		

CONFEDERATE STATES OF AMERICA—1862 ISSUE

(Essay Note, Printed Signatures.)

"KEATINGE & BALL, COLUMBUS, S.C."

TYPE 48

Face Design: Ceres holding sheaf of wheat. R.M.T. Hunter right.

CRISWELL	NOTE	A.B.P.	GOOD	UNC.
□346	$10	EXTREMELY RARE		

CONFEDERATE STATES OF AMERICA—1862 ISSUE

$90,000,000 authorized by "Act of Oct. 13th, 1862"

"KEATINGE & BALL, COLUMBIA S.C."

TYPE 49

Face Design: Fancy green reverse. Lucy Holcombe Pickens. George W. Randolph right.

CRISWELL	NOTE	A.B.P.	GOOD	UNC.
□347-349	$100	110.00	275.00	1000.00

CONFEDERATE STATES OF AMERICA—1862 ISSUE "KEATINGE & BALL, RICHMOND, VA." (THIRD SERIES)

TYPE 50

Face Design: Black and green. Ornate green reverse. Jefferson Davis.

CRISWELL	NOTE	A.B.P.	GOOD	UNC.
□350-356	$50	110.00	220.00	1500.00

"KEATINGE & BALL, COLUMBIA, S.C." (THIRD SERIES)

CRISWELL	NOTE	A.B.P.	GOOD	UNC.
□357-362	$50	70.00	180.00	720.00

CONFEDERATE STATES OF AMERICA—1862 ISSUE "KEATINGE & BALL, COLUMBIA, S.C."

TYPE 51

Face Design: Fancy blue reverse. State Capitol at Nashville, Tennessee. A.H. Stephens.

CRISWELL	NOTE	A.B.P.	GOOD	UNC.
□363-368	$20	70.00	130.00	675.00

CONFEDERATE STATES OF AMERICA—1862 ISSUE

TYPE 52

Face Design: Fancy blue reverse. State Capitol at Columbia S.C., R.M.T. Hunter. Printed on pink paper.

"B. DUNCAN."

CRISWELL	NOTE	A.B.P.	GOOD	UNC.
□369-375IB	$10	30.00	55.00	160.00

"EVANS & COGSWELL"

CRISWELL	NOTE	A.B.P.	GOOD	UNC.
□376-378	$10	30.00	55.00	160.00

TYPE 53

Face Design: Fancy blue reverse. State Capitol at Richmond, VA., C.G. Memminger. Printed on pink paper.

There are many varieties of printers names on notes of this issue, though all have the same engraver's names. In general, the only valuable ones are those with two "Printers" names.

CRISWELL	NOTE	A.B.P.	GOOD	UNC.
□379-390	$5	25.00	45.00	160.00

TYPE
59

Face Design: Blue back. State Capitol at Columbia, S.C., R.M.T. Hunter.

CRISWELL	NOTE	A.B.P.	GOOD	UNC.
☐429-447	$10	25.00	45.00	180.00

Engravers' names on lower margin.

TYPE
60

Face Design: Fancy blue reverse. State Capitol at Richmond, VA. C.G. Memminger.

CRISWELL	NOTE	A.B.P.	GOOD	UNC.
☐448-469	$5	25.00	45.00	180.00

Pink Paper.

TYPE
61

Face Design: Judah P. Benjamin.

CRISWELL	NOTE	A.B.P.	GOOD	UNC.
☐470-473	$2	85.00	80.00	400.00

TYPE 62

Face Design: Clement C. Clay. Pink Paper.

CRISWELL	NOTE	A.B.P.	GOOD	UNC.
□474-484	$1	25.00	50.00	260.00

"ARCHER & DALY. RICHMOND, VA."

TYPE 63

Face Design: Bust of Jefferson Davis. Pink Paper.

CRISWELL	NOTE	A.B.P.	GOOD	UNC.
□485-488	50 Cents	20.00	41.00	72.00

CONFEDERATE STATES OF AMERICA—1864

$200,000,000 was authorized by "Act of February 17th, 1864." All notes of this year are dated "Feb. 17th, 1864."

The actual amount issued was probably ten times the figure given above and the amount printed even greater. Thus there are many minor varieties of each type including color variations, flourishes, and more signature combinations than any other year. The authors list only the **important** types. The most common Confederate Notes appear in this year.

"KEATINGE & BALL, COLUMBIA, S.C."

TYPE 64

Face Design: Reddish horizontal line background. Equestrian statue of Washington and Confederate flag at left. Gen. T.J. "Stonewall" Jackson right.

CRISWELL	NOTE	A.B.P.	GOOD	UNC.
☐489-489A	$500	170.00	325.00	800.00

"A CONFEDERATE COUNTERFEIT."

Same as $100 Note illustrated on the next page, but 1/4 inch narrower, and 1/4 inch shorter. This note only exists in Serial Letter "D."

CRISWELL	NOTE	A.B.P.	GOOD	UNC.
☐ 492	$100	60.00	80.00	200.00

Although a counterfeit, this note was listed in Bradbeer as a genuine, and evidence exists proving that it was accepted as such in the Confederacy. It is an excellent copy, in some ways better engraved than the genuine, but is easily distinguishable by its small size. The authors list it herein with the regular issues because few collectors desire to be without one. It is by far the most popular Confederate counterfeit.

TYPE 65

Face Design: Reddish network background. Intricate blue reverse with "Hundred" in large letters. Lucy Pickens. Two soldiers left. George W. Randolph right.

CRISWELL	NOTE	A.B.P.	GOOD	UNC.
□490-494	$100	45.00	100.00	225.00

TYPE 66

Face Design: Reddish network background. Intricate blue reverse with "Fifty" in large letters. Jefferson Davis.

CRISWELL	NOTE	A.B.P.	GOOD	UNC.
□495-503	$50	40.00	75.00	195.00

TYPE 67

Face Design: Reddish network background. Intricate blue reverse with "Twenty" in large letters. State Capitol at Nashville, TN. A.H. Stephens right.

CRISWELL	NOTE	A.B.P.	GOOD	UNC.
□504-539	$20	25.00	35.00	80.00

"KEATINGE & BALL, COLUMBIA, S.C."
("PTD. BY EVANS & COGSWELL" On left end)

TYPE 68

Face Design: Reddish network background. Intricate blue reverse with "Ten" in large letters. Horses pulling cannon. R.M.T. Hunter at right.

CRISWELL	NOTE	A.B.P.	GOOD	UNC.
□540-553	$10	20.00	25.00	65.00

"KEATINGE & BALL, COLUMBIA, S.C."

TYPE 69

Face Design: Reddish network background. Intricate blue reverse with "Five" in large letters. State Capitol at Richmond, VA. C.G. Memminger at right.

CRISWELL	NOTE	A.B.P.	GOOD	UNC.
□558-565	$5	20.00	25.00	60.00

TYPE 70

Face Design: Reddish network background. Judah P. Benjamin.

CRISWELL	NOTE	A.B.P.	GOOD	UNC.
☐500-571	$2	35.00	65.00	160.00

TYPE 71

Face Design: Reddish network background. Clement C. Clay.

CRISWELL	NOTE	A.B.P.	GOOD	UNC.
☐572-577	$1	40.00	80.00	210.00

"ENGRAVED BY ARCHER & HALPIN, RICHMOND, VA."

TYPE 72

Face Design: Bust of Jefferson Davis. Pink Paper.

CRISWELL	NOTE	A.B.P.	GOOD	UNC.
☐578-579	50 Cents	18.00	35.00	70.00

HOUSE OF COLLECTIBLES SERIES

Title	ISBN	Price	Author
The Official® Price Guides to			
America's State Quarters	0609807706	$6.99	Ganz
Collecting Books, 4th ed.	0609807692	$18.00	Tedford/Goudey
Collector Knives, 13th ed.	0676601898	$17.95	Price
Collector Plates, 7th ed.	0676601545	$19.95	Rinker Ent.
Costume Jewelry, 3rd ed.	0609806688	$17.95	Miller
Dinnerware of the 20th Century	0676600859	$29.95	Rinker
Glassware, 3rd ed.	067660188X	$17.00	Pickvet
Hake's Character Toys, 4th ed.	0609808222	$35.00	Hake
Hislop's International Fine Art	0609808745	$20.00	Hislop
Military Collectibles, 6th ed.	0676600522	$20.00	Austin
Mint Errors, 6th ed.	0609808559	$15.00	Herbert
Overstreet Comic Book Grading Guide	0609810529	$24.00	Overstreet/Blumberg
Overstreet Comic Books, 33rd ed.	1400046688	$25.00	Overstreet
Overstreet Indian Arrowheads, 7th ed.	0609808699	$24.00	Overstreet
Pottery & Porcelain, 8th ed.	0876378939	$18.95	Duke
Records, 16th ed.	0609809083	$25.95	Osborne
Vintage Fashion and Fabrics	0609808133	$17.00	Smith
The Official® Guides to			
Flea Market Prices	0609807722	$14.95	Rinker
How to Make Money in Coins Right Now, 2nd ed.	0609807463	$14.95	Travers
Directory to U.S. Flea Markets, 8th ed.	0609809229	$14.00	Werner
One-Minute Coin Expert, 4th ed.	0609807471	$7.99	Travers
Stamp Collector's Bible	0609808842	$22.00	Datz
The Official® Beckett Sports Cards Price Guides to			
Baseball Cards 2003, 23rd ed.	0609810375	$7.99	Beckett
Basketball Cards 2003, 12th ed.	0609809849	$7.99	Beckett
Football Cards 2003, 22nd ed.	0609809857	$7.99	Beckett
The Official® Blackbook Price Guides to			
U.S. Coins 2003, 42nd ed.	1400048052	$7.99	Hudgeons
U.S. Paper Money 2003, 36th ed.	1400048060	$6.99	Hudgeons
U.S. Postage Stamps 2003, 26th ed.	1400048079	$8.99	Hudgeons
World Coins 2003, 7th ed.	1400048087	$7.99	Hudgeons